Warm Regards:

INSPIRATION 365

Warm Regards:

INSPIRATION 365

ELVIE GUTHRIE-LEWIS

XULON PRESS

Xulon Press
2301 Lucien Way #415
Maitland, FL 32751
407.339.4217
www.xulonpress.com

© 2017 by Elvie Guthrie-Lewis

All rights reserved solely by the author. The author guarantees all contents are original and do not infringe upon the legal rights of any other person or work. No part of this book may be reproduced in any form without the permission of the author. The views expressed in this book are not necessarily those of the publisher.

Unless otherwise indicated, Scripture quotations taken from the New King James Version (NKJV). Copyright © 1982 by Thomas Nelson, Inc. Used by permission. All rights reserved.

Printed in the United States of America.
Edited by Xulon Press.

ISBN: 9781545614822

A Gift Presented To:

_____

From:

_____

Date:

_____

TABLE OF CONTENTS

Day 1: A Call to Worship 1
Day 2: Just Walk Away 2
Day 3: God Is Reaching Out 3
Day 4: Best Friends 4
Day 5: You Asked and I Answered... Now What? 5
Day 6: When God Said No 6
Day 7: Raising a White Flag 7
Day 8: Some Much Needed Rest 8
Day 9: One, Two, Three! 9
Day 10: Eyes to See 10
Day 11: Oh, the Wonder of it All 11
Day 12: Perfect Peace... Where? 12
Day 13: What's the Delay? 13
Day 14: Ahh! 14
Day 15: When Is It A Good Time? 15
Day 16: A Time and a Place 16
Day 17: Empty Promises 17
Day 18: Setbacks and Comebacks 18
Day 19: Preparing for Tomorrow 19
Day 20: The True Meaning of Courage 20
Day 21: Standing in the Gap 21
Day 22: Determining the Outcome 22
Day 23: Entering into Another's Experience 23
Day 24: Drawing on Reserves 25
Day 25: Digging in the Weeds 26
Day 26: From the Heart 27
Day 27: Jesus... The Lamb That Was Slain 28
Day 28: The Arms of Jesus 29
Day 29: A Trustworthy God 30
Day 30: If The Shoe Was On The Other Foot 32

Day 31: I Knocked and I Waited 33
Day 32: Perfect in Form 34
Day 33: A Person of Integrity 35
Day 34: Wash-day Praises.. 36
Day 35: Church Hill & Cotton Tree... 37
Day 36: Don't Cry, Meme Rose 38
Day 37: Morning Song 39
Day 38: One of a Kind 40
Day 39: New Growth 41
Day 40: You Are Killing Me!... 42
Day 41: Relinquishing Control 43
Day 42: Vertigo and Dream of a Lost Car 44
Day 43: Where is Your Trust?.. 45
Day 44: Only a Child 46
Day 45: Imitations 47
Day 46: When Things Are Not What They Appear to Be.......................... 48
Day 47: Zestful Living 49
Day 48: When Self Becomes an Idol 51
Day 49: When to Dim the Lights 52
Day 50: Just for a Fleeting Moment.. 53
Day 51: Who is He? 54
Day 52: My Thoughts or Yours?... 55
Day 53: "At-one-ment" 56
Day 54: Sufficient 57
Day 55: Just a Prayer Away.. 58
Day 56: Conform or be Transformed? 59
Day 57: Pay Attention to the Signals.. 60
Day 58: The Longest Trip Home 61
Day 59: Who You Can Become, Not Who You Are................................. 62
Day 60: After You... 63
Day 61: The Closest Thing to Heaven... 64
Day 62: Divine Appointments 66
Day 63: Wandering Mind.. 68
Day 64: Betrothed 69
Day 65: The Sound of Thunder.. 70
Day 66: Saying it With More Than Words 71
Day 67: Dancing Waters 72
Day 68: Success?.. 73
Day 69: Wrapped in Trials 74
Day 70: Alone... No, Never!... 75
Day 71: Bloom Where You Are Planted... 76
Day 72: Eyes on Jesus... 77

Table Of Contents

Day 73: Five Loaves and Two Fish 78
Day 74: Don't "But" Me! 79
Day 75: A Shelter in the Storm 80
Day 76: Detour 81
Day 77: If for You Alone 82
Day 78: Enjoy Them While You Can 83
Day 79: Anxiety Will Kill You 84
Day 80: Immeasurable Gifts 85
Day 81: Flowers for My Table 86
Day 82: Phobias 87
Day 83: So They Won't Forget 88
Day 84: Obedience: Yielding to God's Will 89
Day 85: Only One Door! 90
Day 86: Broken People 91
Day 87: Too Good to be True? 92
Day 88: Speak Lord... and Help Me to Listen 93
Day 89: Sold Out from Within 94
Day 90: The Alpha and the Omega 95
Day 91: Calm 96
Day 92: Under His Wings 97
Day 93: Take It Back 98
Day 94: Relationship Building for Jesus Christ 99
Day 95: Seventy Times Seven 100
Day 96: Words That Heal 101
Day 97: Don't Rob Me of My Blessing 102
Day 98: Someday Syndrome 103
Day 99: Making My Father Proud 104
Day 100: Our Personal Witness 105
Day 101: Beauty Out of Ashes 106
Day 102: The Pain Behind the Anger 107
Day 103: Patience to Bloom 108
Day 104: Close to the Broken-hearted 109
Day 105: An Experience of the Heart 110
Day 106: Taking the Lesser Seat 111
Day 107: One Day at a Time 112
Day 108: A Foretaste of Heaven 113
Day 109: Living a Life of Excellence 114
Day 110: Making Disciples for Jesus 115
Day 111: At the Name of Jesus 116
Day 112: Trust Him with All Your Heart 117
Day 113: The Devil is on the Prowl 118
Day 114: Does God Really Love Me? 119

Day 115: Comforted to Be of Comfort 120
Day 116: Life's Laughable Moments 121
Day 117: Your Biggest Disappointment - Your Biggest Blessing. 122
Day 118: Your Pit or Mine?................................123
Day 119: Fragrant Prayers 124
Day 120: Knowing that God is God 125
Day 121: Just Do It!................................126
Day 122: Tear Down the Wall................................127
Day 123: No Barriers................................128
Day 124: Waiting with Expectancy 129
Day 125: Unconditional Love................................130
Day 126: Little Deeds of Kindness 131
Day 127: Above All Other Gods 132
Day 128: Giving My Best to this Moment................................133
Day 129: On the Horizon 134
Day 130: New Beginnings 135
Day 131: Trapped................................136
Day 132: Limited Potential or Limited Expectation?................................137
Day 133: Bitter to the Core................................138
Day 134: Finding Joy................................139
Day 135: Paralyzing Fear 140
Day 136: Advocate and Judge 141
Day 137: Stretch Yourself!................................142
Day 138: Will the Real You Please Stand Up? 143
Day 139: Contamination and Purification 144
Day 140: The Peace of Jesus Christ 145
Day 141: Devotion, not Emotion 146
Day 142: Mama's "Sweets" Cabinet 147
Day 143: The Rock that is Higher than I 148
Day 144: I Choose to Bless You 149
Day 145: Confused, Shocked, and Furious 150
Day 146: The All-Wise God 152
Day 147: Strength Enough for Today 153
Day 148: Courage for the Journey 154
Day 149: My Needs are Supplied................................155
Day 150: Roslyn's Close Call................................156
Day 151: Boyce's Friend Ross 157
Day 152: His Plans Are Better Than Mine 158
Day 153: A New Beginning................................159
Day 154: Quicksand 160
Day 155: Surprised?................................161
Day 156: A Bold Move................................162

Day 157: Surrendering all to Christ ... 163
Day 158: Living Harmoniously ... 164
Day 159: Jesus Cares ... 165
Day 160: Standing Up and Standing Out ... 166
Day 161: Limitless Possibilities ... 167
Day 162: Yes, You Can ... 168
Day 163: Not Beyond Reach ... 169
Day 164: We Prayed for You Today ... 170
Day 165: Our Omnipotent Lord ... 171
Day 166: "Just Chill!" ... 172
Day 167: You Should Have Told Me ... 173
Day 168: Created for a Special Purpose ... 174
Day 169: Sharing in Your Sorrows ... 175
Day 170: Traveling Companion ... 176
Day 171: Forever and for Always ... 177
Day 172: Omnipresent ... 178
Day 173: Let Go of the Door ... 179
Day 174: Pray First ... 180
Day 175: Gethsemane ... 181
Day 176: A Forgiving God ... 182
Day 177: Alive for Evermore ... 183
Day 178: God's Amazing Grace ... 184
Day 179: The Priceless Value of True Friendship ... 185
Day 180: Diamond in the Rough ... 186
Day 181: A Way Out of No Way ... 187
Day 182: One Pint vs Every Drop ... 188
Day 183: Love Without Measure ... 189
Day 184: Life's Difficult Moments: Opportunities for Growth ... 190
Day 185: The Best Way to Heal is to Serve ... 191
Day 186: "Son-Beam" ... 192
Day 187: Prove Me Now ... 193
Day 188: Convicted on False Evidence ... 194
Day 189: The Case Has Been Settled ... 195
Day 190: Getting to the Heart of the Matter ... 196
Day 191: The Terrible Price of Disobedience ... 197
Day 192: Broken ... 198
Day 193: One Day Closer ... 199
Day 194: It's Not Over Yet ... 200
Day 195: Vigilance ... 201
Day 196: The Trip of a Lifetime ... 202
Day 197: You've been Chosen ... 203
Day 198: Only Believe ... 204

Day 199: Taking the Pledge 205
Day 200: Pack Your Bags. 206
Day 201: For Every "Yes" a "No" Is Required Somewhere. 207
Day 202: Paralyzed by Fear 208
Day 203: The Anointing. 209
Day 204: Defeated. 210
Day 205: Grafted into the Vine 211
Day 206: Things to Do, Places to Go, and People to See 212
Day 207: Lured into Sin 213
Day 208: The Way 214
Day 209: Love Me Back. 215
Day 210: Each Life Has Meaning 216
Day 211: The Appian Way 217
Day 212: Let Hope, Not Hurt. 218
Day 213: Bring Me Your Brokenness. 219
Day 214: For the Pleasure of Your Company 220
Day 215: Who's Watching You? 221
Day 216: Hidden Treasure 222
Day 217: Repurposing Me 223
Day 218: His Eyes Are on You. 224
Day 219: Comforted to be of Comfort 225
Day 220: It Is All Mine. 226
Day 221: Our Sovereign God 227
Day 222: He's Able. 228
Day 223: Release Me 229
Day 224: God Knows Best. 230
Day 225: My Mother and Me 231
Day 226: A Room Full of Stuff 232
Day 227: Preparing for The Battle 233
Day 228: Emptied and Waiting to be Filled 234
Day 229: The Good You Do Follows You, As Does The Evil. 235
Day 230: His Perfect Timing 236
Day 231: Implicit Trust. 237
Day 232: Standing Firm 238
Day 233: Not Double-Minded 239
Day 234: Two Faces 240
Day 235: Healthy Self: Heal Thyself. 241
Day 236: His Promise to Feed Me 242
Day 237: Lord, Show Yourself Strong Today. 243
Day 238: Christ the Restorer. 244
Day 239: The Power of the Tongue. 245
Day 240: Addicted to the Word 246

Table Of Contents

Day 241: Cast Your Net On The Other Side 247
Day 242: His Beauty In Me................................248
Day 243: An Acceptable Religion 249
Day 244: Righteous Before the Lord........................250
Day 245: Living With Eternity In View.....................251
Day 246: The Future... Today!.............................252
Day 247: Giving Thanks Always For You.....................253
Day 248: Unmerited Favor..................................254
Day 249: Practicing Forgiveness: Life's Best Medicine 255
Day 250: One Fork, One Knife and One Spoon 256
Day 251: Living Above Your Circumstances 257
Day 252: Lord, Make Me The CEO............................258
Day 253: Overcoming The Odds..............................259
Day 254: With Wings Like Eagles...........................260
Day 255: Confession: The First Step to Pardon 261
Day 256: The Publican's Prayer............................262
Day 257: I Win Either Way 263
Day 258: Teach Them How to Fish...........................264
Day 259: What is Your Purpose for Living?.................265
Day 260: Not Again!.......................................266
Day 261: Is Your Boat Unsinkable? 267
Day 262: Pray More and Worry Less.........................268
Day 263: His Peace for Your Worries 269
Day 264: The Lamb Who Died is The Lord Who Lives 270
Day 265: Overcoming or Becoming?..........................271
Day 266: If Riches Would Change Me 272
Day 267: Walking in His Amazing Grace 273
Day 268: Pray First.......................................274
Day 269: Whatever You Are, Be a Good One..................275
Day 270: To Die For 276
Day 271: Worrier or Prayer Warrior?.......................277
Day 272: Do More Than Just Survive: Thrive 278
Day 273: Walking Alone or Following the Crowd?............279
Day 274: Love, Not Judge!.................................280
Day 275: No Mistakes......................................281
Day 276: In Pursuit of Happiness 282
Day 277: By Beholding We Are Changed 283
Day 278: The Wrong Door 284
Day 279: An All-Forgiving God 285
Day 280: Captain of My Ship 286
Day 281: Heard, Acknowledged, Understood 287
Day 282: Rejoice! 288

Day 283: Living Holy Lives 289
Day 284: Separation Anxiety 290
Day 285: Wisdom's Power 291
Day 286: Victory in Jesus 292
Day 287: Changed into His Image 293
Day 288: Father God 294
Day 289: He's True to His Word 295
Day 290: Repentance or Despair? 296
Day 291: Mindful Awareness 297
Day 292: Tell Me, Teach Me, Involve Me. 298
Day 293: A Position of Trust 299
Day 294: For This I Could Have Saved One More 300
Day 295: My Constant Companion 301
Day 296: Touching Lives for Eternity 302
Day 297: Reconciled 303
Day 298: Transformed 304
Day 299: Sin by Any Name 305
Day 300: The Midnight Cry 306
Day 301: Hope Keeps The "Ticker" Going 307
Day 302: The Many Faces of a Mother 308
Day 303: My Anxieties Stymie Me 309
Day 304: Prayer: It's the Best We Can Do 310
Day 305: Living Worry-Free 311
Day 306: An Extraordinary God 312
Day 307: A Promise Kept 313
Day 308: Over Yonder, Down By The Crystal Sea 314
Day 309: He Specializes in Cleaning up Messy Lives 315
Day 310: Countdown to Friday 316
Day 311: I Want to Get to Know You 317
Day 312: Head Over Heels in My Trust of You Lord 318
Day 313: Tender Moments 319
Day 314: He Is Still My Savior 320
Day 315: He Would Not Go In 321
Day 316: Giving Your Life to and for Christ 322
Day 317: The Wind and the Waves Obey Him 323
Day 318: Never Alone 324
Day 319: Check Your Pulse 325
Day 320: God Already Knows 326
Day 321: Making the Crooked Paths Straight 327
Day 322: What Is It About Hope? 328
Day 323: Resigned to Her Fate 329
Day 324: The Clock is Ticking 330

Table Of Contents

Day 325: Run!..331
Day 326: Love at Any Age 332
Day 327: He Couldn't Do It Alone and Neither Can We 333
Day 328: Maybe Tomorrow...................................334
Day 329: Exceeding All Expectations 335
Day 330: Celebrating the Successes of Others............336
Day 331: Stop Stretching the Truth.......................337
Day 332: Give to God What Is Right, Not What Is Left 338
Day 333: A Sign of God's Providence 339
Day 334: Surviving or Thriving?..........................340
Day 335: Finding What Is Real..............................341
Day 336: Snatched 342
Day 337: Finding Common Ground 343
Day 338: Road Rage 344
Day 339: Respect 345
Day 340: Worship Him With The Psalms...............346
Day 341: Enduring Loss 347
Day 342: The Command to Love 348
Day 343: Stand Up!...349
Day 344: I Gave My Life for You 350
Day 345: Outnumbered Two to One 351
Day 346: Lord, Please Change Me........................352
Day 347: Caught in the Rain 353
Day 348: Your Path Was Specially Chosen for You 354
Day 349: Praying for Grace and Mercy..................355
Day 350: Locked Out 356
Day 351: In the Path of the Storm 357
Day 352: What Would You Do With It?...............358
Day 353: Sitting on the Edge of Disaster 360
Day 354: There'll be Sunshine in the Morning 361
Day 355: When the News is not Good..................362
Day 356: You Are Here!......................................363
Day 357: Rest Only When the Work is Done 364
Day 358: Stay On The Path With Me....................365
Day 359: Setting the Stage for Success 366
Day 360: Speak to Me, Lord................................367
Day 361: Time Cannot Be Bought or Sold 368
Day 362: Oh, For The Peace That Christ Offers 369
Day 363: Banking Your Riches Higher Than the Attic....................370
Day 364: Who Said You Couldn't?......................372
Day 365: Warm Regards.....................................373

FOREWORD

Dear Readers,

One morning, I was running late for church and so the rest of my family went on ahead of me. About three miles from church, I saw a car ahead of me with a license plate that said Advent2. Wow, I thought, someone who believes in the second coming of Christ. I was immediately intrigued and I knew right away that I was late for a reason. I felt absolutely sure that the person in that car was heading to my church and that I was going to be the first to greet him or her. I drove behind the car for a while. However, as I am a little heavy-footed with my driving, I overtook the car but kept it in my rearview mirror. Sure enough, the car turned where I did and I was waiting at the door to meet Elvie Guthrie-Lewis.

She came up to me, confident, well dressed – everything matching as in a *Vogue* catalog – and she had the biggest, friendliest smile on her face. I immediately saw the friendship potential that was being extended with that first hello. I was not wrong. 1 Samuel 18:1 said of Jonathan and David:" As soon as he had finished speaking to Saul, the soul of Jonathan was knit to the soul of David, and Jonathan loved him as his own soul." I think that God puts us in each other's lives, because He sees that we need them and they need us. Elvie and I are alike in so many ways, and in just as many ways we are very different. In her, I recognized that God sent me a friend who was not afraid to challenge me to make my love for God, and my faith, a priority. A friend who was generous in sharing: her physical belongings, her compliments, and her life experiences. I have learned so much from her; and so, when she shared her love of writing and her dream of writing a series of devotionals, I was very impressed with her ambition, and I knew she would get it done. I was confident that God was going to use her to touch lives.

This devotional, *Warm Regards*, is full of her life stories. As her friends, we recognize ourselves in some of her writing; and in what she writes, we are further blessed by the words she has chosen to tell our stories. Our stories: our successes, and even some of our sorrows, are being used to glorify our Lord and Savior. What a blessing. What a joy. What an honor.

Each meditative story concludes with Words of Love. As you read, you can imagine what Jesus is trying to say to each of us, what He is trying to teach us in His loving, contemplative way. There is no judgment, just stories to which we can each relate; stories that will warm our hearts; stories that will nurture us, and encourage us, as we grow in our faith.

As you read this devotional each day, I challenge you to find the friend or relative in your life who epitomizes the message, and share that message with them. I pray that the thoughts from these pages, written from the heart, will change lives in profound ways. Ask God to open your heart to receive exactly what He needs you to have for the moment; and to help you boldly live out the lessons in your daily walk with Him.

Delane Lesh, Ed.D

ACKNOWLEDGMENTS

Warm Regards is dedicated to my parents, Maurice and Ernestine Guthrie. I am forever indebted to them for the sacrifices they made to provide me with the foundation of a good education. My father, who died twenty years before my mother, did not live to see me achieve the educational level to which I have attained; but he was immensely proud when I graduated teachers' college. My mother, in particular, fostered in me a love of books. They would both be ecstatic to see me achieve this dream that I have had since the young age of five years.

I am blessed to have a loving and supportive husband, Felton Lewis, who encourages me to pursue every goal I set for myself. To my sister, Joy, and my friends, especially my prayer partners, thank you for encouraging me when doubts began to set in. To my dear friend, Dr. Delane Lesh, thanks for writing the Foreword, and for your supply of ideas about which to write. I am indebted to my friends who have given me permission to include some of your stories. I have changed names, where necessary, to protect your privacy.

I thank You, Lord, for the warmth of Your love that I feel every day, and for the daily inspiration You gave me throughout the seven months of writing. You are the best Partner with whom to work; Your blessings to me are beyond measure.

I am honored to have had the privilege to retire and spend the first several months of my retirement on this project. My prayer is that it will be a blessing to every reader, and that you will be eager for the other projects that I pray will follow.

INTRODUCTION

I often feel that I hear the voice of our heavenly Father speaking to me, saying things like, "I want you to know how much I love and treasure you. You are the apple of My eye, and I want you to keep that in mind as you go through life's journey. Know that you are not alone. I left heaven and came to earth to redeem you, because My Father and I want to spend eternity with you." His inaudible voice continues, "You have been adopted into Our family, which makes you a joint heir of Our eternal home. I came to earth on a mission from the Father; to redeem you to Him. I fulfilled that mission at Calvary. When He called Me back to heaven, I left you the Holy Spirit to walk with you, instruct you and guide you; and help you to the journey's end."

Although His voice is not audible, He speaks to my heart, and He often reiterates: "Please know how much you are loved, and all I desire is your love in return. May you love Me more than life itself, and your brothers and sisters likewise." And then, His inaudible voice concludes with words like, "Warmest regards, My beloved."

These "conversations" leave me with such an inner warm glow that I have developed an affinity for "Warm Regards" as the conclusion of correspondence to loved ones and close friends. I pray that either in the words of each day's reading, or in the selected scripture texts, you will hear the Savior's voice speaking to you, saying, "Until then, My Beloved, know that you are secure in My love for you.

Warm regards, Jesus."

DAY 1
A CALL TO WORSHIP

Scripture: Today, if you will hear His voice, do not harden your hearts... Hebrews 3:7-8.

The first worship gathering of the New Year was a very rich experience for me. The early morning lesson study focused on the war that broke out in heaven, causing Lucifer, the angel of light, to fall from grace, and be cast to the earth, where he works day and night to accuse humanity. Had Lucifer's heart been focused on worship of the Creator, instead of pride and self-glory, jealousy would not have sprung up within him and set him on a path of destruction. Having lost favor with God, Satan has purposed in his heart that God will not enjoy the worship that He so desires from mankind, created in His image.

God longed to enjoy fellowship with the crown jewel of His creation; and for a period of time, scripture does not say how long, He met with Adam and Eve in the Garden of Eden, in the cool of the day, and enjoyed time with them. How beautiful must have been this time of worship and fellowship. It was a time of communion between Creator and creature, but also a time of bonding between friends.

The enemy, Satan, could not stand to see this kind of worship and adoration being given to the God of the universe. He wanted to claim the territory of our hearts for himself, so he devised a plan. He would get mankind to doubt God, and to question His directive. He implemented his plan, and it worked. Eve listened to the lies of the devil, and disobeyed God's explicit commands. Adam followed suit.

How heartbroken our Father God was, that the next time He came for His special time with His children, instead of them eagerly awaiting His usual visit, they were hiding from His presence. The deceiver of our souls has won on too many occasions, and has gotten too much time with us. Our Savior longs to restore our special time together, and so He is extending His arms of love and mercy to us, calling us back to worship, which belongs only to Him.

Words of Love: Make a joyful shout to the Lord, all you Lands! Serve the Lord with gladness; Come before His presence with singing.... Psalm 100

DAY 2
JUST WALK AWAY

Scripture: Do not offer any part of yourselves to sin as instruments of wickedness, but rather offer yourselves to God as those who have been brought from death to life; and offer every part of yourselves to Him as instruments of righteousness. Romans 6:13

Mankind suffers from all kinds of addictions: some seemingly more damaging than others, but all having negative impacts on others and/or the addict. How I hate to hear the word "addict," and never thought it would ever be applied to me, but I am not immune. No, I am not an alcoholic, and neither am I a drug addict. I am not addicted to porn, food, exercise, computer or work. Maybe to work... for over forty years, but that is not the addiction that afflicts my very soul.

A dear friend once described me as a "Benevolent Shopaholic." She was very gracious with that description, because I will buy for anyone I believe can benefit from the bargains that I see. She jokingly said she would not pray for me to gain victory, because she would be cutting off her source of blessing. The problem is that she, like me, and many others for whom I shop, can do just fine without my purchases. Another friend more accurately describes such a habit as "redundant buying."

I have prayed for victory many times, and I wish I could tell you that success has been achieved; but it is a daily battle. We have been admonished to lay up treasures in heaven, where moth and rust cannot destroy. Yes, I may be a generous giver, but what good does it do for God's kingdom to give where it is not needed, and sometimes not even wanted, while the needs of the poor go unmet?

So, I invite you to join me in this day's commitment to walk away from that sin (addiction) that so easily besets us. Is it easy? Absolutely not... but is it possible? A profound **yes**. With God, all things are possible, and so we pray for His help... just for today. We will take it one day at a time and remember to thank Him each time He strengthens us to just walk away.

Words of Love: If the Son therefore shall make you free, you shall be free indeed. John 8:36

DAY 3
GOD IS REACHING OUT

Scripture: For of this I am sure, He who started a good work in you will carry it on to completion, until the day of Christ Jesus. Philippians 1:6

Where are you in your faith journey? Do you feel like a baby, needing the milk of God's Word, and needing a caregiver to feed you and prevent starvation at worst, but malnutrition at best? Are you progressing to solid food, but still need it soft to prevent choking? Or, have you matured to all textures? Do you know where the food is, and how to obtain it to satisfy your hunger? Wherever you are in your Christian development, God has just what you need to enhance your spiritual growth.

Christ's hands are not short. He is eager to connect with you, and is willing to make the first move. When you are weak, He wants to strengthen you; when you are weary and tired, He is begging you to rest in Him; when you are hungry, Christ the bread of life offers you food; when you are thirsty He says, "Come drink from the fountain of life;" when you feel dejected and hopeless, He offers you hope; when you are faint from life's struggles, He picks you up and carries you to a place of safety.

The Savior is waiting to enter your heart, why don't you let Him come in? He is reaching out, gently knocking and eagerly desiring entrance so that He can improve your situation, but respectfully refusing to force His way in against your will. Jesus wants to bring restoration to your broken life; to restore your broken relationships as well as your broken dreams. Take hold of His outstretched hands… He is reaching out today.

Words of Love: Praying always with all prayer and supplication in the Spirit, and watching thereunto with all perseverance and supplication … Ephesians 6:18

DAY 4
BEST FRIENDS

Scripture: Behold, I stand at the door, and knock: if any man hears My voice, and open the door, I will come in to him, and will sup with him, and he with Me. Revelation 3:20

What have your friendship experiences been like? Do you have someone on whom you can call when you are sad, someone who will pray with you; someone with whom you can share a silly moment and who will laugh with you; or someone who will lovingly point you in the right direction when you have messed up, or to prevent you from messing up? I am blessed to have some very dear friends. They all impact my life in different, yet profound ways, and I value the contributions of each one to our relationship. I would be hesitant, therefore, to single out any one as my best friend.

Some of these friends are prayer partners; some are traveling companions. Some shop for me, others are shopping buddies, and others I shop for, because they don't like to shop. My friends and I laugh and cry together, and provide each other with honest counsel that is sometimes hard to hear, but always a blessing to accept.

I place great value on the friendships I enjoy with these ladies and the others in my network of friends. One thing is certain: we are confident in our friendship and the love we have for each other.

When I am hurting, some of my friends hurt so much for me that they would be quick to challenge those who have caused me pain. Some friends I talk with daily, others weekly, and others will just call periodically to say, "You have been on my mind and I love you." We are all created for relationships with others, and we are a happier people for these friendships. A special "Thank You" to all my beloved friends.

Jesus wants to be our Best Friend, our "Bosom Buddy;" closer than a brother, a sister, or any earthly friend, no matter how close they are. The scripture tells us that even when a mother will likely forget her sucking child, our Heavenly Father will not forget us. Jesus longs for the kind of relationship with us where we can lay on His breast, and share our simplest thought and our greatest dream. He promises never to leave us or forsake us. He is only a whisper away. Yes, He simply wants to be our Best Friend.

Words of Love: Come unto Me all you who labor and are heavy laden, and I will give you rest. Take My yoke upon you, and learn of Me; for I am meek and lowly in heart: and you will find rest unto your souls. Matthew 11:28-29

DAY 5
YOU ASKED AND I ANSWERED... NOW WHAT?

Scripture: Trust in The Lord with all your heart and lean not on your own understanding. In all your ways acknowledge Him, and he shall direct your path. Proverbs 3:5-6

Have you ever prayed earnestly about something, truly desiring God's leading, and then when you proceeded as you thought He was guiding, you fell flat on your face? You cried out, Lord, what was Your purpose? How could You stand by and let things go the way they did? Lord, I thought we had an understanding. I kept my part of the agreement, but You have not kept Yours.

What a patient, kind, loving and merciful Savior we have, who will allow us to vent our frustrations with Him. Instead of "zapping" us for insubordination to Deity, He strives with us and gently says, "You asked, and I have answered." "True, it does not look like what you asked for, and thought I approved, but wait and see the fulfillment of your request. What I have in store will blow your mind."

Lord, that was an earful, and I receive it with gratitude. Your ways are truly higher than my ways, and Your thoughts than my thoughts. I will obediently stand still, and watch to see how You work things for my good, and the glory of Your kingdom.

Words of Love: Now to Him who is able to do exceedingly abundantly above all that we ask or think, according to the power that works in us, to Him *be* glory in the church by Christ Jesus to all generations, forever and ever. Amen. Ephesians 3:20-21

DAY 6
WHEN GOD SAID NO

Scripture: My God, My God, why have You forsaken Me? Matthew 27:46

Christ was agonizing in the Garden of Gethsemane, and begging the Father to take away the impending death that was facing Him. He prayed until His sweat was as drops of blood; but the Father said a firm "No." Think for a moment, after the initial horror of the thought that a child is begging a parent to come to his rescue, and the parent turns his back, the real reason that God said "No."

I am reminded of a commercial where a family's home was on fire. The parents watched from the lawn as their little girl, standing at an upstairs window, begged them to save her. They refused, stating that she was not the dutiful child she should have been. This was not the reason that our Father God said no to the pleading of His Son and our Savior, Jesus Christ. It was actually out of love for a desperate and destitute humanity that God said no. Had He rescued His Son, He would not have been our Savior. Instead, we would have been a lost people, with no hope of eternal salvation.

So, the next time you think that "no" is such a bad word, pause for a moment and ponder your need for a savior. Then thank God for suffering through the heartbreak of having to turn His back on the cries of His Only Begotten Son, and watching Him die on an old rugged cross, for people who did not know their need for, or want, a savior. After you have thanked the Father, then thank Jesus, whose prayer did not stop with a request to escape the cross. With a firm resolve to go through with the mission for which He came to earth, He concluded with the words, "Not my will but Thine Father be done."

The next time you pray for something and God says no, trust Him that in His wisdom, He sees the big picture and is working out your "salvation," doing what is best for you. The scripture reassures us that, could we see the end of our journey, we would ask to have been led no other way than God has led us. What a comforting feeling to know that someone loves us so much, and takes such a personal interest in our lives, that He is willing to endure our wrath and indignation to save us by saying no to requests that are not in our best interest. Even if it is difficult, stop and thank Him. Tell Him that although you don't understand it, you are going to trust Him with childlike faith. What joy that will bring to His heart.

Words of Love: When Jesus heard that, He said to them, those who are well have no need of a physician, but those who are sick. Matthew 9:12.

DAY 7
RAISING A WHITE FLAG

Scripture: I have been crucified with Christ; it is no longer I who live, but Christ lives in me; and the life which I now live in the flesh I live by faith in the Son of God, who loved me and gave Himself for me. Galatians 2:20

In a war, when the enemy raises a white flag, it is usually a sign of surrender. This gesture indicates that one army knows the other army is effectively victorious and they are defeated. Instead of holding out any longer, delaying needed relief and possibly even increasing the casualties, the defeated side says, "We are putting down our weapons and surrendering to you."

Christ is waiting for us to hold up the white flag of total surrender to His control. Unlike the devil, whose desire is to enslave us, when we surrender to Jesus Christ, He will set us free.

I visited a detention camp in Denmark, close to the border with Germany. If the story is true, Denmark established that camp to prevent the Germans from taking Danish prisoners to concentration camps in Germany, where their fate would be worse. It has been said that we are all slaves to one force or another. Let us run to the camp of Christ Jesus. We will find safety there.

Words of Love: For whoever desires to save his life will lose it, but whoever loses his life for My sake and the gospel's will save it. Mark 8:35

DAY 8
SOME MUCH NEEDED REST

Scripture: And He said, "My Presence will go with you, and I will give you rest." Exodus 33:14

Sometimes, what we need to rejuvenate and restore us is a little rest and relaxation. We can then return to the business at hand with new vigor and direction, and a clearer sense of purpose. Christ Himself frequently needed physical rest. He would sometimes leave His disciples and go off alone to spend time with His Father. At other times, after He had met the demands of the crowd that thronged Him, He would invite His disciples to "come aside and rest."

Rest is one of the elements of a healthy life. I believe all of God's creation was meant to rest. Even the ground, if overworked in farming, tends not to yield as it could, and in Bible times they were encouraged to give the earth a season of rest. Many diseases are exacerbated by the body's lack of rest.

There is an equally significant rest that is needed for that wellness that we aspire to attain. It is an emotional rest. Studies have shown that emotional stress has a lasting negative impact on the human body. You sometimes hear people say that situations in their lives are causing them "duress." What we need is the presence of Christ, who calmed the storm on the Sea of Galilee. When He enters into our circumstances, He provides the calm we need. As the well-known song *Peace Be Still* says, "Master the tempest is raging, the billows are tossing high." Just as Jesus was able to rest in the boat amidst the raging storm, He calls you and me to both a physical and an emotional rest in Him.

Words of Love: Come to me, all of you who are weary and carry heavy burdens, and I will give you rest. Matthew 11:28

DAY 9
ONE, TWO, THREE!

Scripture: So teach us to number our days, that we may gain a heart of wisdom. Psalm 90:12

What is to be gained from numbering our days? I believe it is the reality of how fragile and fleeting life really is. With this reality comes a greater appreciation for the days we have been given, "The line between the dots." We have had myriad opinions on the subject; i.e., live each day as though it was your last; it is not what you take from life, but rather what contributions you have made to it that will be remembered, etc. Each of us is a unique creation, made for a special purpose. We have been equipped with special talents and abilities to accomplish the tasks we have been called to fulfill.

The question we must each ask ourselves is whether or not we have accepted the charge to carry out our special assignment. None of us is asked to fulfill duties assigned to someone else. The story is told of a man traveling to a far country, who called his servants and gave each one assigned property (talents) according to his ability. On his return, they were called to give an account of their handling of the master's goods entrusted to them.

The one who had been given the greatest amount had invested it wisely and had doubled the master's holdings; the second servant had done likewise, and had earned an increase for the master. The third servant, however, was jealous and slothful. He felt that the master deserved no more than he had left behind. His thinking was that he had not lost anything, he had simply kept the master's goods locked away safe and sound.

Life was not intended to be lived "safely," sitting in the pews, and feeding on manna every day. There is work to be done that requires our talents, wisely used, to accomplish them. There is a song titled, "Work for the night is coming," by Anna Coghill, which alludes to the fact that we will no longer be able to work at that time. When will your night be? None of us know the hour of that second dot; the close of our day...so what are we waiting for, to make a difference? Let's not waste another precious day, as the countdown to the final dot begins: three... two... one.

Words of Love: Since his days are determined, the number of his months is with You; You have appointed his limits, so that he cannot pass. Job 14:5

DAY 10
EYES TO SEE

Scripture: Jesus said to her, "Did I not say to you that if you would believe you would see the glory of God?" John 11:40

Pause for a moment and look around you. Put on your goggles of faith. God's glory is everywhere. There are miracles unfolding before your eyes, waiting to be discovered and shared. This morning I woke up to rain, and I was reminded of how rain is formed as the result of water droplets gathering together in the clouds, and gravity causing them to fall to the ground as rain. That is a miracle that we often overlook. Then my mind turned to the beautiful trees all around me; the oak tree being one example.

A small acorn falls to the ground, having the DNA of a mighty tree, and with the right elements of nutrient-rich soil, water, and sunlight, the Almighty performs another miracle, and from that seed springs a small twig that grows into a magnificent tree. What about the miracle of the natural sleep cycle... amazing by any stretch of the imagination. Our eyelids become tired and close, then without any help from us, they open and we are awake... simply a miracle. Don't overlook the small miracles of love and kindness expressed in numerous ways. It is not the natural tendency of man to be and do good, so each act of mercy and kindness is a miracle orchestrated by God.

Let me share with you a story of the miracle of a changed heart: Jimmy was a privileged and rebellious teenager, who made many wrong choices, influenced by peers who were equally privileged. They caused many annoyances at best, and some real destruction of the neighborhood at the worst. An encounter one day turned Jimmy's heart around. Forgiveness was sought and obtained, restitution was made, and a life on a trajectory of failure was redirected to God and a life of service. That is what I call miraculous.

Miracles... they are everywhere, just waiting for eyes to be opened to them, through faith. Lord, my prayer today is, please give me eyes to see all that you have done for me, and may the wonder of it all cause me to sing Your praise.

Words of Love: For it is the God who commanded light to shine out of darkness, who has shone in our hearts to give the light of the knowledge of the glory of God in the face of Jesus Christ. 2 Corinthians 4:6

DAY 11
OH, THE WONDER OF IT ALL

Scripture: Many, O Lord my God, are Your wonderful works which You have done; And Your thoughts toward us cannot be recounted to You in order; If I would declare and speak of them, they are more than can be numbered. Psalm 40:5

When was the last time you stopped and considered God's great love for you? Rachel was a woman on a mission to spread an awareness of the love of Christ for His trying and dying children. She could not contain herself, and wanted to tell everyone of the joy she had found in God's forgiveness.

Rachel had felt God's calling on her life at an early age, and she had even considered going overseas as a student missionary, but the pull of the world had gotten in the way, and she had walked away from God. For years, she lived the fast life: alcohol, drugs and even prostitution. She is the first to admit that she had fallen far from what her life ambition had been, as a new Christian in her teen years.

Thanks to a praying family, and a loving and forgiving God, Rachel could feel the struggle for her soul. At times, it seemed as though the devil had a firm grip, and was dragging her down to utter destruction; but just when it seemed that all hope was lost, she felt the gentle but firm grasp of the Savior, and heard His tender voice wooing her back to His arms.

Finally, in an act of desperation, Rachel ran to a treatment center, where she received the help she so desperately needed. Her broken and emaciated body was healed; but more importantly, her broken spirit and wounded soul were restored. Today she is fulfilling her missionary dreams close to home. She is ministering to the people among whom she once lived; and seeing the joy in her changed life, many are being drawn into a relationship with Jesus Christ.

Words of Love: The Lord has appeared of old to me, saying: "Yes, I have loved you with an everlasting love; Therefore, with lovingkindness I have drawn you..." Jeremiah 31:3

DAY 12
PERFECT PEACE... WHERE?

Scripture: You will keep him in perfect peace, whose mind is stayed on You, because he trusts in You. Isaiah 26:3

Life is infiltrated by trials and temptations, wars and strife; and there does not seem to be peace anywhere. A recent documentary chronicled some of the most beautiful places on earth; places of "peace and tranquility." One such place was the Seychelles. To maintain the natural feel of the island paradise, cars are discouraged, and ox carts or bicycles are the preferred mode of transportation. But even there, perfect peace is not attained. One article states that the Seychelles attracts some wealthy visitors, making it a prime target for pirates.

Find your choicest place on the planet for peace and serenity, then research it for crime, ecosystem, etc.; what you will quickly find is the disappointing fact that every place has its challenges. So where does one find perfect peace? There is only one place, and that is in the arms of Jesus Christ.

Peace is not found in people, places or things; but rather in an experience with the Master Peace Giver, Jesus Christ. An encounter with people, places and things often leaves one empty, but an experience with Jesus Christ is filling, invigorating, and all-sustaining. The pirate of our soul is always in the periphery, looking for weak spots where he can penetrate. Once he is allowed to enter, the Holy Spirit will not entertain co-occupancy, so we will have to make a choice. Satan does not take eviction graciously, and will fight to retain residency. If you want peace, however, you will have to employ all resources at your disposal to get him out. Once he is out, fill that space quickly by inviting the Holy Spirit to take up permanent residence there.

Words of Love: I have told you these things, so that in Me you may have peace. In this world, you will have trouble; But be of good courage, I have overcome the world. John 16:33

DAY 13
WHAT'S THE DELAY?

Scripture: So, Jacob served seven years for Rachel, and they seemed only a few days to him because of the love he had for her. Genesis 29:20

Patience is a virtue. That is all well and good when you are not the one who has to wait. Isn't that how most of us feel? The story is told of a father whose child was in a crisis, for which the family wanted immediate relief. The medical team explained that they were awaiting the results of some additional tests, to determine the best course of action.

The impatient family insisted on a quick fix, using only the results of the first test as the basis for their decision. After raising a ruckus, with threats of malpractice lawsuits for negligence, the hospital had them sign documents declaring their choice, and releasing the facility and providers of any wrongdoing. The procedure was done and a measure of relief was obtained. Victory achieved for the family, you say. But, wait... not so fast. The results of all the other tests indicated that such a drastic and permanent measure as was chosen by the family was not necessary, and certainly was not the best option.

Patience is truly a virtue, and one to be embraced, especially when it comes to issues of our eternal salvation. The all-knowing God has warning signs all along the path of life, and encourages us to patiently observe them to navigate treacherous paths more easily. He never promised that there would be no delays, but simply asked that we follow His guidance. Don't rush after the quick fixes of life. There are no shortcuts to true happiness. What may seem like a delay may just be the right elements being put in place to ensure the best outcome.

Words of Love: Wait on the Lord; Be of good courage, and He shall strengthen your heart; Wait, I say, on the Lord! Psalm 27:14

DAY 14
AHH!

Scripture: The heavens declare the glory of God; And the firmament shows His handiwork. Psalm 19:1

The beauty of God's creation takes my breath away. One evening a friend came to dinner and brought me four of the most gorgeous roses in multiple shades of orange. We all "oohed and aahed" at their magnificent form and spectacular beauty. They would soon fade and be discarded, however. When compared to all the beauty of this earth, they were miniscule.

There is no denying that this earth has been scarred by sin, and that what we see now is nothing compared to what Eden lost was like, or what Eden restored will be. But there is still enough beauty around us to fill us with a sense of awe, and create in us a longing for an eternity of wonders to explore.

Take an imaginary walk with me to a few places that are sure to take your breath away: Niagara Falls, with its cascading water of some 9 million gallons per minute; the Grand Canyon with its colorful striations of rock; the Alps filled with snow-covered peaks surrounded by jutting spires of rock and deep valleys with pristine lakes.

There is one awesome wonder that does not require much, if any, travel from wherever in the world you live. It is the wonder of sunrise and sunset. There is only one thing more awe-inspiring to me than the scenes we have just explored. It is the knowledge that the Creator of all these spectacular beauties prepared them for the crown jewel of His creation to enjoy, because of His great love for us. Today, be awed by the beauty that surrounds us; but ultimately, be awed by how much God loves you and me, and let us be inspired to love Him in return.

Words of Love: Let the heavens rejoice, and let the earth be glad; Let the sea roar, and all its fullness; Let the field be joyful, and all that is in it. Then all the trees of the woods will rejoice before the Lord. Psalm 96:11-12

DAY 15
WHEN IS IT A GOOD TIME?

Scripture: For He says "In an acceptable time I have heard you, and in the day of salvation I have helped you." Behold, now is the accepted time; behold, now is the day of salvation. 2 Corinthians 6:2

Are you a procrastinator, always putting off for tomorrow what you do not want to do today? The following have been cited as some of the reasons why people procrastinate:
- Fear
- Self-doubt
- Intimidation
- Feelings of inadequacy
- Lack of resources

And what is one of the solutions to resolve this grave defeater? It seems too simple a solution: Begin. Whatever the task that lies ahead of you, small or great, there must be a starting point, a groundbreaking, as it were. A plan must be developed, the ground must be broken, the foundation must be laid, and brick upon brick the structure must be framed.

It is as true for our prayer life as it is in any other area or task to be accomplished. The plan is the path to salvation, and the beauty is that the Savior has already done not only the blueprint, but He has laid the foundation for us. There was the First Advent; thirty-three years of exemplary living for us to follow; Gethsemane; Calvary; the Resurrection and the Ascension.

Salvation is free, but I must take hold of it. I build on the foundation that Christ has laid through daily prayer and a study of God's word. The foundation sometimes lies bare for days, weeks, months, or years. The progress we make on that "building" is up to each of us. The Master Builder is always available, and He will never leave us apprentices alone, but neither will He usurp our rights as homeowners. So, when do you want to start on your building? Today is as good a time as any.

Words of Love: Then He said to him, "A certain man gave a great supper and invited many, and sent his servant at supper time to say to those who were invited, 'Come, for all things are now ready'..." Luke 14:16-24

DAY 16
A TIME AND A PLACE

Scripture: To everything there is a season, a time for every purpose under heaven...
 Ecclesiastes 3:1-8

All my life, I have been very structured, sometimes even perceived as being regimented. It has taken me a while, but I have been learning gradually to go more with the flow. I still believe in a place for everything and everything in its place, and I still believe in timeliness, even though I am adjusting nicely to a "new normal" in my retirement.

It is not news, though, that God desires to meet with us. He is not really worried about the place, but He loves to meet with us often. As a matter of fact, He would treasure a 24/7 relationship with us, and it is possible through the person of the Holy Spirit. I can just imagine His excitement when we invite Him in to spend time with us. Where do you like to "chill," to get your anxiety level down, and your heart quieted? Is it by the sea, watching the waves crest, or by a mountain brook, listening to the trickling water? Is it in a park, watching children swing, and walkers meander along the trails? Does your life prohibit much or any quiet time, as you merge into busy traffic or jostle for shoulder space on packed busses and commuter trains?

Whatever your circumstances, and wherever your special place may be, make it a priority to incorporate Christ into your daily life. He is an awesome companion, and He enjoys spending time with us.

Words of Love: And if I go and prepare a place for you, I will come again and receive you to Myself; that where I am, there you may be also. John 14:3

DAY 17
EMPTY PROMISES

Scripture: Again, the devil took Him up on an exceedingly high mountain, and showed Him all the kingdoms of the world and their glory. And he said to Him, "All these things I will give You if You will fall down and worship me." Matthew. 4:8-9

Satan offered Christ what did not belong to him. Jesus Christ created the universe. He owns and sustains everything.

Nathan was introduced to Jane by a mutual friend. He was handsome, well-dressed, smooth-talking, and a "ladies' man." The truth is, he was a wolf in sheep's clothing, a con artist. But how was Jane to know? She was immediately smitten.

Jane was well-educated, accomplished, and making strides up the corporate ladder, but she was lonely. She had several failed relationships, and she was feeling desperate. Nathan pursued her. He was from another state and frequently flew into town to visit her. He brought her beautiful gifts and flowers, and took her to elaborate places to dine. After a short while, some unnerving signs presented themselves, but Jane brushed them aside. Eventually the unpleasant truths about Nathan was revealed.

There are many in world like Nathan and Satan himself, making empty promises and offering things that do not belong to them. Father God, You alone are trustworthy, and offer us that which belongs to You, including eternal life. May we be quick to accept your offer, knowing that You will never disappoint us.

Words of Love: For all the promises of God in Him are Yes, and in Him Amen, to the glory of God through us. 2 Corinthians 1:20

DAY 18
SETBACKS AND COMEBACKS

Scripture: Therefore, do not cast away your confidence, which has great reward. For you have need of endurance, so that after you have done the will of God, you may receive the promise. Hebrews 10:35-36

There is great truth in the saying, "Every setback is a setup for a comeback."

Marlin's life is a testament to that saying. He was harassed on the job and eventually left. At first, he was heartbroken, and questioned God as to why He had led him in that direction, when he had prayed for His guidance. In a period of intense prayer and seeking after God, Marlin was led to the story of the Israelites who had to leave Egypt because of Pharaoh's harsh treatment. They did not want to leave, but the treatment they endured was so harsh that God knew leaving was the only way to save them, and return them to the Promised Land. Through a series of orchestrated events, it came time for their departure.

When they came to the Red Sea, there were obstacles before them and on both sides. Then they looked behind and their hearts sank as they saw the Egyptians bearing down on them. They felt trapped and cried out to Moses, "Why have you brought us here to die?" The word of the Lord came back saying, "Stand still and see the salvation of your God, for the Egyptians that you see today, tomorrow you will see them no more." What seemed like a failure to God's people was an opportunity for them to see God work strong and mightily on their behalf.

Marlin was encouraged, and he sought God for guidance and direction. He asked God to close every door that would prevent him from glorifying the Creator. Before long, God opened opportunities that far exceeded Marlin's expectations. His severance package was better than he expected, and he obtained work at rates beyond what he had ever earned in his long professional career.

Words of Love: Blessed is the man who endures temptation; for when he has been approved, he will receive the crown of life which the Lord has promised to those who love Him. James 1:12

DAY 19
PREPARING FOR TOMORROW

Scripture: Sow for yourselves righteousness; Reap in mercy; Break up your fallow ground, For it is time to seek the Lord, till He comes and rains righteousness on you. Hosea 10:12

When Allie was young, she wanted to learn to play the piano, but she did not want to put the time in to practice. She whined when her mother made her practice the same notes repeatedly when she messed up. Mother had a favorite saying that she repeated many times throughout the years, "The greatest preparation for tomorrow is doing your best today." Allie grew older and wanted to play on the varsity team, but again, she complained that she was not good enough; the practice was too long, too hard, too boring or some other concocted reason to get out of putting in the required time. Once again, Mother repeated her "overused" saying as Allie perceived it.

Mother would not let up, however. She held Allie accountable for putting in the time required to be the best she could be. She did not compare her to anyone else's standard, and measured her ability only by the level of effort she had demonstrated. Allie soon learned that mediocrity would not be accepted by her parents. Her dad did not say very much, but wholeheartedly supported the standards set by the mother.

Allie not only led her varsity team to a successful championship season, but she eventually became the CEO of a very successful company, and an accomplished concert pianist. Over the years of achieving many successes, Allie said she could literally hear her mother's voice in her head saying, "Allie, the greatest preparation for tomorrow is doing your best today." Extend yourself to your fullest capability today, and depend on Christ alone to set the limits of your achievements.

Words of Love: Every good gift and every perfect gift is from above, and comes down from the Father of lights, with whom there is no variation or shadow of turning. James 1:17

DAY 20

THE TRUE MEANING OF COURAGE

Scripture: Have I not commanded you? Be strong and of good courage; do not be afraid, nor be dismayed, for the Lord your God is with you wherever you go. Joshua 1:9

I watched a posthumous award to a young man who had shown tremendous courage to save the lives of others, for which he paid the ultimate price: his young life. There were not many dry eyes in the audience, and I want to believe not many were dry in homes around the county. I know I could not contain my tears.

What does it take to show the kind of courage where you voluntarily run into a burning home or car, jump into raging floodwaters, or put your life at risk in any manner to save the life of another? I tell you what it takes: it takes love; the love of Christ that surpasses the love of self.

Christ has set the example for us to follow. There is no fear in love, for perfect love casts out all fear. Christ did not want to go to Calvary, but His great love for humanity gave Him the courage to face His darkest hour. Many human beings have walked the road of sacrifice for others, but only the sacrifice of Jesus Christ offers us eternal life.

I sometimes wonder about the lives for which others have courageously and lovingly sacrificed theirs. How do those who were saved then live their lives? I always follow up those moments of questioning with the self-searching question: How am I living, loving and serving to show my gratitude for the courageous sacrifice Christ made for me on the cross? He took my place and yours: so, ask yourself the same question. I pray that it makes a difference as to how you live the rest of your life.

Words of Love: Be strong and of good courage, do not fear nor be afraid of them; for the Lord your God, He is the One who goes with you. He will not leave you nor forsake you. Deuteronomy 31:6

DAY 21
STANDING IN THE GAP

Scripture: I looked for someone among them who would build up the wall and stand before me in the gap on behalf of the land so I would not have to destroy it, but I found no one. Ezekiel 22:30

Standing in the gap for others has gotten me in plenty of trouble during my younger years, and I was often told that I should be an attorney or a union representative. There are a vast number of people who live in the shadows, feeling downtrodden by others in authority or those who have a stronger voice. Someone had to stand in the gap for them, even if that someone was me.

I was a freshman at an all-girls boarding school. Under the clock, on the quadrangle, was a notorious spot for student punishment and public humiliation. On this particular day, the punishment was meted out by the principal herself. The unfortunate student had to stand under the clock, in her uniform, during supper; while the entire student body ate, and gawked at her, wondering what she had done.

A cardinal rule of the school was that, for the evening meal, everyone had to be changed out of their uniform. Having suffered a similar experience, I had empathy for my fellow student and decided to intervene. The intervention was intense, but successful.

We have an Advocate, in the person of Jesus. He is familiar with all our suffering and grief, and He can empathize. He stands before the Father, and vets every accusation hurled at us by the devil. He does not make excuses for our sins, but says, "For him, and for her, I died. With my very blood, I paid the ransom. Their debt has been fully compensated. Their sins are forgiven."

Words of Love: My dear children, I am writing this to you so that you will not sin. But if anyone does sin, we have an advocate who pleads our case before the Father. He is Jesus Christ, the one who is truly righteous. 1 John 2:1

DAY 22
DETERMINING THE OUTCOME

Scripture: For I know that my Redeemer lives, And He shall stand at last on the earth; And after my skin is destroyed, this I know, that in my flesh I shall see God, Job 19:25-26

It has been said that life is ten percent what happens to you, and ninety percent how you handle what actually happens. It is all about attitude.

Karen and Josie were in a major accident that left them both equally scarred on the outside. What was different, however, were the internal scars, or lack of them, that they each carried.

Karen purposed in her heart that she would give her circumstances to God. She would not be defined by her external appearance. She maintained an attitude of gratitude, and lived each day believing that there was a purpose to her life. Her positive attitude and zest for life were a testimony to all who met her. It did not take long for people to look beyond her physical appearance and embrace the personality of confidence, love and kindness that she exuded.

Karen entered college, where she applied herself with the same attitude she approached other aspects of her life, and she excelled and succeeded at the top of her classes. Later, some procedures became available to help her conditions, and she was a prime candidate. Today, Karen shares her testimony with all who will listen: "when life gives you lemon, make the best lemonade or lemon meringue pie that you can."

Josie, on the other hand, was bitter and blamed God. She became a recluse and took up habits that led to her rapid decline. She could not get past her external appearance and physical handicaps. Her self-imposed limitations, substance abuse, and depression made her ineligible for the procedures from which Karen benefited. Regrettably, Josie's attitude was what led to her early demise.

We are told in the word of God that trials will come to His children, as they did to Biblical characters like Joseph, Daniel, and the three Hebrew boys, among others. We are not immune to suffering. What we are promised, however, is that God will remain by our side, and His companionship gives us hope for a better and brighter day ahead. Let faith and hope change the outcome for you.

Words of Love: For to this you were called, because Christ also suffered for us, leaving us an example, that you should follow His steps: 1 Peter 2:21

DAY 23
ENTERING INTO ANOTHER'S EXPERIENCE

Scripture: Then Jesus answered and said: "A certain man went down from Jerusalem to Jericho, and fell among thieves, who stripped him of his clothing, wounded him, and departed, leaving him half dead.... On the next day, when he departed, he took out two denarii, gave them to the innkeeper, and said to him, 'Take care of him; and whatever more you spend, when I come again, I will repay you.' Luke 10:30-35

The Golden Rule states, "Do unto others, as you would have them do unto you." The word "empathy" means to psychologically identify with the feelings, thoughts or experiences of another person. Both of these expressions are captured in the story of the Good Samaritan.

I am always impressed with heroic stories of people who overextend themselves to do a good deed for someone else. What saddens me is when the person who has been rescued or saved makes light of the second chance they have been given; especially if the hero lost his or her life in the process. Like the Good Samaritan in the Bible story, heroes do not think of the consequences to themselves, and they shy away from the spotlight and accolades. They simply see a need and jump into action to help. When they live to be interviewed, they are quick to say that they do not consider themselves as heroes. Sometimes, unfortunately, though unsuccessful, they die trying to help prevent a tragedy.

Like the hero in the story of the Good Samaritan, Casey rushed to the scene of the disaster, left by the earthquake, in a neighboring community. He did not ask questions about the victims' race, religion, caste, gender, age, culture, or sexual orientation, before volunteering his service. It did not matter to him who they were. Casey recognized that we are all brothers and sisters, created by Christ in His image, and having the same life blood running through our veins. He worked tirelessly alongside first responders in the search and rescue efforts.

Casey used up the little leave that he had on his job and went into unpaid leave, but he refused to quit until the job was done. One day Casey was observed standing a short distance away from the operation center, very emotionally distraught. His long hours and arduous efforts to save a small child did not produce the desired result. He knew that another family who was so hopeful would be utterly heartbroken; and he felt like he had personally failed them.

There were many successes attributed to Casey's and the other volunteers' tireless and selfless efforts. When the incident commander finally called off all rescue efforts, and went into recovery mode, the volunteers were dismissed with many thanks for their assistance and support. Casey hung around for a while longer, still hoping for one more rescue. In the stillness that ensued, God blessed Casey's keen hearing with the sound of a weak voice crying, "Someone, please help me." The rescue efforts resumed, and one last lone survivor was found in an area which had a small air pocket, after more than a week of rescue efforts. She had been in and out of consciousness, which may have helped her survive for so long.

Casey was tired and sore from the physical nature of the disaster relief efforts, but his heart was light with the joy of service. He credited his perseverance to his strong relationship with the Creator and Redeemer, who left the comforts of heaven to rescue a dying world. In an effort to save us, Christ entered into our experience, and now He extends His loving arms to us daily, gently encouraging us to hold on, for His help is on the way.

Words of Love: To do righteousness and justice is more acceptable to the Lord than sacrifice. Proverbs 21:3

DAY 24
DRAWING ON RESERVES

Scripture: Cast thy bread upon the waters: for thou shalt find it after many days. Give a portion to seven, and also to eight; for thou knowest not what evil shall be upon the earth. Ecclesiastes 11:1-2

"Daniel," Jane called hesitantly from the kitchen counter, where she was reading the mail, "how much do we have in the bank?"

"Why do you ask?" Daniel called back to her.

Jane went on to explain that they had just gotten a request for assistance from an organization that did a lot of good for the needy in their community.

Daniel and Jane lived on a fixed income, but believed in putting away something each month for that "rainy day." This was one of those days, and thankfully they had a little reserve from which to draw. There was a time in Daniel and Jane's life when they needed a hand to reach out to them, and they received the help they needed from others. They pledged then to always put something away to assist the less fortunate. They have been faithful to that promise, and many have been the recipients of their spirit of giving.

Something else comes to mind when I think of drawing on reserves. I think of the times when I was in school and diligently preparing for exams. I would read, take pop quizzes and mock exams, listen to tapes and watch videos, employing multiple means, based on the subject matter. I would include prayer; asking God to bring to my recollection what I had studied. At the time of the exam, I would draw on the reserves from the deposits I had made over days, weeks and months. Had I not put anything into my memory bank, there would have been nothing from which to draw.

So it is with our spiritual bank account. We must constantly make deposits through the reading of God's word; through listening to or watching doctrinally sound messages; through praying to our Creator God; through encouraging interpersonal relationships. We must build a bond of trust with our Best Friend Jesus. Then when life's struggles get really rough; when the tests come that we would otherwise fail; when there is barely enough to meet our own needs, but the needs of others are greater; we find that we have some reserves in the bank from which to draw. Father, may we be faithful in making frequent deposits in Your eternal bank. We are confident that You will supply rich dividends.

Words of Love: My son, attend unto my wisdom, and bow thine ear to my understanding. Proverbs 5:1

DAY 25
DIGGING IN THE WEEDS

Scripture: A froward man soweth strife: and a whisperer separateth chief friends. Proverbs 16:28

Mrs. Armstrong was on her way to the corner store, when she noticed young Mark sitting amidst the weeds in the overgrown lawn. What was even more strange was that he had small garden tools and what appeared to be a large magnifying glass. He was intently digging and looking, oblivious to the elderly neighbor's greeting. Mrs. Armstrong paused and called out to Mark several times before she got his attention.

"What are you doing?" she asked Mark.

"Just looking," was the casual reply.

"Just looking, with a shovel and magnifying glass?" Mrs. Armstrong probed.

"Yes, just seeing what I find," was Mark's response, as he continued his pursuit of weed digging.

Mrs. Armstrong smiled warmly at Mark as she went on her way to the store. Later that day, she was spending some quiet time with her Best Friend. It was time that she cherished and made accommodation for every day. She began to reflect on the discord that was taking place between some dear friends of hers. The conflict had torn the group apart, and was breaking her heart. She thought about some of the stories that were being passed around, and her mind went back to young Mark's activity, and the comment that he had made, he was just "digging in the weeds to see what he could find."

Now, isn't that the work of the devil? she thought. *Always digging in the weeds to see what "dirt" can be found on someone in an effort to stir up strife.*

God's Word encourages us to think good thoughts, and speak kind words of others. Exodus 20:16 admonishes us not to bear false witness against our neighbors. Mrs. Armstrong purposed in her heart to intervene. Over the ensuing months, through prayer and divine intervention, she began to see small but positive improvements in the interactions of these once close friends.

Words of Love: You shall not bear false witness against your neighbor. Exodus 20:16

DAY 26

FROM THE HEART

Scripture: But this I say: he who sows sparingly will also reap sparingly, and he who sows bountifully will also reap bountifully. 2 Corinthians. 9:6

Henry was not rich, but he was blessed to be able to help many who sought his assistance. As time passed, Henry felt that he was being taken for granted. Some borrowed and never repaid, others were late in repaying, and others forgot how much they owed. Henry said on several occasions that he was going to stop lending and doing, because he was not lucky with borrowers.

Henry received two pieces of advice from well-meaning family and friends. One was not to lend what he could not afford to give; and the second was to do, give or lend without expecting gratitude for the act. Do good for no other reason but because it is the right thing to do. If the motive for doing good deeds is wrong, then there is no blessing in the act.

Henry took some time to process the advice he had been given, and his attitude changed. He realized that he had been blessed in order to be a blessing to someone else. He further realized that he was only a steward of the resources he had been privileged to manage. He took a completely different approach to utilizing the blessings he had, whether it was time, talent or treasure. He lent with more joy, not expecting any profit from his lending. He became a more generous giver, expecting nothing in return. He gave his talent without a price.

What Henry discovered in this process of metamorphosis was joy, peace, and love. He welcomed each experience as a gift from God to him. When his attitude toward giving, and doing changed, he gave as though it was being done for Christ. Both the giver and the receiver experience the fullness of joy, where neither feels superior or subservient, but as partners joining forces to accomplish a mission.

Today, be genuine in your acts of mercy and benevolence. Be sure that they are from the heart.

Words of Love: And whatever you do in word or deed, do all in the name of the Lord Jesus, giving thanks to God the Father through Him. Colossians 3:17

DAY 27

JESUS... THE LAMB THAT WAS SLAIN

Scripture: The next day John saw Jesus coming toward him, and said, "Behold! The Lamb of God who takes away the sin of the world!" John 1:29.

Justin, who lived in the city, was visiting relatives who owned and operated a sheep farm in another state. The family arrived late in the evening, after all the sheep had been corralled for the day. Justin had never been on a farm before. He awoke early the next morning, excited about the prospects of seeing, and possibly getting in on the activities of sheep farming with his cousins.

As the family gathered for the morning worship before breakfast, they reflected on the sacrificial gift of Jesus Christ. He was the Lamb that was slain for the forgiveness of sins, and the redemption of a lost world.

Justin enjoyed his summer on the farm, and the story of the sacrificial lamb was never far from his mind. The seed of truth had been sown, and began to germinate and take root in his heart. He asked many questions, and began to search the scriptures for himself.

On his return home to the city, Justin's parents noticed a growth and maturity that was nothing short of miraculous and transformational. He went on to finish high school and entered a Christian university, where he pursued medicine, becoming a medical missionary upon graduation.

Words of Love: Oh, that they had such a heart in them that they would fear Me and always keep all My commandments, that it might be well with them and with their children forever! Deuteronomy 5:29

DAY 28
THE ARMS OF JESUS

Scripture: For they did not gain possession of the land by their own sword, nor did their own arm save them; But it was Your right hand, Your arm, and the light of Your countenance, because You favored them. Psalm 44:3

Have you had days when the battles are fierce and your strength wanes from the fight? Daisy was experiencing one too many of those days. It was a constant struggle on the job, and she began to question God. Faithful to her Christian values, and secure in her relationship with her Savior, Daisy knew that she could cry out to God with her questions. He was not the kind of friend who was intimidated or offended by her questioning. When all was said, and done, however, she knew she had to trust Him, even in the darkest of hours.

Daisy read the scripture, she fasted and prayed, and she sought the intercessory prayers of her friends. As she searched the scripture, she was led to verses like Psalm 89:20-23, where God, speaking of His servant David, said, "With My holy oil I have anointed him; with My hand shall he be established: mine arm also shall strengthen him. The enemy shall not exact upon him, nor the son of wickedness afflict him."

The more Daisy sought God, and placed her shortcomings before Him, the more strength she gained for the journey. Her life did not become struggle-free, but she learned to turn things over to God, where she rested securely in His loving arms, knowing that the battle was not hers to fight. Joy filled Daisy's heart, where before there was only sadness. The smile returned to her face, and her shoulders, once drooping from burdens she was not meant to bear, became straight again. What a place of comfort... the arms of Jesus.

Words of Love: The Lord will fight for you, and you shall hold your peace. Exodus 14:14

DAY 29

A TRUSTWORTHY GOD

Scripture: And it will be said in that day: "Behold, this is our God; We have waited for Him, and He will save us. This is the Lord; We have waited for Him; We will be glad and rejoice in His salvation." Isaiah 25:9

"Today I am struggling," Evan said, thinking aloud. Marigold turned and looked at him, perplexed by his words, which came out of nowhere. "What are you talking about," she asked, "and what brought that on?"

The conversation that followed revealed that Evan was having some internal struggles, and the Lord had orchestrated this outburst, so that he could get the help he needed. Evan was a hard-working man who loved the Lord and his family. His hard work was not bringing the necessary income to meet the family's needs and they were falling behind on some of their bills. The couple had discussed the principle of tithing before, and believed it was the right thing to do, but Evan did not see how they could give one tenth of their meager income, when they were experiencing such financial hardships. Marigold thought differently. She believed that they should put God first, and trust Him.

Evan and Marigold paused from their activities and sought God in prayer. Together they put on paper all their expenses, and their income. This time, unlike previous budgets, they placed their tithes at the very top. They then began to trim their expenses, to bring them in line with what was left after tithing. As they expected, there were not enough funds remaining to meet their needs. Once again, they raised their voices to God in prayer, telling Him of their commitment to faithfulness.

Rising from their knees, Marigold hurried to answer the phone, which had been ringing. She missed the call, and not having caller ID, had no idea who had called. She resumed her activities with a song of praise in her heart, eager to see how her Loving Savior was going to work in their lives. Just then the phone rang again. This time she quickly answered and, greeted the warm voice of Evan's boss. He apologized for calling at that time, and asked if it was convenient to talk with Evan.

It was a lengthy call, which Evan took in Marigold's hearing. The company for which Evan worked was opening a new branch in a nearby town, and they wanted Evan to manage it. His salary would more than double, and with management status, he would enjoy many cost-saving perks. God had been waiting to open the windows of heaven and pour out His blessings on this family, but He waited to see if they would be faithful and trusting in His faithfulness and His trustworthiness. As always, He never fails.

Words of Love: Your mercy, O Lord, is in the heavens; Your faithfulness reaches to the clouds. Psalm 36:5

DAY 30
IF THE SHOE WAS ON THE OTHER FOOT

Scripture: Bear one another's burdens, and so fulfill the law of Christ. For if anyone thinks himself to be something, when he is nothing, he deceives himself. Galatians 6:2-3

Many cultures are familiar with this or a similar saying, indicating that we should stop and reflect on the outcome we would desire if the circumstances were reversed. We have also heard of the Golden Rule: Do unto others as you would have them do unto you; and the less familiar Platinum Rule, which says: Do unto others as they would have you do to them.

Renza was a loyal friend who always went the extra mile for anyone needing her assistance. She was well-known for her generous ways; so much so that acquaintances began to take advantage of her generosity. One day a favor was asked of Renza, and she had to say no. Her practice of catering to the needs, or rather the wants, of others had become such an expectation, that her "no" was met with resentment. What was not known to these "friends" was that Renza was experiencing some life challenges that had not yet become common knowledge.

Renza needed understanding friends who would look beyond the external vibrant facade, and see the fragile person who was trying to give life everything she had, until she literally had nothing left to give. It was not long afterwards that Renza had to stop working, due to her serious medical condition. Some of those who had passed judgment and made unkind remarks, when she could not do what suited their interests, were too embarrassed or proud to make amends. Others made their apologies and had an opportunity to restore broken relationships before Renza passed away.

Words of Love: Therefore comfort each other and edify one another, just as you also are doing. 1 Thessalonians 5:11

DAY 31
I KNOCKED AND I WAITED

Scripture: Trust in Him at all times, you people; Pour out your heart before Him; God is a refuge for us. Psalm 62:8

This picture of Christ knocking at a door has always been a very vivid one for me. Of course, being a still photograph, no one knows how long He had been waiting or how much longer He waited. Jesus Christ, the Savior of the world, has been knocking at the door of our heart, and waiting to gain entrance. He promises to come in and dine with us, if we will let Him. He is one of those guests who always bring something with them, and His gifts are always a blessing. He never leaves us empty; we are always better off for His visit.

So, the questions I want to ask are these: "What are you waiting for? Why are you not running to open the door? Do you realize what you are missing out on, by delaying His entrance?" I don't know about you, but like Mary, I long to sit at His feet. I may even forget that there is a meal to be fixed, but then if we lose track of time and get hungry or thirsty, He is the Living Water, and the Bread of Life. He will fill us up so that we never hunger or thirst again.

The next time He visits, invite Him in, and offer Him living quarters. He would like nothing better than to take up permanent residence within each of our hearts.

Words of Love: Behold, I stand at the door and knock. If anyone hears My voice and opens the door, I will come in to him and dine with him, and he with Me. Revelation 3:20

DAY 32
PERFECT IN FORM

Scripture: Then God said, "Let the waters abound with an abundance of living creatures, and let birds fly above the earth across the face of the firmament of the heavens." ... and God saw that it was good. Genesis 1:20-25

It was a beautiful Saturday afternoon, and the family was enjoying a walk along the sandy shores of the lake, enjoying all the scenes of nature that surrounded them. The mother bent to pick up something and mused, "It is perfect in form." The entire family was avid nature lovers, and the two girls, ages eleven and thirteen, ran to their mother's side, eager to explore the find. The shell was simply gorgeous. The colors, shape and intricate design were a testament of great artistry.

The parents, Tom and Jeanie, used every opportunity as teaching moments to draw the girls' attention to Christ. Both girls had many questions and the parents provided answers to the best of their ability.

God the Creator, whose artistic ability supersedes that of all the great artists of the world combined, designed a beautiful world for mankind to enjoy and care for. At creation, He looked at everything He had made and pronounced it good.

Tom and Jeanie's daughters had tender, malleable hearts, and they loved to share the stories of the Bible with them. They told them that sin was the reason for the blight and blemish that the world experiences today, and that God never created or intended any kind of imperfection. He, however, does expect us to respect all creatures, great and small, perfect and imperfect, love them and care for them, until He comes again to restore all things to their original state: perfect in form.

Words of Love: The Lord is good to all, and His tender mercies are over all His works. Psalm 145:9, 17

DAY 33
A PERSON OF INTEGRITY

Scripture: The integrity of the upright will guide them, but the perversity of the unfaithful will destroy them. Proverbs 11:3

*W*hat does integrity look like? The following story will help to unwrap that for us. Mr. Jones was the night watchman at a company where large deposits were made at the close of business each day. He was struggling financially, and had been praying for God to open up a way for him to improve his family's financial situation.

One evening it was storming outside when one company made their last deposit. There were several money bags, and in their haste to get out of the pelting rain and hail, one of the bags dropped, unnoticed by the company employee making the deposit. Mr. Jones had been watching the monitors, and knew that it was the last deposit for the evening. He later went to make his final round of the area, before settling in for the night, as the weather forecast predicted even worse weather before daylight.

Something impressed Mr. Jones to take a closer look at the area around the night depository. There was so much water in the area that he had to abort his first attempt and retrieve his galoshes. When he was finally able to get to the area, he found a large money bag, stuffed with what appeared to be bills. Mr. Jones retrieved the bag and retreated to the safety of the building where he locked all the doors securely, and called both his manager, and the manager of the company that had made the deposit.

Although he had the opportunity, and the need, not for a moment did Mr. Jones think of doing anything that could possibly tarnish his reputation. Even more importantly, however, he would not do anything to bring disrepute to the name of Christ, whose name he bore as a Christian. He reflected on the scripture in Luke 8:17, which says that what is done in the dark will be brought to light; and in Matthew 5:16, which says to let your light so shine before men, that they may see your good works, and glorify your Father which is in heaven.

Words of Love: Finally, brethren, whatever things are true, whatever things are noble, whatever things are just, whatever things are pure, whatever things are lovely, whatever things are of good report, if there is any virtue and if there is anything praiseworthy—meditate on these things. Philippians 4:8

DAY 34

WASH-DAY PRAISES

Scripture: I will praise the Lord according to His righteousness, and will sing praise to the name of the Lord Most High. Psalm 7:17

I must tell you some stories of my childhood, and share how in everyday simple tasks, we can find reasons to praise and glorify the Almighty God. I am from one of the beautiful Caribbean islands, and my home was nestled close to one of the most gorgeous strips of lily white sand beaches with water that was mostly clear aqua blue. But not so when the force of the river water was stronger where it met the waters of the sea. In this area where salt water and fresh water met, "brackish" water was found.

In what was then a sleepy fishing village, the women washed clothes in the riverbed, where the water was mainly fresh. A stone's throw away, in the sea, the men could be observed hauling nets, which they had cast in the predawn hours of the morning. Sometimes the catch was good, and at other times it left much to be desired. But that is another story.

When we were not in school, we loved to watch our mothers wash, and listen to them sing songs of praise as they beat clothes on the rocks, and rinsed them in the clear river water. I did not know then, as we waded in the shallow waters around the women, that the foundation was being laid for my life of gratitude. They never grumbled about their hard lot in life, but instead thanked God for the daily provisions that He gave them.

When the nets were drawn ashore, the women walked the short distance, collected and cleaned their husband's portion of the catch, then returned to their clothes lying in wash tubs, or on some smooth rocks close by. I was motivated to load the washing machine with some towels and bed linen from overnight guests, when I was writing this devotion. I paused and lifted up my heart, which was humbled by God's goodness. Then I prayed to Him for women everywhere, who still take time to praise Him, whatever their task; whether their "wash day" is in the laundry room, by a river bed, or wherever it may be.

Words of Love: Rejoice always, pray without ceasing, in everything give thanks; for this is the will of God in Christ Jesus for you. 1 Thessalonians 5:16-18.

DAY 35
CHURCH HILL & COTTON TREE

Scripture: For the living know that they will die; But the dead know nothing, and they have no more reward, for the memory of them is forgotten. Ecclesiastes 9:5

I don't know how many of you had a church hill or a large cotton tree you had to pass at nights during your childhood, but my memory of the famous church hill followed by the large and foreboding cotton tree in my neighborhood is reminiscent of ghost stories. There was a sharp and dangerous corner as you ascended the hill, and drivers would have to blow their horns in both directions to notify vehicles coming in the opposite direction to wait as they navigated the corner. The parish church sat on top of that hill.

My aunt lived in the old homestead on the beach road, now a boulevard, and my parents lived about three or four miles away in the "mountain." It did not require much for us to walk from one home to the other, but we had to pass church hill and the cotton tree, on opposite sides of the road. I remember jumping from one side of my mother to the other as we passed those two "haunted spots" on the way home from my aunt's house, in the dark of night. I would look in the direction of the sea, as I passed church hill, and then I would quickly look in the direction of the mountain, as I passed the cotton tree; sometimes putting my hand up to my face, so that I would not get any glimpses from the periphery.

Now that I have grown both in years and in my relationship with Christ, I often reflect on the state of the dead, and the promises of God, that one day He will come back to redeem His faithful children. Scripture reminds us that the dead in Christ, who are sleeping the 'sleep of death,' will rise first, and we who are alive will be caught up together with them to meet Him in the air. There will be no more fears of the "Church Hills or Cotton Trees" of the world, because there will be no more death. How I long for that day to come. Don't you?

Words of Love: Also, their love, their hatred, and their envy have now perished; Nevermore will they have a share in anything done under the sun. Ecclesiastes 9:6

DAY 36

DON'T CRY, MEME ROSE

Scripture: For His anger is but for a moment, His favor is for life; Weeping may endure for a night, but joy comes in the morning. Psalm 30:5

It was sudden and unexpected. Ted was young and vibrant; full of life, and had so much living left to do. He was engaged to be married to a beautiful young lady. His mother Rose, not having any girls of her own, was looking forward to having her more as a daughter than a daughter-in-law.

"So, what went wrong?" I asked Rose, when I felt comfortable interrupting her sobs.

Ted had developed a very rare and fast-growing cancer, and he was given one month to live. "He did not even last a full month," Rose sobbed.

Rose's little granddaughter sat in a corner, quietly crying her little heart out as well. It was a pitiful sight, and the best I could do was just be there for my dear friend. I had flown in for the memorial service, and was getting more of the details that were left out over short telephone conversations. The trip home had been planned to attend Ted's wedding. Instead, all the family and friends were gathered for his memorial service.

As we sat and talked, hugged and cried, little Caroline walked over to her grandmother, and with the composure of an adult, she wrapped her arms around Rose and said, "Don't cry, Meme Rose, we will see Uncle Ted in heaven, when Jesus comes back."

Rose embraced her granddaughter tightly, and for her words of wisdom and encouragement, I had to give her a warm embrace as well.

How sad that a parent has to bury a child, and how sad that any of us have to be separated by death. But how comforting to know that for the children of God, death is only temporary, and there is hope beyond the grave. Truly, we may have to endure weeping and sadness for a season, but there is great joy for the redeemed, in the promises of eternity with Christ.

Words of Love: But rejoice to the extent that you partake of Christ's sufferings, that when His glory is revealed, you may also be glad with exceeding joy. 1 Peter 4:13

DAY 37
MORNING SONG

Scripture: Blessed be the Lord God of Israel from everlasting to everlasting! And all the people said, "Amen!" and praised the Lord. 1 Chronicles 16:36

I woke up this morning to a beautiful bird song, and my heart sang along with its song of praise. I wish I knew what kind of bird it was, but in the crisp air of this winter morning, with the sun shining and the breeze blowing, this bird did not have a care in the world. The song was not a sound of fear, but of calm assurance and confidence that its needs were being met.

Oh, that we would learn from the birds. God's word tells us that they do not plant or reap, yet they have enough food to eat; and a sparrow which is sold for less than a penny does not fall to the ground without our Heavenly Father's knowledge. If He takes such a personal interest in the care of birds, how much more He will care for you and me.

The next time you hear a bird sing, pause and remember the promises of God, that you are worth far more than many sparrows, and any bird for that matter. Reflect on all that He has done for you. When placed in the right perspective, I believe you will realize that the blessings outweigh the trials, and sometimes the trials themselves are blessings in disguise. So, find your song today, and sing like there is no tomorrow. My song is, "I'll go where You want me to go, Dear Lord," by Mary Haughton Brown. May you find the song that speaks to your heart, and may it remind you of the providence of our Almighty God.

Words of Love: For the Lord God is a sun and shield; The Lord will give grace and glory; No good thing will He withhold from those who walk uprightly. Psalm 84:11

DAY 38

ONE OF A KIND

Scripture: I will praise You, for I am fearfully and wonderfully made; Marvelous are Your works, and that my soul knows very well. Psalm 139:14

The framed artwork hanging on the wall caught my attention. Among them were two paintings of vases. Each had multiple vases, which were all very different; some fairly plain, and others bearing intricate designs. I was fascinated with the artist's work, and the more I looked, the more captivated I became; so much so that I began to smile subconsciously.

I began to see the work of the Master Potter in a fresh new light. Some of the vases had beautiful shapes, but others had more striking colors. The intricate designs of some were breathtaking, and strategically placed beside them were others that dimmed in their beauty. I saw humanity in those two paintings, and understood that Christ created each of us as a "one-of-a-kind" piece of pottery, each unique in our form and our purpose. He has placed us in positions to co-exist with each other.

As different as each vase was, there were some foundational similarities. They were all made of clay; they were all fashioned by the same designer and bore his name; and they each had a purpose. Displayed in the right setting to highlight their best qualities, they could all serve very useful functions for which they were designed. The life lesson in those paintings was what brought the smile to my face. God has created a masterpiece in each of us. We are one of a kind.

Today, I pray to see the beauty in each of my fellow men; to affirm them, and work to highlight their best assets, so that their uniqueness will not be viewed as a liability but a wonderful asset to be celebrated. For, in so doing, we are acknowledging the work of the Artist, Creator of the universe, whose designs cannot be replicated. Like a snowflake and a thumbprint, you and I are truly one of a kind.

Words of Love: But the very hairs of your head are all numbered. Matthew 10:30

DAY 39
NEW GROWTH

Scripture: Now may He who supplies seed to the sower, and bread for food, supply and multiply the seed you have sown and increase the fruits of your righteousness. 2 Corinthians 9:10

The winters are very hard on some of my tropical plants. As much as the outdoors are brutal to their survival, they do not fare much better when brought inside. Even with the right amount of water and nourishment, the leaves fall profusely and they are often left with bare stems, which are pitiful to behold. This past winter I decided to do something a little different. I left a little light close to some of the plants. The result was amazing: new growth began to spring up in several of the plants.

This reminded me of the life of the Christian. There are some "winters" when the bitter chill of life's trials leaves us bare, stripped of all the foliage that had previously protected the inner core of our spiritual existence. We continue going to church and receiving the nourishment of the spoken word, but we still seem to be dying. Then there is a nudging from the Holy Spirit who whispers, "Plug into the Source and get the Light."

Finally, the message sunk in. What we need is an experiential relationship with the Light of the world: Jesus Christ. We need to have one-on-one time with Him, and let the current of His love energize our lives. In the same way sunlight is important to the process of photosynthesis, one of the basic elements of plant growth, Christians need the "Son-light" to produce new growth in us.

Words of Love: That Christ may dwell in your hearts through faith; that you, being rooted and grounded in love, may be able to comprehend with all the saints what is the width and length and depth and height— to know the love of Christ which passes knowledge; that you may be filled with all the fullness of God. Ephesians 3:17-19

DAY 40
YOU ARE KILLING ME!

Scripture: Do not be deceived: "Evil company corrupts good habits." 1 Cor. 15:33

Faith was one of the most negative persons I have ever known. There was hardly a conversation in which she was not "spewing venom" at someone or something. The glass was always half-empty, and the world "out to get her." She was beautiful on the outside, and people were always drawn to her. It would not take a fifteen-minute conversation, however, before they were desperately looking for a quick retreat. These fast starts, and equally fast exits in her interpersonal relationships, left her even more bitter towards the world.

If the sun was shining, Faith would be emphatic that it would not be long before there would be overshadowing clouds, followed by torrential rain. Colleagues referred to her as "Miss Kill-Joy," and people began to avoid her like the plague.

I grew up with Faith, and I was very saddened by the change in her demeanor, because as a child she was as beautiful on the inside as she was on the outside.

I decided to make my friend's desperate need for intervention an issue of prayer. I am very honest with those I love, and my honesty sometimes results in resistance from those loved ones. My desire to see Faith happy, however, was worth the risk of igniting her wrath.

We planned to meet for dinner one evening, and over a delicious meal, with which she found many faults, I explained to Faith that she was draining the life out me, and everyone else with whom she had an encounter, because of her negative spirit. I had arranged for a secluded corner booth, so that we could talk in privacy. Faith shared a lot, and I listened. She agreed to see a therapist, and is receiving necessary help. She has a long road to overcome the circumstances that brought about the negative changes in her; but, with the support of a small band of prayer warriors, who are mentoring her, and a God who loves her more than anyone else, her inner beauty will be restored.

Words of Love: But exhort one another daily, while it is called "Today," lest any of you be hardened through the deceitfulness of sin. Hebrews 3:13

DAY 41
RELINQUISHING CONTROL

Scripture: In all your ways acknowledge Him, and He will direct your paths. Proverbs 3:6

I was planning for retirement, with a goal to concentrate on writing, an interest I have had for many years. In the months leading up to the December retirement date, I became aware of three consultant opportunities that would provide some supplemental work as I wrote. Two were in one location in the capitol city where I had an apartment; and the other was three hours away, but only ten minutes from my home.

It seemed a no-brainer, right? Take the one closest to my home. Not so fast though; there were pros and cons to all of the positions, so I sought the Lord in prayer. I pleaded with Him to close every door that would get in the way of me doing what I believed He had called me to do, even if it meant closing the door on all three opportunities.

During the week between Christmas and New Year's, I received a call indicating that one of the opportunities would not materialize, due to limited grant funding. On the morning of January 20, I had a call from one of the two remaining opportunities, stating that the contract was ready for signing. Later that same day, the administrator of the third opportunity called to say that the consultant they had on staff had agreed to stay on if they could be flexible with her schedule.

Now, isn't God great? He had worked out all the details, once I relinquished control to Him. The one opportunity left available to me was the one which best fit my interest, and allowed me more time to write.

Words of Love: The Lord has appeared of old to me, saying: "Yes, I have loved you with an everlasting love; Therefore, with lovingkindness I have drawn you. Jeremiah 31:3

DAY 42
VERTIGO AND DREAM OF A LOST CAR

Scripture: Set up signposts, make landmarks; Set your heart toward the highway, the way in which you went. Turn back, O virgin of Israel, turn back to these your cities. Jeremiah 31:21

I woke up one morning with one of the worst episodes of vertigo I had ever had. It began the day before in the dentist's chair, but even after taking the prescribed medication, the problem had not resolved itself overnight. At the same time, I was beginning to have a sore throat.

Feeling that the vertigo might be the initial symptom of an upper respiratory infection or the flu, I took some multi-symptom cough medicine and a second dose of the vertigo medicine. I went into a long five-hour sleep, during which I had all kinds of "nightmares."

The dream that finally woke me up was one in which I had parked my car and gone to a function a short distance away. Forgetting something important for the function in the car, I went to retrieve it, only to realize that the car was nowhere to be found. The remote broke, and with it I lost hope of finding the car without divine intervention. Imagine the panic.

In the dream, I prayed to God for assistance, retraced my steps by following identifying landmarks I had observed earlier, and found the car. This dream reminded me of a song by F.E. Belden to "Look for the way-marks."

As pilgrims on a journey through life, we must look for and remember the way-marks, to help keep us on track and prevent us from losing our way. I am still praising God that it was only a bad dream.

Words of Love: Call upon Me in the day of trouble; I will deliver you, and you shall glorify Me. Psalm 50:15

DAY 43
WHERE IS YOUR TRUST?

Scripture: Some trust in chariots, and some in horses; But we will remember the name of the Lord our God. Psalm 20.7

It was a cold evening at the teen summer camp. The campers were playing around when one sustained some serious, though non-life-threatening injuries. The parents were notified, and the camp nurse, assisted by a visiting physician, treated the injuries.

After the campers had settled down for the evening, the camp leadership team gathered for the day's reflection and prayer. They gave God thanks for His leading and protection over the camp and campers for the past week and a half. They interceded for the injured camper, and prayed that this incident would not leave a "black mark" on an otherwise stellar camp.

It was a somber evening as the shadows fell, and all hearts were turned heavenward for divine intervention in the recovery of the young camper. It took one of the youngest on the leadership team to bring a sense of focus to the group, when she asked the sobering question, "Where is your trust, everybody?" She went on to point out how unusual it was for them to have a physician visit during a camping trip, and for him to be there the afternoon of the accident was divine intervention.

A time of prayer and praise like they had not experienced during that camp followed. They gave God thanks for hearing their cries before they called, and for answering their prayers before they even opened their mouths to utter them. Everyone on the leadership team retired that night having a deeper relationship with Christ, in which their faith and trust were strengthened.

During the remaining days of camp, many campers gave their hearts to Jesus, including the young camper who was injured. He recovered fully from the accident, and became a camp counselor the next year.

Words of Love: Thus, says the Lord: "Cursed is the man who trusts in man and makes flesh his strength, whose heart departs from the Lord. Jeremiah 17:5

DAY 44
ONLY A CHILD

Scripture: Out of the mouth of babes and nursing infants You have ordained strength, because of Your enemies, that You may silence the enemy and the avenger. Psalm 8:2

One of my prayer partners called me with a funny story about her great-granddaughter. She had picked the child up from school, and they had several stops planned along the way to her house, where she had a full schedule of homework assistance. They had only made it to their first stop, when the little girl called out from the back-seat window to an unsuspecting passerby, "Do you know that Jesus died for your transmission? Yes, Jesus died for your transmission." The kind woman who was greeted with this unusual question from a seven-year-old child, paused and responded gently, "Yes sweetheart, I know that Jesus died for my transgressions, and I am so thankful."

The story was funny and I chuckled briefly. The chuckle was followed with deep introspection. "When was the last time you shared that piece of good news with someone else?" I asked myself, and I am now asking you the same question. There is a dying world out there, desperate for someone to share the truth of God's saving grace. You and I need to join the children of all ages in spreading this life-saving message: that Christ died to save mankind from Satan's grip.

The Holy Spirit still has some work to do with me, so that my desire to labor for souls in God's harvest field will outweigh any hesitation about getting out of my comfort zone. I want others to be ready when Jesus comes, and share the joy that I am looking forward to. Thanks to little Carmen for reminding us to shout it from the mountain top, or the back seat of a van.

Words of Love: And they said to Him, "Do You hear what these are saying?" And Jesus said to them, "Yes. Have you never read, 'Out of the mouth of babes and nursing infants You have perfected praise'?" Matthew 21:16

DAY 45
IMITATIONS

Scripture: For He satisfies the longing soul, and fills the hungry soul with goodness. Psalm 107:9

I love the sound of gentle flowing water, such as a brook or a small waterfall. So, to create this desired atmosphere, I have bought multiple electronic waterfalls, but gave up on them when they failed to deliver what they promised. Then I saw an LED Candle Fountain, and decided to give imitation fountains one last try.

To my pleasant surprise, it delivered better than expected, but still not quite what I have longed for. Imitations may satisfy for a while, but nothing fills the longing of your heart like the real thing. It's been said that there is a hole in every human heart that only Jesus Christ can fill.

My imitation candle fountain fills a temporary gap, but I long to open the window of my home and enjoy waterfalls, which are the handiwork of the Creator. Likewise, I want to open the window of my heart and enjoy the recreated wellspring of my soul.

Words of love: Blessed are those who hunger and thirst for righteousness, for they shall be filled. Matthew 5:6

DAY 46
WHEN THINGS ARE NOT WHAT THEY APPEAR TO BE

Scripture: Judge not, that you be not judged. For with what judgment you judge, you will be judged; and with the measure you use, it will be measured back to you. And why do you look at the speck in your brother's eye, but do not consider the plank in your own eye? Or how can you say to your brother, 'Let me remove the speck from your eye'; and look, a plank is in your own eye? Hypocrite! First remove the plank from your own eye, and then you will see clearly to remove the speck from your brother's eye. Matthew 7:1-5

I read a story in my childhood about a beloved dog that was left to watch a baby while the father took care of business away from the home. The man returned home to find things in disarray. Blood was everywhere, and the infant was nowhere in sight. In his anger and disappointment, he shot the dog, believing it had harmed the infant. He discovered later that the faithful dog had removed and hidden the infant as it fought off the intruding animal that had sought to make a meal of the child. The man was saddened that in haste he had rushed to judgment and destroyed his most loyal and trusted friend.

Sometimes we are blessed with opportunities to rectify wrongs; to make amends for the harm we have caused others unjustly. There are other times when pride and arrogance, or sometimes even a sense of shame, prevent us from doing the right thing. Then there are times when we have simply lost that window of opportunity to correct the injuries we caused, and we have to live with the guilt of our actions.

My prayer for all of us is that we will pause before we act, and think before we speak; that we will gather all the evidence before we pass judgment. May we realize how difficult it is to undo or reverse damage done carelessly. Finally, may we be slow to rush to trial, remembering the scripture above, which says that the same measure you use on others will be used to measure you.

Words of Love: Judge not, and you shall not be judged. Condemn not, and you shall not be condemned. Forgive, and you will be forgiven. Luke 6:37

DAY 47
ZESTFUL LIVING

Scripture: Therefore, if anyone is in Christ, he is a new creation; old things have passed away; behold, all things have become new. 2 Corinthians 5:17

I have met many people in my lifetime who are "off the chain" with energy. Their zest for life is contagious, and when you are in their presence, there is a sense of joy and happiness, and general wellbeing. They speak hope, and their actions abound with hopefulness. They surround themselves with an atmosphere of positivity, and they make it very clear that "negaholics" and their negativity are not welcome in their space.

Some qualities observed in the lives of ZESTFUL people are:
- Zeal - These are people who are zealous for Christ. They have experienced His abundant life and they are not afraid to tell it to the world.
- Expectancy – People who practice zestful living expect good things from the Lord. They are not presumptuous; they simply live a life of faith.
- Service – A life of service is embedded in the DNA of people who are living a zestful life. They find joy in serving others, and are always seeking out opportunities to lend a helping hand. You can find them volunteering at the soup kitchens; collecting clothes and supplies for disaster victims; offering to pick up someone without transportation; helping an embarrassed person clean up a mess that he made, while assuring him that they have similar accidents quite frequently.
- Trust – People living a zestful life trust God for their existence. They expect the sun to shine and good things happen, because their confidence is in the Eternal Giver of good gifts. If today was not so good, they look for tomorrow to be better; and if today is great, they are exuberant about the prospects for tomorrow.
- Forgiveness – People living a zestful life do not harbor grudges, and readily forgives. They understand that an unforgiving spirit drains the very life of a person.
- Unity – Zestfully living people promote unity in all their encounters. They are mediators, not dividers; and they work for the greater good.

- Love – The ultimate quality of people living a zestful life is love. They love freely and never count the cost. Their love for humanity is only surpassed by their love for Christ.

So, what are we waiting for? There is a world out there to love; factions to unite, and people to forgive; a God to trust; more people to serve; good things to expect; and by God's grace, the zeal to inspire us to action.

Words of Love: Never be lacking in zeal, but keep your spiritual fervor, serving the Lord. Romans 12:11

DAY 48
WHEN SELF BECOMES AN IDOL

Scripture: You shall not make idols for yourselves; neither a carved image nor a sacred pillar shall you rear up for yourselves; nor shall you set up an engraved stone in your land, to bow down to it; for I am the Lord your God. Leviticus 26:1.

We sometimes become so obsessed with our own sense of accomplishment that we forget the true source of our successes. Lucifer was a beautiful and talented being. The Bible describes him in Ezekiel 28:14 as "the anointed cherub, with brightness, beauty and wisdom far surpassing that of any other created being." Then the scripture goes on to say, "his heart was lifted up because of his beauty, and he corrupted his wisdom by reason of his brightness." (v. 17)

What do you have that is taking the place of God in your life? What is preventing you from giving the Creator first place in your heart? Why are you lifted up with pride and arrogance? Is it beauty or brain; possession or position; statue or station; talent or treasure?

Remember, all good gifts come from God above, and He has been generous in bestowing these "gifts" on us. The pride that filled Lucifer's heart permeates the soul of too many of God's children today. We behave as though the world owes us homage. This elevated sense of self causes us to expect from our fellowmen more than we are rightfully due; and when they fail to deliver to our expectations, we rant and rave, and treat them with less care and respect than we do our four-legged friends.

The cure for self-idolization is to get a fresh glimpse of Jesus. Make Him the center of our world. Recognize His self-sacrifice on our behalf, and acknowledge sin as the great equalizer of all mankind. The scripture says it clearly in Isaiah 53:6, "All we like sheep have gone astray; we have turned everyone to his own way; and the Lord hath laid on him the iniquity of us all." None of us have just cause to think too highly of ourselves; and as His creatures, none of us can claim a rightful place over the Creator. So, let's honor Him with first place in our hearts.

Words of Love: You shall have no other gods before Me... Exodus 20:3-6

DAY 49
WHEN TO DIM THE LIGHTS

Scripture: In him was life; and the life was the light of men. John 1:4

Some of the light fixtures and lamps in my home have dimmer switches. This feature creates ambiance; and it also hides the glaring dust that often settles on the furniture. Then there is a dim and a bright light feature in our automobiles. Each serves a valuable purpose, when used appropriately.

When I think of those lights, I think about my life. When is it appropriate to have the dimmers on, and when does the bright light need to be on? The following story helps to illustrate that for me: I tuned in to the weather station as I prepared to get on the road early one morning. The weatherman stated that the fog was dense and the visibility was almost zero. He encouraged drivers to slow down, and drive with the dim lights on. Apparently, the bright light causes a glare when it hits the fog, which poses a hazard to oncoming traffic. Sometimes the glare of our "religiosity" can be a hindrance to new believers, and we cause them to "run off the road" or stray from the path, possibly never to return.

On the other hand, the low beam does not produce enough light for nighttime driving on dark roads. There is a time and a place for the dimmer switch to be adjusted to bright or dim, and I am giving the control of that switch to the Holy Spirit. I want just the right amount of light to shine from me to reflect Jesus Christ; enough to point others to Him, "The Way, the Truth and the Life;" enough to create an atmosphere of the warmth of God's love, so that all people feel welcome, and are drawn into His presence.

Words of Love: Let your light so shine before men, that they may see your good works and glorify your Father in heaven. Matthew 5:16

DAY 50

JUST FOR A FLEETING MOMENT

Scripture: Lord, what is man, that You take knowledge of him? Or the son of man, that You are mindful of him? Man is like a breath; His days are like a passing shadow. Psalm 144:3-4

There were predictions of possible light snow overnight and into the early morning hours. Snow, though not totally atypical, was not a regular occurrence in the central part of this southern state, so I rushed to the window upon awakening, to see if there had been any accumulation. There was none. I participated in our morning prayer call, and then I began my personal time with the Lord.

I was sitting up in my bed, my favorite "prayer closet," and facing the balcony with a view of the trees and the next-door parking lot, when at 8:10, beautiful snow flurries began to fall. I hurried to the window for a closer experience, but it lasted for exactly two minutes. At 8:12 the snow flurries were replaced with raindrops.

How much like life and the small windows of opportunity that we often have to capture and embrace the special blessings that God sends us. In just the blinking of an eye, if we don't tune in to Him, we can miss these wonderful moments.

Thankfully, God is a God of grace and second chances.

On multiple occasions during the morning, there were short periods of snow, and each time I was equally drawn, not taking any of those moments for granted, knowing that I might blink and they would be gone. Just like life itself; not to be taken for granted, as it can be gone in a flash, "in the twinkling of an eye." Let us, therefore, value and treat each moment of life as a special gift from God, because it is.

Words of Love: Behold, I tell you a mystery: We shall not all sleep, but we shall all be changed—in a moment, in the twinkling of an eye, at the last trumpet. For the trumpet will sound, and the dead will be raised incorruptible, and we shall be changed. 1 Corinthians 15:51-52

DAY 51
WHO IS HE?

Scripture: And God said to Moses, "I AM WHO I AM." And He said, "Thus you shall say to the children of Israel, 'I AM has sent me to you.'" Exodus 3:14

What a seemingly strange answer. Jesus had heard this question asked multiple times: after He had performed some miracle, or made some statement about His place in the Trinity. He was labeled by some as a blasphemer, and a troublemaker.

On the other hand, there were those who saw Him for who He truly was, and called Him: Master, Savior, Redeemer, King of kings, and Lord of lords; Light of the World, The Bread of Life, The True Vine, among other names of honor. Who did Jesus Himself say He was? How did He describe Himself?

Jesus said to Moses in the text above: I Am Who I Am, and in response to the Pharisees, He had this to say, "Your father Abraham rejoiced at the thought of seeing my day; he saw it and was glad." 'You are not yet fifty years old,' the Jews said to him, 'and you have seen Abraham.' 'I tell you the truth,' Jesus answered, 'before Abraham was born, I Am.'"

Yes, Jesus is all that He claimed to be and more, but in a more personal sense, He is my Best Friend. There is room at the table and in His heart for you as well, so, it would be my honor and privilege to introduce Him to you. I hope this book helps to make that introduction, if He is not already your Best Friend, too.

Words of Love: No longer do I call you servants, for a servant does not know what his master is doing; but I have called you friends, for all things that I heard from My Father I have made known to you. John 15:15

DAY 52
MY THOUGHTS OR YOURS?

Scripture: For My thoughts are not your Thoughts, neither are your ways My ways, says the Lord. Isaiah 55:8

"What are you thinking?" I asked myself, as my mind began going down many 'rabbit trails.' This was happening quite frequently, as my mind wandered back to some of the experiences that I have had over the years: little injustices that have chipped away at my confidence, and left blotches of paint on the fabric of my life.

Then on one of those mind-wandering occasions, I began to question God as to who He really was. He sat me down for a conversation that drew me into a closer relationship with Him than I had before. He reminded me that He, the great I AM, had used each painful life experience to create the special fabric of my life that it was at the time: one with God-confidence in place of self-confidence; one in which empathy for others replaced mere sympathy.

He said He had to take me into the wilderness of hurt and pain, like Moses, so I could be a better servant. Best of all, He reminded me that He had paved the way for me, and remained to walk it with me to eternity. I was humbled that the Creator would take so much time with me, and my questionings have turned into praises. My desire is to reflect on the outside the work He is doing on the inside.

Words of Love: For what man knows the things of a man except the spirit of the man which is in him? Even so no one knows the things of God except the Spirit of God. 1 Corinthians 2:11

DAY 53
"AT-ONE-MENT"

Scripture: For if when we were enemies we were reconciled to God through the death of His Son, much more, having been reconciled, we shall be saved by His life. And not only that, but we also rejoice in God through our Lord Jesus Christ, through whom we have now received the reconciliation. Romans 5:10-11

I have always been intrigued by words that have double meanings, or offer a meaning or explanation beyond what is believed to have been initially intended. Atonement is one of those words. Among the dictionary definitions for the word a-tone-ment are: reparation for a wrong or injury and, the reconciliation of God and humankind through Jesus Christ.

The same word, broken differently: at-one-ment, although not an official word, gives the warm feeling of being one with Christ. While He is making atonement for our sins, and interceding to restore our broken relationships with the Father; He takes a very personal interest in our wellbeing and desires an intimate connection with each of us. He is so personally involved in the intricacies of our lives, He knows the number of hairs on our heads, every tear that we cry, and every heartache that we feel.

Our God is not an absentee landlord, who leaves the care of His children to a caretaker. He remains involved in our daily lives, and invites us to call on Him any hour of the day or night. He is a 24/7 kind of friend, and He is never tired of us calling on Him. He wants to give us the kind of peace that being one with Him brings.

In a world that has so much chaos, what is holding you back from having this kind of oneness with that special "Someone" who loves you so much? He is the "Soul Mate" of soul mates. I am crying out to Him today to hold me close in this bond of love. Won't you join me in asking Him to hold you close as well, and never let you go? He has enough room for all.

Words of Love: But he who is joined to the Lord is one spirit with Him. 1 Corinthians 6:17

DAY 54

SUFFICIENT

Scripture: And my God shall supply all your need according to His riches in glory by Christ Jesus. Philippians 4:19

My husband and I had an elderly friend who we loved to have over for meals. You would think that I was a gourmet cook, because every meal I prepared was described as the best he ever had. His favorite thing to say after he had eaten to his satisfaction was, "I have dined sufficiently."

I miss Brother Ben. He lived a simple life, and God was sufficient for all his needs. He did not have much of this world's goods, but if you asked him, he was quick to tell you that God was taking care of his needs, and there was nothing that he lacked. When he died, he had enough to take care of his burial expenses; and since he did not believe in accumulating debt, there were no bill collectors to be paid. The only family he had was his church family, where he had served God faithfully, and they all mourned his loss, like any loving family would.

How is your life? Is God sufficient for all your needs? Are you dining sufficiently at His table daily, or are you going through the day on an empty stomach? God has provided a banquet table loaded with what you need to nourish mind, body and soul, and He invites you to come eat bread and drink "wine," without money or price.

So, pull up a chair. Actually, there is one with your name on it. Enjoy what has been prepared for you by the hand of a loving Father. You are invited to return daily; and when all is said and done, I hope you and I can say like Brother Ben, "I have dined sufficiently," and "Lord, You have been sufficient for all my needs."

Words of Love: And He said to me, "My grace is sufficient for you, for My strength is made perfect in weakness." Therefore, most gladly I will rather boast in my infirmities, that the power of Christ may rest upon me. 2 Corinthians 12:9

DAY 55
JUST A PRAYER AWAY

Scripture: O You who hear prayer, to You all flesh will come. Psalm 65:2

You have heard people say, "Call me any time," or "I am only a phone call away." Try calling them a couple times when it is inconvenient, however, and those words will have little truth to them. If they are polite, they may offer to call you back at a convenient time. If they are not, they may even tell you to call them back at a more convenient time, as though you can always predict what time that might be.

I had a friend who would call me any hour of the night if she needed to talk, and I could do the same with her. Then I got married, and she began to withdraw, believing I would no longer be available to her, even though I tried to convince her that I was.

With Jesus, we do not have to guess at His availability. He sees our needs, and He is waiting to meet those needs, but He wants to hear from us. He wants us to ask, not beg; there is no need for that. Then when we receive from His gracious hands, He wants to hear words of gratitude from our lips.

There are times when our Heavenly Father simply wants us to curl up beside Him, and share whatever is on our hearts: the events of the day; the words He sent us through a speaker or a preacher; the kindness we saw or experienced from others; the pain and injustices we observe around us. We can tell Him our fondest dreams, and ask if they are in His will for our lives; and we can intercede on behalf of humanity. Whatever has been laid on your heart, bring it to the Savior. Remember, He is only a prayer away.

Words of Love: The eyes of the Lord are on the righteous, and His ears are open to their cry. Psalm 34:15

DAY 56
CONFORM OR BE TRANSFORMED?

Scripture: And do not be conformed to this world, but be transformed by the renewing of your mind, that you may prove what is that good and acceptable and perfect will of God. Romans 12:2

Davey graduated high school at the top of his class, with a full scholarship to an Ivy League college, and a very promising future. He grew up with loving parents who were leaders in their church. In his early teens, Davey had shown a streak of rebellious behavior, but with counseling he had settled down, and had begun showing great interest in church activities. Although very smart, he was more of a follower than a leader.

Several members of Davey's graduating class decided to spend a week together at a popular resort, before going their separate ways to college. His parents agreed; a decision they regretted for the rest of their lives. A bright and promising future slipped away from Davey that week. The misuse of alcohol and multiple drugs landed Davey in the hospital, and finally in a psychiatric facility where he spent months, and never recovered to his full potential.

The Word of God, such as in the text above, provides many warnings for His children to not be conformed to the practices of the world. When we are hesitant to take a firm stand against wrong, the devil takes note of that weakness, and he uses all kinds of cunning devices to erode our last resolve. We cannot depend on our own strength to fight conformity to the things of the world. Instead, we must keep our eyes on Jesus to be transformed into His likeness.

Words of Love: He who says he abides in Him ought himself also to walk just as He walked. 1 John 2:6

DAY 57
PAY ATTENTION TO THE SIGNALS

Scripture: Therefore, we must give the more earnest heed to the things we have heard, lest we drift away. Hebrews 2:1

On my way home from work one afternoon, I stopped at a traffic light that had just turned red. There were two traffic lanes in each direction, plus a turning lane, and I was in the right lane heading north. There was a car to my immediate left, and one in the left turning lane. After a short wait, I noticed in my peripheral view that the car in the turning lane was moving forward, and without looking up at the signal, I proceeded through the intersection. It did not take long to realize that I had done something very wrong, as all the cars behind me and those in the lane beside me were still at a complete stop. I had run the red light.

Embarrassment, as well as panic, flooded me. "Was there a police officer close by; and what if I get a ticket?" These and other thoughts raced through my head, as my heart pounded in my chest. Then the thoughts of what could have happened, had there been a car turning from the opposite direction, further added to my distress. My inattentiveness could have resulted in a collision as I went through the intersection.

One of the lessons that I learned from that experience is that we cannot go through life on autopilot; not paying attention to the warning signals all around us. God has provided numerous signals in His Holy Word, but the problem is that we are entangled by the distractions of the world, and we misread the signs. I was very fortunate on two fronts that afternoon: I did not cause an accident, and I did not get a ticket.

Misreading the signals that Christ has set for us could cause a head-on collision with the destroyer of our soul, resulting in the loss of our eternal salvation. Christ bids us, "Watch the lights, and wait for the signal." He wants us to make it safely to our eternal home.

Words of Love: But concerning the times and the seasons, brethren, you have no need that I should write to you. For you yourselves know perfectly that the day of the Lord so comes as a thief in the night. 1 Thessalonians 5:1-2

DAY 58
THE LONGEST TRIP HOME

Scripture: O death, where is your sting; O grave, where is your victory...? 1 Corinthians 15:55-57

The year was 1997, and spring had just arrived when I got the call from home that my mother was not doing very well. I was in frequent communication with her doctor, who made house calls. I made plans to go home for a visit, and the day was nearing for the trip. It seemed as though her condition was stabilized, and I was looking forward to some quality time with her during the two-week visit.

The doctor called me from her bedside over a weekend, stating that if I wanted to see her alive, I was to come immediately. I called the airline and was able to change my ticket to leave in a couple of days. Just before leaving for the airport for the early morning flight, I received a call from home saying she had just passed away. I questioned God as to why He did not allow her to remain alive for twelve more hours; so that I could be the one to cradle her in my arms or hold her hands in those final moments.

Although I have not heard His audible voice quieting my aching heart, I have felt His comforting assurance that He did what was best for her and for me. She was my "baby" as I was her baby, and that trip home was the longest and most heart-wrenching one for me. You see, she was not there to hug me tight and offer me a seat on her lap, as she did on other visits. All I can do is hold on to those beautiful memories and wait for her greeting at the first resurrection.

Do you have loved ones who have passed away, and their absence still breaks your heart? If they died in Christ, you just have to live for Him, and you will meet them again.

Words of Love: And now, dear brothers and sisters, we want you to know what will happen to the believers who have died so you will not grieve like people who have no hope... Then we will be with the Lord forever. So, encourage each other with these words. 1 Thessalonians 4:13-18

DAY 59
WHO YOU CAN BECOME, NOT WHO YOU ARE

Scripture: So he said to Him, "O my Lord, how can I save Israel? Indeed my clan is the weakest in Manasseh, and I am the least in my father's house." Judges 6:15

There are many stories in the Bible of people feeling inadequate for a task that the Lord called them to perform. Among them are Moses and Gideon. The story in Judges tells us that after Deborah the prophetess died, Israel enjoyed peace for forty years, then the Midianites decided that their respite was long enough, and they planned an invasion.

God had a plan of deliverance, which He intended to implement using the weak and fearful Gideon, whose fear caused him to hide and thresh wheat in the winepress. That is where the angel found him, and addressed him as a "mighty man of valor." I imagine that Gideon's excuses were met with the assurance that whom God calls, He equips. The story tells us that God reduced the number of the Israelite army from 32,000 men to 10,000, and finally to 300. Armed only with trumpets, but led by the Mighty Captain, King Jesus, the Israelites defeated the great Midianite army.

What "battle" are you being called upon to fight? What "army" must you defeat? Rest assured that in your own strength, it might be impossible; but with God, all things are possible. God sees that with His equipping, the weak and fearful man or woman that you are can become a mighty warrior for His cause. Are you up to the challenge? Wouldn't you like to see the person of confident humility that God can create out of your weak vessel? Yield to Him, and watch Him work a miracle in and through you.

Words of Love: The bows of the mighty men are broken, and those who stumbled are girded with strength. 1 Samuel 2:4

DAY 60
AFTER YOU

Scripture: And everyone who has left houses or brothers or sisters or father or mother or wife or children or lands, for My name's sake, shall receive a hundredfold, and inherit eternal life. But many *who are* first will be last, and the last first. Matthew 19:29-30

Alex was a very polite young man. He was raised that way. Then came the day of the big test, and Alex nearly failed it.

It was a beautiful summer day, and Alex was running errands in town. He had been laid off from one job, and was waiting on the results of a couple new job openings for which he had interviewed. Funds were running low and bills were mounting. He had prayed for God's intervention, but the long wait was not helping his weakening faith.

A large business had opened up in town the year before and was celebrating their one year anniversary. They were awarding the 100th customer who walked in the store that day with $1,000. When Alex got to the door of the business, a well-dressed gentleman came up behind him. Alex said, "After you," and let the man precede him through the door. Just then confetti fell from the ceiling and shouts rang out from the employees, followed by the announcement that the gentleman Alex had just allowed to walk in the door before him had won the prize. Alex's heart sank, and he asked God why, seeing how desperate his financial situation was. God showed him that His plan was bigger than the prize he had just lost.

Unknown to Alex, people in the store who knew his situation, and observed his kind action, stepped in to help. The gentleman who won the prize, because of Alex's politeness, was the president of one of the companies he was waiting to hear from. Through the intervention of the store manager, Alex was called for a second interview. He was offered the job, with a $1,000 signing bonus, and a salary which was better than he expected.

Alex worked hard and earned the respect of everyone on the job. He received stock options, and quickly achieved management status. He later became vice-president, but never lost sight of the importance of deferring to others, regardless of their station in life.

Words of Love: God will repay each person according to what they have done. Romans 2:6 (NIV)

DAY 61
THE CLOSEST THING TO HEAVEN

Scripture: And he showed me a pure river of water of life, clear as crystal, proceeding from the throne of God and of the Lamb. In the middle of its street, and on either side of the river, was the tree of life, which bore twelve fruits, each tree yielding its fruit every month. The leaves of the tree were for the healing of the nations. And there shall be no more curse, but the throne of God and of the Lamb shall be in it, and His servants shall serve Him. Revelation 22:1-3

A friend, whom I had not seen for a while, told me of being blessed to purchase a home at a desirable location in a country he considers paradise. He spoke with such passion and love for the place, elaborating on the peace and tranquility at the water's edge, that I began to be caught up in the imagery. There was evident nostalgia, as his eyes told the story more than his words.

When we talk about heaven, what story do our words and our eyes tell? With the picture of faith that we paint, do people long to be there? Can they see excitement and longing in our eyes?

My friend told me about the home; they had purchased it only about six months earlier, and the family had already visited three times, with plans to make the trip three to four times each year. He expressed how "lucky" they were to have acquired such a jewel of a place, and explained plans for expansion in the years to come.

I know the area, and it is truly beautiful, but I doubt it comes close to the beauty of heaven. The country is marred by crime, and no location is immune. Then there is always the threat of natural disasters, as well as man-made inconveniences.

Heaven will have a sea of glass, and streets paved with gold. There will be no inconveniences. In this tropical paradise that my friend spoke about, there are numerous seasonal fruits to be enjoyed all through the year. In the paradise of God, one tree bears twelve fruits, which will never be out of season. Because there is no night there, according to scripture, our eyes will constantly behold its beauty.

There is one thing more about heaven, with which no earthly paradise can compare; the presence of the Trinity will be constant. We will have the companionship of our Creator and Savior always, throughout the ceaseless ages of eternity. What a paradise to look forward to. I hope you can hear the longing in my words. What a day of rejoicing that is going to be, when you and I are welcomed home.

Words of Love: For behold, I create new heavens and a new earth; And the former shall not be remembered or come to mind. Isaiah 65:17

DAY 62

DIVINE APPOINTMENTS

Scripture: Now an angel of the Lord spoke to Philip, saying, "Arise and go toward the south along the road which goes down from Jerusalem to Gaza." This is desert. So he arose and went. And behold, a man of Ethiopia, a eunuch of great authority under Candace the queen of the Ethiopians, who had charge of all her treasury... Acts 8:26-31

Have you heard people say, or said yourself, that an encounter was coincidental, or that it was being in the right place at the right time? While the latter is true, being in the right place at the right time is providential rather than coincidental. God orchestrates these divine appointments in response to prayers, either ours, or someone else's, to meet our needs, or those of others who are being encountered.

My friend Jane is a firm believer in divine appointments, and relates the following story. She had been preparing for a retreat, and had forgotten to arrange for the refreshments, a necessary part of any successful retreat. On the morning of the retreat, she was walking down the hall at work when she encountered another mid-level manager coming from the room she was about to enter.

The two ladies exchanged a warm greeting, and the other lady said to Jane, "I apologize for all the food still left in the room; our meeting did not have the expected attendance, and we have all this leftover to get rid of. Do you know of anyone having a meeting today, who might be able to use all this food?" she asked. Jane explained her predicament, and they thanked God for taking care of both their needs with the same encounter.

God had appointed their meeting at the perfect time, before the lady had the opportunity to offer the food that Jane needed to anyone else. When we trust our gracious Father, He always orders our steps, placing us in places, and situations where our needs can be met, or where He can use us to meet the needs of others.

Prayer: Father, we thank You today for the divine appointments You have made for us. Help us to be obedient and to get up, dress up, and show up. In Jesus' name, we pray. Amen.

Words of Love: For if you remain completely silent at this time, relief and deliverance will arise for the Jews from another place, but you and your father's house will perish. Yet who knows whether you have come to the kingdom for such a time as this? Esther 4:14

DAY 63
WANDERING MIND

Scripture: But you, when you pray, go into your room, and when you have shut your door, pray to your Father who is in the secret place; and your Father who sees in secret will reward you openly. Matthew 6:6

Are you someone who, like many of us, sometimes finds it difficult to focus when you are praying? It would be nice if simply closing our doors on the distractions around us would rein in our wandering thoughts.

One of the things that I have found beneficial in defeating the devil in this problem is to turn every wandering thought into a prayer. If my mind wanders to shopping, I pray that shoppers will be good stewards of the resources the Father has given them; if it wanders to past hurts, I pray for the perpetrators to learn to do justly, love mercy, and love others as themselves. With God's help, I am defeating the devil at his own game, and instead of feeling guilty for not being more focused, I am accepting divine intervention in directing me to pray for people and circumstances that needed prayers, which otherwise might not have come to my thoughts to pray for them. This has actually enriched my prayer time, and makes the encounter with God more personal.

So, the next time your mind begins to wander during a time of prayer, thank God for reminding you of that particular person or situation, and make that a focus of your prayer. I guarantee you will begin to enjoy your prayer experiences, and they will be more meaningful.

Scripture: Be sober, be vigilant; because your adversary the devil walks about like a roaring lion, seeking whom he may devour. 1 Peter 5:8

DAY 64

BETROTHED

Scripture: Then I, John, saw the holy city, New Jerusalem, coming down out of heaven from God, prepared as a bride adorned for her husband. Revelation 21:2

What an anticipation a girl has after her "Prince Charming" proposes; after all the preparations; and finally, the big day of the wedding celebration. The event hall is decorated and scrumptious cultural fare has been prepared for invited guests. The main attraction, however, is the bride, dressed more beautifully than she has ever been. The groom sweats or shivers with excitement as he awaits the entrance of his betrothed. His thoughts extend beyond the festivities of the day to a future with her; and then she appears, taking his breath away.

The scripture tells us that the holy city, where Christ will reign with His redeemed, will be more beautiful than the most beautiful bride ever to walk the aisle into the hands of her waiting bridegroom. The millennium with God in heaven will only be the first course of a feast with endless courses to be enjoyed throughout the ceaseless ages of eternity. The holy city, New Jerusalem, will be our final home; and its beauty can only be imagined. My imagination is limited to the greatest beauty I have so far beheld in real life or in pictures. I can't wait to see what that beautiful city will be like. Best of all is the knowledge that I will share it with my beloved Savior for all eternity.

Scripture: When everything is ready, I will come and get you, so that you will always be with me where I am. John 14:3

DAY 65
THE SOUND OF THUNDER

Scripture: Now all the people witnessed the thunderings, the lightning flashes, the sound of the trumpet, and the mountain smoking; and when the people saw it, they trembled and stood afar off. Exodus 20:18

It was a clear day, with no inclement weather forecast. Out of nowhere, there was a sound like a massive explosion. People were on edge, because of recent terrorist activities across the world, and the memory of one like we had never experienced before still haunts us. Some people ran out into the streets, and others tuned in to radio and television, to learn what had generated the sound, and if there were any effects.

That situation reminds me of the second advent. There will be a sound like thunder, or more like a sonic boom, piercing the heavens. It will be the angelic host, sounding the trumpets, and summoning those who are sealed by the blood of Christ, both living and dead, to the marriage feast of the Lamb. Yes, God will speak with trumpet sounds like thunder to beckon His children home.

The question to reconcile within ourselves is whether this sound will bring us joy of great anticipation being fulfilled, or fear that we have rejected the call of the Holy Spirit to repentance, and now it is too late. On that day, there will be no sitting on the fence. We will all be running to, or hiding from, the sound of thunder. I plan, by God's grace, to be running towards Him, shouting, "This is my God, I have waited for Him and He will save me." You should plan likewise.

Words of Love: For the Son of Man will come in the glory of His Father with His angels, and then He will reward each according to his works. Matthew 16:27

DAY 66

SAYING IT WITH MORE THAN WORDS

Scripture: My little children, let us not love in word or in tongue, but in deed and in truth. 1 John 3:18

Carina and Carlotta were twins who were as different as night and day. One was bubbly and spontaneous, while the other was quiet and very reserved. People were drawn to Carina's bubbly personality, and she was always invited to events taking place. Sometimes Carlotta would be invited "just because," but she still felt left out.

As the girls grew, there were some qualities in both that separated them even more distinctly. Carlotta was thoughtful and caring. She processed each request before saying yes, and she kept her commitment. She was genuine, and was quick to come to the aid of anyone needing help. She was a defender of "the underdog," and a friend to the friendless. While she did not say much, one could always feel her unwavering support. Carina was quick to say yes to requests, but often found herself overextended and could not follow through on her promises.

Both girls were smart and successful in their own right, and they chose professions that suited their personality. Not surprisingly, Carlotta went into the health care field, and became a physician. Carina chose a profession in the television and film industry.

As the years went by, the girls became successful in their respective fields, and the parents were very proud. Carina called periodically and expressed her love, but her schedule was always too busy when there was a need requiring her personal attention. Carlotta, recognizing her parents' growing needs, quietly made arrangements for their care; and eventually brought them to live close by, so she could personally oversee their care. For Carlotta, it was not enough to express her love in words, or to send gifts on special occasions. Meeting needs as Jesus would was the best way she could show her love for Him and for her parents.

Words of Love: By this all will know that you are My disciples, if you have love for one another. John 13:35

DAY 67

DANCING WATERS

Scripture: For since the creation of the world His invisible attributes are clearly seen, being understood by the things that are made, even His eternal power and Godhead, so that they are without excuse. Romans 1:20

It was a crisp winter morning in January when a friend called and asked me to take care of some business for her, as she was in a conference and could not do it herself. I had not planned on going to the store, but went to the closest one, which overlooked the gulf. How glad I was that I went.

As I turned the corner on a side street from the store, I beheld a sight that caused a smile to break out on my face. The shimmering sunlight on the still water was causing it to "dance." My heart joined in the melody of the songs I imagined being played in the dancing waters. I paused and thanked God for the beautiful gift He had just given me: a glimpse of His matchless love.

Such a peace came over me that I wanted to fall asleep. "Dear God, how I praise You for Your blessing of such beauty around me." It took a force of will to pull me out of my dreamlike state, and on to my next errand. I reluctantly drove away, promising myself to take every opportunity to enjoy more of the magnificent beauty of God's creation.

Words of Love: The heavens declare the glory of God; And the firmament shows His handiwork. Day unto day utters speech, and night unto night reveals knowledge. There is no speech nor language where their voice is not heard. Psalm 19:1-3

DAY 68
SUCCESS?

Scripture: Now a certain ruler asked Him, saying, "Good Teacher, what shall I do to inherit eternal life?" So, Jesus said to him… Sell all that you have and distribute to the poor, and you will have treasure in heaven; and come, follow Me." But when he heard this, he became very sorrowful, for he was very rich. Luke 18. 18-23

The rich young ruler, in the Bible story above, had achieved great success by this world's standard: Prestige, Power, and Possessions. He had it made. In today's society, he would have been quite a catch; a very eligible and sought-after young man. He was evidently from the upper strata of society: educated, privileged and well respected. A "ruler," the Bible calls him.

I sense that this young man, for all his wealth and affluence, was yearning for a deeper fulfillment. So, He sought Jesus, the One who has all the answers, and wants more than anything to draw us to the Father. He says that to follow Him we must relinquish our hold on the things of this world; or maybe it is to free ourselves of the hold that these things have on us.

Sadly, the wealthy young man, like so many of us, wanted Jesus, but only if he could hold on to Him with one hand, and the world with the other. Jesus says that while we must live in this world until He comes or calls us to sleep, we must not allow the world to live in us. He, only, wants to have residence in our hearts. The price was too steep for the rich young ruler; the grasp of the world was too strong. Two people were sad that day: the young man who thought that too much was being asked of him, and the Savior whose heart was broken that one with such promise would love the gifts more than the Giver.

Is that same battle waging within you? Where does your allegiance lie? When you choose the Giver over the gifts, He promises a rich reward that only He can supply.

Words of Love: Then Jesus said to His disciples, "Assuredly, I say to you that it is hard for a rich man to enter the kingdom of heaven. Matthew 19:23

DAY 69
WRAPPED IN TRIALS

Scripture: My brethren, count it all joy when you fall into various trials, knowing that the testing of your faith produces patience. James 1:2-3

"Lord," she cried, "I cannot take it anymore; this is too much for anyone to bear." Kadie was burdened by the multiple trials in her life. She was at a breaking point: job loss due to downsizing in her company; a broken marriage; a wayward son; and now there was the diagnosis of a stage three malignant tumor.

Kadie sank into despair. She was already hitting rock bottom, and the threat of losing her home to foreclosure because of her inability to keep up with her mortgage payment was the last straw. She finally did what she should have done in the first place; she took her burdens to the feet of Jesus. She confessed her weaknesses, and prayed for forgiveness for her shortcomings.

The Father did not add condemnation and scolding of her already dejected spirit. He opened His arms wide and invited her to rest and find solace there. Through heartfelt confessions and the study of God's Word, she found that His grace was sufficient. She trusted Him like she had never done before, and in her new-found love relationship with Jesus, Kadie found that He was enough. Wrapped in the trials that beset her, she found God's amazing grace, and His matchless love.

Kadie gradually climbed out of her pit of despair. Her cancer went into remission, medical disability helped to stabilize her financial woes, and she did not lose her home. She is not without struggles, but she had this to say: "I would not trade the experience for anything. Wrapped in those trials was my Savior's love, and what a wonderful relationship I have developed with Him."

Words of Love: And He said to me, "My grace is sufficient for you, for My strength is made perfect in weakness..." 2 Corinthians 12:9.

DAY 70
ALONE... NO, NEVER!

Scripture: And the Lord, He is the One who goes before you. He will be with you, He will not leave you nor forsake you; do not fear nor be dismayed. Deuteronomy 31:8

This scripture was Moses' encouraging words to Joshua as he prepared him to take the helm in leading the children of Israel into the Promised Land. Joshua felt inadequate and alone, as he sensed the prospect of losing Moses' leadership, but Moses reassured him that with Father God leading the way, he would never be alone.

Have you ever felt like Joshua: fearful of forging ahead with something for which you felt ill-prepared or simply had a lack of self-confidence? Be assured that with a call from the Master comes the promise of His companionship. His call is an opportunity to follow His lead. It does not guarantee freedom from resistance and opposition; what it does promise is that the outcome will be what He desires.

Martinez struggled with this philosophy. If God had placed her on this path, and she was leaning and depending on Him, why did things seem to go awry? She felt abandoned by the One who called her. She sought and listened to wise counsel; and in the end, she acknowledged that God always knew what He was doing, and she could not be more pleased with the outcome.

Words of Love: I will not leave you orphans; I will come to you. John 14:18

DAY 71

BLOOM WHERE YOU ARE PLANTED

Scripture: Whatever your hand finds to do, do it with your might; for there is no work or device or knowledge or wisdom in the grave where you are going. Ecclesiastes 9:10

When Samuel the prophet went to Jesse's house to anoint the next king, David was not brought forth, because his father Jesse considered him insignificant. He was out in the fields caring for the sheep, and was not invited to the anointing ceremony; at least not until God, through Samuel, rejected all the other brothers, and Samuel asked if there was any other, insisting that he be brought into his presence.

Instead of fuming over his lot in life, David served well where he was placed, faithful to his assignment. He was so committed to his task that he destroyed a lion and a bear to protect his flock. Because he was faithful to the "little duties," God used this "seemingly insignificant" boy to perform a big job of killing the giant Goliath, who was feared by everyone else. In the same way David fearlessly killed the lion in defense of the sheep in his care, he was eager to defend the honor of Almighty God, of whom Goliath spoke disrespectfully.

Where has God placed you at this point on your journey? Are you serving to your full potential? Are you fuming because you have been passed over again? Are you being asked to train the person who is going to get the promotion you deserve? Is the new staff member being compensated at a higher rate of pay than you are?

Be faithful to the tasks you accepted and for the wages you agreed to. Give a hundred percent of your time and talent. God is watching, as are those around you. The spirit with which you serve will be rewarded; if not now, then in eternity.

Words of love: His lord said to him, 'Well done, good and faithful servant; you have been faithful over a few things, I will make you ruler over many things. Enter into the joy of your lord. Matthew 25:23

DAY 72

EYES ON JESUS

Scripture: Therefore, we also, since we are surrounded by so great a cloud of witnesses, let us lay aside every weight, and the sin which so easily ensnares us, and let us run with endurance the race that is set before us, looking unto Jesus, the author and finisher of our faith, who for the joy that was set before Him endured the cross, despising the shame, and has sat down at the right hand of the throne of God. Hebrews 12:1-2

There is so much distraction in the world around us, and so many things vying for our attention that it is hard to stay focused. A friend shared a story about a group of athletes who were representing their country in an event. The team had been making great strides until one member became distracted by events around them, causing the team to lose the race.

I imagine the emotions of the group, as well as the country being represented. Much time and resources had been invested in their preparation and participation in the event. I can also imagine the young athlete's shame; the hurt of the team members; the frustration of the trainer and sponsors, and even the anger of some fans.

The lesson of this story is that we are all in a race. For some it is a sprint, while for others it is a marathon. Some of us have the course set uphill and around winding trails; others have a straight course ahead. I cannot run your race and you cannot run mine. Each of us has different challenges and different expectations to meet. Sometimes there are others running in the lanes beside us, and sometimes there are even other events taking place along the way. We may be tempted to take our eyes off the road ahead, looking to the right, to the left, or even behind. That could be disastrous, however, as the devil is always waiting for opportunities to cause us to stumble, veer out of our lane, miss a turn, or simply become discouraged.

Christ is standing at the finish line, and He is encouraging us every step of the way. Visualize the look of love on His face; hear the excitement in His voice. He says, "As long as you keep your eyes on Me, I will provide you with all the support you need to successfully run this race: The Bread of Life to satisfy your hunger and give you the spiritual energy to keep running, and the Living Water to quench your thirsty soul." Stay the course. The prize will be worth it.

Words of Love: Let your eyes look straight ahead, and your eyelids look right before you. Proverbs 4:25

DAY 73
FIVE LOAVES AND TWO FISH

Scripture: Cast your bread upon the waters, for you will find it after many days. Ecclesiastes 11:1

Many of you know the story of Jesus feeding the multitude with the lunch of a small boy. We must do nothing to detract from that miraculous event. But I beg to take a moment and wonder about the boy who had the five loaves and two fish. I believe neither the loaves nor the fish were of large sizes; not that the size would have made any difference to the validity of the miracle.

Not much more, if anything, is known about the child who provided the means for this miracle; the only person in a crowd of more than five thousand to have been prepared for an outing to listen to the Great Teacher. Was he alone? Did he come from afar? What must have been going through his mind as the disciples sought food among the crowd, and then found his lunch? What happened to him after being part of such a miracle? Not being a Bible scholar, I don't have the answers to these questions, and maybe the questions are not even relevant.

There are some deeper truths about this story and the young boy that speak to my heart, however:
- This young boy did not leave home with the expectation to be used by the Master, but he was prepared
- He was willing to give all that he had for the greater good
- In his hands, his lunch was only enough for his day's needs; but in the hands of the Master, it fed the multitude, with some to spare

What do you have at your disposal? Are you willing to make your meager "loaves and fish" available to the Savior? He wants to use what you have, and multiply it to satisfy the needs of those who lack. He will give you more than you could ever ask or need in return.

Words of Love: You shall surely give to him, and your heart should not be grieved when you give to him, because for this thing the Lord your God will bless you in all your works and in all to which you put your hand. Deuteronomy 15:10

DAY 74
DON'T "BUT" ME!

Scripture: And so it was, when Jesus had ended these sayings, that the people were astonished at His teaching, for He taught them as one having authority, and not as the scribes. Matthew 7:28-29

In the Caribbean where I grew up in the 1950s, the adults had a problem with children who argued with them, and using the conjunction "but" was considered to be very argumentative. My mother was one of those ladies with that belief, and using that word landed me in big trouble one afternoon after school. I related a story of something that happened at school to the family, and my mother insisted it could not have happened the way I told them it did. I dared to say the forbidden word, "'But,' Mamma." I did not even get to finish the statement with, "you were not there."

Unlike my beloved mother, who was sometimes wrong in her opinions, as we often are, when God the Father, or Christ Jesus, speak, Their Word should not be challenged. Their Word is the authority; it is dependable and absolutely trustworthy. They will never have to tell me that no "buts" are accepted. If Their Word says it, I believe and accept it, for they are the same yesterday, today, and forever. Their Word is their character; and Their character does not change.

Words of Love: For I am the Lord, I do not change; therefore, you are not consumed, O sons of Jacob. Malachi 3:6

DAY 75
A SHELTER IN THE STORM

Scripture: For You have been a strength to the poor, a strength to the needy in his distress, a refuge from the storm, a shade from the heat; For the blast of the terrible ones is as a storm against the wall. Isaiah 25:4

Hurricane Katrina, for those of us living in states bordering the Gulf of Mexico, is a storm etched in our memories forever. There were mandatory evacuations in many low-lying areas, and others were encouraged to seek shelter further inland. As the twenty-four-hour warning period arrived, a contra flow of traffic was initiated and no traffic was allowed to go south.

My husband, who had resisted evacuating for previous storms, was ready at daybreak the day prior to the storm, and so we headed north. Friends, three hours inland, were gracious enough to offer us shelter; and we spent a week there before we were able to return to our home.

The storms of life are raging all around us, and they often threaten us with annihilation. We need a safe shelter; and the only place of true safety is in Jesus Christ. He is our Rock, our hiding place, our firm foundation, and our stronghold. He encourages us to run to Him. During Katrina, the shelters along the way filled up quickly, and many people were turned away.

Vernon J. Charlesworth wrote the lyrics to the beautiful song, "A Shelter in the Time of Storm," in 1880, with the first verse which reads: "The Lord's our Rock; in Him we hide, A shelter in the time of storm; Secure whatever ill betide, A shelter in the time of storm." We need the confidence of those words. During the storms that toss us to and fro; and threaten to untie our mooring, we need to find the safe harbor that only Jesus guarantees. Let us not wait for mandatory evacuations. The Holy Spirit encourages and gently nudges us, but He will never force us against our will. Let us heed the call before the flood waters begin to rise, and it is too late to find refuge.

Words of Love: Take heed, watch and pray; for you do not know when the time is. Mark 13:33

DAY 76
DETOUR

Scripture: And we know that all things work together for good to those who love God, to those who are the called according to His purpose. Romans 8:28

It hardly matters what country, state, city or town you live in, there seems to be constant road construction going on, and it is often accompanied by signs which say, "Detour ahead." Sometimes the detour sign is without warning, and it takes you by surprise. Life is somewhat like road construction; unexpected detours frequently pop up along the way. Most times we are not prepared for them: we are running late for some encounter, or we have inadequate fuel for extra distance.

Connie and Chester had recently gotten married. They were working on advanced degrees, and talked about starting a family right away. What they had not planned on was the diagnosis of a possible terminal illness. The plans for children were put on hold, as medical care was sought for this fast-progressing disease.

An aggressive treatment plan was implemented. Connie's doctoral studies were sidelined, and Chester struggled to go on with his studies, as they had planned to complete this journey together.

A friend gave them a wonderful gift, which refocused them and got them back on track. It was the gift of wise counsel. She told them, "This is called life, and there are numerous detours you will have to face while you live it; so prayerfully follow the outlined path, and the detour signs will take you back to the main thoroughfare." They took this well-meaning advice to heart, and the struggles became easier to bear.

Words of Love: Therefore, we do not lose heart. Even though our outward man is perishing, yet the inward man is being renewed day by day. 2 Corinthians 4:16

DAY 77
IF FOR YOU ALONE

Scripture: The Spirit of the Lord is upon Me, because He has anointed Me to preach the gospel to the poor; He has sent Me to heal the brokenhearted, to proclaim liberty to the captives, and recovery of sight to the blind; To set at liberty those who are oppressed. Luke 4:18

Christ loves us with an everlasting love, and would have gone to the cross for any of us alone. Pauline was feeling the weight of her sinfulness, when a friend invited her to church. The minister preached a sermon that touched her heart, and gave her hope that she was not beyond the mercy and grace of God. He said that if she or any one of us was the only sinner needing to be rescued from this sinful world, Christ would have come and died.

Pauline could not believe her ears; she was loved that much, that Jesus would have come and died to save her alone. The thought "blew her mind" and sent her searching for more truths. She discovered that the message was a simple one:
- She had sinned - the crime
- She deserved death - the penalty
- She needed a rescuer - Jesus, Savior
- The price He paid for her rescue - His blood

Pauline called the pastor and told him she wanted to commit her life to Christ. "No one has ever loved me this much," she said. "I have always been made to feel obligated when someone did something nice for me," Pauline went on to say, "but this time I want to love my Sweet Jesus with all my being."

When it truly sinks in how much Jesus loves each of us, and what our salvation cost Him, how selfish it is not to love Him in return. My girlfriend puts it this way, "I am abundantly blessed and highly favored to have a God who loves me to that extent;" and I say, "Amen."

Words of love: For God so loved the world that He gave His Only Son, that whoever believes in Him should not perish, but have eternal life. John 3:16

DAY 78

ENJOY THEM WHILE YOU CAN

Scripture: To everything *there is* a season, a time for every purpose under heaven. Ecclesiastes 3:1

There are a few fruits and vegetables that grow year-round, but most are seasonal in nature. The best time to enjoy them is when they are in their peak season.

Some life experiences are "seasonal" as well. There is an old adage which says, "Strike while the iron is hot." This implies that opportunities will not always be available, so we should take advantage of them while we can.

Susan's siblings had made the trip home for a visit from their respective posts overseas. There had been some family feud that had driven a wedge between the siblings over the years. Susan felt an overwhelming need to let bygones be bygones, and enjoy the family togetherness while she had the opportunity, but she resisted. She was cordial, but she never joined in the festivities, always making excuses for her absence and inability to participate.

The time came for them to leave and return to their "homes." The siblings expressed how sad they were not to have had more time with Susan, but hoped next time would be different. Disaster struck shortly thereafter, however, and the family was never complete again.

Susan was heartbroken and riddled with guilt. She had missed the opportunity to enjoy her siblings while she could. She begged forgiveness of God, and the rest of the family, for her selfish and unforgiving ways. Although she received the forgiveness she sought, she still misses the privilege she forfeited of having a good time with everyone when the opportunity was presented.

Tomorrow is not promised to any man, so, enjoy every blessed moment of today. Find ways to say more "Thank You," "I Love You," and "I Appreciate You." When the opportunity is no longer available, you will be glad you did.

Words of Love: And whatever you do in word or deed, do all in the name of the Lord Jesus, giving thanks to God the Father through Him. Colossians 3:17

DAY 79
ANXIETY WILL KILL YOU

Scripture: Be anxious for nothing, but in everything by prayer and supplication, with thanksgiving, let your requests be made known to God; and the peace of God, which surpasses all understanding, will guard your hearts and minds through Christ Jesus. Philippians 4:6-7

The scripture goes on to say that prayer and supplication, with thanksgiving, bring peace that passes all understanding. A weight is lifted from your shoulders when you relinquish your cares and anxieties to the Lord.

Damian was working on a project in his home office when something happened beyond his knowledge or expertise. All he knew was that he had apparently lost all his work to that point. His computer had recently been repaired, and it was doing some strange things with which he was not familiar. Being unsure of the automatic file backups, as he was used to it doing before the repair, and not doing frequent manual saves, Damian became anxious. He researched various options, but nothing seemed to work, resulting in a full-blown panic attack.

Frantic, Damian ceased his futile efforts and sought God in prayer. He was directed to resources that helped him restore the file and resolve the glitch that caused the problem, to prevent it from happening again. Damian ended up having to seek medical attention for the heart palpitations that his anxiety produced.

There is a song written by Joseph M. Scriven as a poem in 1855 which says, "Oh what peace we often forfeit, Oh, what needless pain we bear; all because we do not carry, everything to God in prayer." When we fail to make prayer our first step, we take many steps backwards, and the resulting anxiety can have lasting health consequences.

Words of Love: And let the peace of God rule in your hearts, to which also you were called in one body; and be thankful. Colossians 3:15

DAY 80
IMMEASURABLE GIFTS

Scripture: But as for me, I would seek God, and to God I would commit my cause—Who does great things, and unsearchable, marvelous things without number. He gives rain on the earth, and sends waters on the fields. He sets on high those who are lowly, and those who mourn are lifted to safety. Job 5:8-11

God allowed Satan to rob Job of just about everything he had: his children, possessions, and his health. His wife and friends, instead of being the support that he needed, blamed him for bringing such distress on himself, and encouraged him to curse God and die. Job himself, in a moment of weakness, questioned God, but he refused to blame or dishonor Him.

When God restored Job, He did it in a big way. Job was one of the wealthiest men, if not the wealthiest, of his time, before his tremendous loss. He was even more prosperous after his restoration. That is the God we serve; the One who delights in bestowing immeasurable gifts and blessings on His faithful children.

God's gifts to us surpass material gains. They are gifts of favor, family, friends, health of body and a sound mind. There are gifts of peace, joy, contentment, and service. Then there are the gifts of grace, sharing, generosity and hospitality, sympathy and empathy. There are the gifts of laughter and happiness; and oh, the gift of loving, even those who do not love us in return. The list is inexhaustible, if we consider all the "little ones" that we so often take for granted.

A popular song admonishes us to count our blessings 'gifts,' name them one by one, and see all that God has done. He is a Big God, with a storehouse of unlimited gifts, and a tremendously generous heart, ready to bestow upon us more than we have room to receive.

Words of Love: Bring all the tithes into the storehouse, that there may be food in My house, and try Me now in this, says the Lord of hosts, if I will not open for you the windows of heaven and pour out for you such blessing that there will not be room enough to receive it. Malachi 3:10

DAY 81
FLOWERS FOR MY TABLE

Scripture: But you are a chosen generation, a royal priesthood, a holy nation, His own special people, that you may proclaim the praises of Him who called you out of darkness into His marvelous light. 1 Peter 2:9

A dear friend came to visit me one evening. She had taken a job close by, and had not visited my home before. I made a simple dinner and invited another friend to join us.

The friend who was visiting for the first time brought the most gorgeous bouquet of yellow roses. To display them justly, I found a crystal and silver goblet that was a gift from hosts in Denmark. They were the perfect centerpiece for my dinner table.

Those flowers made me think of who we are to God: 'precious flowers that adorn His table.' He loves us so much that He desires to have us in His presence for all eternity. The God of the universe desires to gaze upon us forever; and what a price He paid. What matchless love. We were filthy with the stain of sin, but He cleaned us up; watered our withered souls, fed us with the bread of life, and nourished us back to spiritual health.

God cherishes the beloved sons and daughters that He created us to be. As the poetic words in the book of Solomon describe: we are God's bride. He wants to make us more beautiful than anything else He has created, especially on the inside: more beautiful than any lily of the field or any bouquet of yellow roses.

Words of Love: For you are a holy people to the Lord your God; the Lord your God has chosen you to be a people for Himself, a special treasure above all the peoples on the face of the earth. Deuteronomy 7:6

DAY 82
PHOBIAS

Scripture: There is no fear in love; but perfect love casts out fear, because fear involves torment. But he who fears has not been made perfect in love. 1 John 4:18

Fear is real and can sometimes paralyze us, preventing us from experiencing life as God wants us to. I have a fear of heights and precipitous roads. My heart palpitates, my legs feel like jellyfish, and my hands become clammy whenever I encounter hilly roads. You got it... leave me in the plains.

There is something wrong with this and other phobias that we have, however. They limit our life experiences. I don't have the space to tell you how my phobias have limited me. I have a friend who will not ride in an elevator, and is almost equally fearful of riding the escalator. She will take the stairs regardless of the floor. Thankfully, she has the stamina to do so.

I'm convinced that God wants us to live a life free of unrealistic fears. This requires unwavering trust in His leading. I don't know that He wants us to be daredevils, but neither does He want us to be paralyzed by phobias that plague this sinful world.

What are your fears? What is preventing you from living life to its fullest? Would you like to begin living a life of freedom? Let us pray and ask God for deliverance.

Prayer: Father God, to us our fears are real, but Your Word says that You have not given us a spirit of fear, but of a sound mind. Please fill us with Your Holy Spirit, and calm our fears, so that we may truly live and serve You as You designed. Amen.

Words of Love: Say to those who are fearful-hearted, Be strong, do not fear! Behold, your God will come with vengeance, with the recompense of God; He will come and save you. Isaiah 35:4

DAY 83

SO THEY WON'T FORGET

Scripture: Only take heed to yourself, and diligently keep yourself, lest you forget the things your eyes have seen, and lest they depart from your heart all the days of your life. And teach them to your children and your grandchildren. Deuteronomy 4:9

Marcia was concerned that her children, who were no longer faithful in their worship of Jehovah, were not sharing the truths about Christ with her grandchildren. Thankfully, they were not opposed to her teaching them, and taking them to church with her. Marcia used every opportunity to plant the seeds of God's precepts in these open and receptive little hearts, not knowing what fruits her efforts would produce.

Moses had led a rebellious and ungrateful group of Israelites through the wilderness for forty years, and his struggles with them were many. He, though imperfect, and having his own struggles with anger and impatience, was faithful in teaching God's people about Him as their loving Father. As he neared the end of his life, he admonished the Israelites to remember God's goodness and teach their children and grandchildren. In chapter 5 of Deuteronomy, he outlined the law, as given to him by God, and encouraged the children of Israel to observe them.

Marcia reflected on the example of Moses. She purposed in her heart to make sharing the love of Christ with her grandchildren and great-grandchildren a part of her life work.

Who has God placed in your life to share His Word with today? Don't ignore the opportunity, even if your efforts appear to be in vain. The truths that seem to be spurned today may have sunk very deep in the hearts of the hearers, and in due season may draw them into the arms of a Savior who has been waiting patiently.

Words of Love: And the covenant that I have made with you, you shall not forget, nor shall you fear other gods. 2 Kings 17:38

DAY 84
OBEDIENCE: YIELDING TO GOD'S WILL

Scripture: I delight to do Your will, O my God, and Your law is within my heart. Psalm 40:8

Joey was a good kid, and he was liked by his teachers and coaches. He was well-rounded, too: having a GPA of 3.75; playing sports; and serving in student government.

One day Joey was put to the test, to see where his allegiance was. It was a tough decision for this seventeen-year-old, who was new in his faith. He struggled for a while, vacillating between two desires; one to maintain his image and prestige in the eyes of man, and the other to stand firm for God. Joey finally decided he would choose God's way. To the disappointment of many, but to the glory of God, Joey yielded to God's will. His obedience to Christ caught the attention of several people, whose admiration and respect he earned.

Joey's strong and unyielding faith ended up being a blessing rather than a barrier. He focused his attention on his goals and earned a full scholarship to a prestigious university. He maintained his obedience to God's will throughout his college years, and went on to enjoy a very promising career. Joey is proud to share his faith, and in humility he exemplifies his strong connection with Jesus Christ.

True happiness comes from yielding to what is right, and resisting what is wrong. Joey did it by God's grace, and so can you.

Words of Love: Now therefore, if you will indeed obey My voice and keep My covenant, then you shall be a special treasure to Me above all people; for all the earth is Mine. Exodus19:5

DAY 85
ONLY ONE DOOR!

Scripture: Most assuredly, I say to you, he who does not enter the sheepfold by the door, but climbs up some other way, the same is a thief and a robber. John 10:1

John chapter 10 paints a beautiful image of the efforts made by a true shepherd to protect and care for his sheep. There is the imagery of the sheepfold, made of rocks stacked on each other and having only one entrance. The shepherd corrals his sheep as the evening draws near, then he positions himself at the opening of the fold. No thief or wild animal can get to the sheep without first contending with him at the door.

When we allow Jesus Christ to secure us in His fold, we may have attacks from every direction, but no harm can come to us without the attacker first battling with our Protector. David said he fought off a lion and a bear to save his sheep; imagine what steps the Good Shepherd will take to ensure our eternal safety.

Something else intrigues me about the imagery of the shepherd, the sheep and the sheepfold. The story states that when a shepherd comes to get his sheep from a communal sheepfold, he goes to the door and calls his sheep; and they follow him, for they know his voice. A robber and a thief would try other means such as scaling the low walls of the fold, and the sheep would run, because they do not recognize him.

Are you secure in fold of the Good Shepherd? He recognizes that like the helpless sheep, we are no match for the traps of the devil; so, He offers us shelter and safety from the thief who would rob us of our eternal joy. Unlike the sheep, however, we were gifted with the ability to make intelligent choices. We can choose to stay in the fold where there is safety, or we can choose to wander off and be prey to the wiles of Satan.

Words of Love: I am the door. If anyone enters by Me, he will be saved, and will go in and out and find pasture. John 10:9

DAY 86
BROKEN PEOPLE

Scripture: Remember therefore from where you have fallen; repent and do the first works, or else I will come to you quickly and remove your lampstand from its place—unless you repent. Revelation 2:5

The world is filled with broken people; many struggling to hold on to the truths of God's saving grace. The consolation is that it is not how many times we have fallen, but how many times we are willing to cry out for mercy and deliverance that makes the difference between being lost or saved.

Many people begin the Christian walk with eagerness; they want everyone to experience the joy they have found in Christ. Very soon, however, their light begins to flicker and quickly goes out. This is because, like the seeds that have fallen into shallow soil, they have not allowed the truths of God's Word to sink deep into their hearts. Then the first obstacle that Satan puts in their path trips them up, and they fall away.

The church is also filled with broken people. It is sometimes referred to as a hospital; and hospitals, we know, are for people who are sick and broken. Even when they heal, scar tissue remains, which itself causes other problems to develop 'down the road.' You may have heard the saying, "Hurting people hurt people." These broken people can inflict some serious pain on others, sometimes causing them give up and turn away from God.

Another imagery that comes to mind is that of a vessel fighting the raging sea. There is still more safety in the boat that is still upright, however, than jumping into the angry tides. Putting our combined energies into saving the ship is more helpful than trying to row away on a makeshift raft, all by ourselves, in shark-infested waters.

Let us remember the truths and the love that first drew us to Christ. They are worth holding on to, through much prayer, study of God's Word, and sharing the light that we have. God will never turn His back on a repentant heart. With outstretched hands, He will keep us from falling.

Words of Love: The sacrifices of God are a broken spirit, a broken and a contrite heart—These, O God, You will not despise. Psalm 51:17

DAY 87
TOO GOOD TO BE TRUE?

Scripture: But Ruth said: "Entreat me not to leave you, or to turn back from following after you; For wherever you go, I will go; And wherever you lodge, I will lodge; Your people shall be my people, and your God, my God." Ruth 1:16

The story of Ruth is a very inspiring one. It reminds us that faithfulness has its rewards. I find a few facts in the story quite interesting:
- Naomi, her husband and her two sons, sought refuge from a famine in Bethlehem, in the land of Moab
- Both sons took Moabite wives
- Neither of the sons had any children
- All three men died, leaving no heirs, and their wives without a protector
- There was news of improved conditions in Bethlehem, so Naomi decided to return home
- She discouraged her two daughters-in-law from following her, but instead to return to their people and their pagan gods.

Naomi's reasoning for discouraging her daughters-in-law from leaving Moab with her seems logical, and done out of love for them, but it lacked faith in a trustworthy God. Orpah heeded her mother-in-law's entreaty, but Ruth would hear none of it. Thus, we have the beautiful passage of scripture above, followed by verse 17 of the same chapter: "Where you die, I will die, and there will I be buried. The Lord do so to me, and more also, If anything but death parts you and me."

The story unfolds that on their return to Bethlehem, Ruth found favor in the eyes of Boaz, a distant cousin of Naomi, in whose field she had gleaned. Through a series of divine interventions, Boaz ends up marrying Ruth, thus setting in place the lineage of David, and ultimately of Jesus Christ.

God says He will reward our faithfulness over the small matters in life, with opportunities for greater things. It pays to be faithful.

Words of Love: My eyes shall be on the faithful of the land, that they may dwell with me; He who walks in a perfect way, he shall serve me. Psalm 101:6

DAY 88
SPEAK LORD... AND HELP ME TO LISTEN

Scripture: Therefore, Eli said to Samuel, "Go, lie down; and it shall be, if He calls you, that you must say, 'Speak, Lord, for Your servant hears.'" So Samuel went and lay down in his place. 1 Samuel 3:9

Samuel mistook the calls of the Lord for Eli's, but Eli assured him that he had not called. After the third time, Eli figured that it must have been the Lord who was calling Samuel, and instructed him how to respond. Not only was Samuel responsive to Eli's instructions regarding how he should answer, but he was obedient to deliver the message that the Lord gave him for Eli.

The Lord speaks to us all the time: through His Word; through the wise counsel of others; through nature, and through the Holy Spirit. The question is, are we listening? Are we waiting to hear a loud audible voice like thunder? Why isn't the gentle chiding of a quiet conscience enough?

According to scripture, Eli had been warned over time about the misconduct of his sons. Wanton behaviors were being displayed; a disregard and disrespect for holy things. Eli, however, was an enabler, and neglected to provide fatherly counsel and punishment for their behaviors. As a result, God exacted His punishment, which was death.

Words of Love: While it is said: "Today, if you will hear His voice, do not harden your hearts as in the rebellion." Hebrews 3:15

DAY 89
SOLD OUT FROM WITHIN

Scripture: Now when they saw him afar off, even before he came near them, they conspired against him to kill him… Come and let us sell him to the Ishmaelites, and let not our hand be upon him, for he is our brother and our flesh… Genesis 37:18-36

It is extremely painful when there is betrayal by those one holds dear; whether it is family, friends, or colleagues. The reason it is so very difficult is that they have knowledge of personal and intimate details that make their stories about you more believable than something coming from a stranger.

Joseph experienced the betrayal of his brothers, who first conspired to kill him, then relented and sold him into slavery. Although his physical life was spared, his life of freedom was sacrificed for many years.

Cooper experienced a situation similar to Joseph. He was far from home, and had welcomed the friendship of some colleagues. They turned on him, misjudged him and lied about him, and although he was not killed or imprisoned, it nearly cost him his career. Those who came to his defense also became targets, and some were even forced from their positions.

The worst example of being sold out from within, however, is the story of our Lord Jesus. Judas sold Him for thirty pieces of silver, and Peter denied knowing Him three times. Christ's forgiveness, and Joseph's, demonstrated what it means to forgive and not seek your own revenge.

Words of Love: Beloved, do not avenge yourselves, but rather give place to wrath; for it is written, "Vengeance is Mine, I will repay," says the Lord. Romans 12:19

DAY 90
THE ALPHA AND THE OMEGA

Scripture: I was in the Spirit on the Lord's Day, and I heard behind me a loud voice, as of a trumpet, saying, "I am the Alpha and the Omega, the First and the Last... Revelation 1:10-11

The words of the scripture above were spoken to John, during a worship experience, while he was exiled on the Island of Patmos. According to the scripture, John falls at the feet of this Being who appeared before him, as though dead. I can only imagine the fear and trembling at the sight of this foreboding figure, who told John not to be afraid. He said He was the One who was dead and was now alive forevermore, and held the keys of Death and Hades (Revelation 1:18).

Who is He who has no beginning and no end, and offers us a life in eternity with Him; if we are faithful? Who better to align ourselves with than the One who has conquered the grave, and is the only One who can both offer and guarantee us eternal life; a life beyond the grave? His name is Jesus, and we call Him Lord.

Christ's message to John for us is a call to holiness and right living. God desires to replicate His character in us who were created in His image.

If we believe the message given to John, and understand the implications, then let us ask Jesus to reign in our hearts, and prepare us to meet the Father. My prayer is: "Restore in me a clean heart, O God, and renew Your Spirit within me."

Words of Love: Do not fear any of those things which you are about to suffer. Indeed, the devil is about to throw some of you into prison, that you may be tested, and you will have tribulation ten days. Be faithful until death, and I will give you the crown of life. Revelation 2:10

DAY 91

CALM

Scripture: He calms the storm, so that its waves are still. Psalm 107:29

I was flying to see my sister in the winter of 2016, for the special occasion of her baptism. It was a beautiful day with crisp air and bright skies. The flight was delayed, which would likely cause me to miss my connection, so, the airline representative took precautionary measures and booked me on a later connecting flight with a three-hour layover. I accepted the announcement since I could not change the circumstances or the outcome.

We finally boarded the plane, went through the usual perfunctory instructions, and settled in for what we anticipated would be a good flight. It was a full flight and all was quiet as some people worked sudoku puzzles, some read, some listened to music on their iPods, and others slept. I engaged my seat mate in a brief conversation, then we turned our attention to our respective interests. All was calm, and I wanted it to remain that way.

I had a moment of reflection as I thought about the turmoil of life, and how most of us wish for things to be calm. It would not take much for this "calm" flight to turn to panic with a little bit of turbulence. Thankfully, we had a smooth flight, and everyone maintained a visible calm.

What upsets your sense of calm? What turns your day "upside down"? Is the ebb and flow of life's turbulent waters knocking you off your feet? Is your stress level "off the chart"? There is one who has the power to calm all storms, and He wants to calm your "troubled seas."

Words of love: God is our refuge and strength, a very present help in trouble. Psalm 46:1

DAY 92

UNDER HIS WINGS

Scripture: He who dwells in the secret place of the Most High shall abide under the shadow of the Almighty. I will say of the Lord, "He is my refuge and my fortress; My God, in Him I will trust." Psalm 91:1-2

On one leg of a trip between Atlanta and West Palm Beach, I was in a window seat directly over the wings of the plane. I could see ahead in the distance, and the same looking behind, but I could not see the sights directly below. It was a clear day with cotton-candy clouds, but my reason for liking window seats, to see the sights below, was hampered by the gigantic wings of the aircraft.

A moment of reflection. The image of Christ as a protective parent, sheltering His children from the storms of life or from the jaws of the foe, is one of awe-inspiring love. His protective wings are never intended to block our view of the world around us, but to shelter us until we are ready to fly.

When life's trials assail you, and you long for safety; run to the Father, and find refuge under His wings, as the words of this beautiful song written by William Cushing in 1823 say, "Under His Wings I am safely abiding; Though the night deepens and tempests are wild. Still I will trust Him, I know He will keep me, He has redeemed me, and I am His child."

Words of Love: Because he has set his love upon Me, therefore I will deliver him; I will set him on high, because he has known My name. Psalm 91:14

DAY 93
TAKE IT BACK

Scripture: Who sharpen their tongue like a sword, and bend their bows to shoot their arrows—bitter words, that they may shoot in secret at the blameless; Suddenly they shoot at him and do not fear. Psalm 64:3-4

Two childhood friends were fighting over hurtful words one had said to the other. One boy could be heard shouting to the other, while holding him in a headlock, "Take it back; you had better take it back." Unfortunately, words spoken cannot be retrieved. Fortunately, these two friends did not stay angry with each other for very long.

More damaging than the words one young friend spoke, unthinkingly, to another, are some of the words I have heard spoken by adults:
- "I curse the day you were born, and wish you had died"
- "You are just like your father, and I hate you"
- "You are nothing but a no-good scoundrel"
- "You are good for nothing"
- "You will never amount to anything good"

I have heard it said that sticks and stones can break your bones, but words do not matter. That saying is without merit. The damage caused by sticks and stones is often more easily repaired than the wounds caused by ill-spoken words. We are encouraged to think of the consequences of our words, and send up a prayer before we speak them.

Words of Love: Set a guard, O Lord, over my mouth; Keep watch over the door of my lips. Psalm 141:3

DAY 94
RELATIONSHIP BUILDING FOR JESUS CHRIST

Scripture: Therefore, if anyone is in Christ, he is a new creation; old things have passed away; behold, all things have become new. Now all things are of God, who has reconciled us to Himself through Jesus Christ, and has given us the ministry of reconciliation. 2 Corinthians 5:17-18

I visited my sister's church for a midweek prayer service, where the reflective study was on Making Friends for Christ. The speaker mentioned that Jesus treated people as One desiring their good. He further stated that Christ accomplished this by showing a genuine interest in the people for whom He labored, and among whom He ministered. He met them where they were, not expecting more of them than it was their capacity to deliver.

I quickly thought about my neighborhood, and acts of kindness that might speak to the hearts of those who live around me, without pushing religion. I asked myself the questions: Have I shown them sympathy in their times of grief? Have I acted to meet known needs without being asked? Have I won their confidence, displaying love and care?

Take a moment to reflect on your neighborhood and your immediate neighbors. Do you know them by their first names, or do you even know their names at all? Do you share in their joy when they are happy, and show your sorrow for them when they grieve? Or do they only know you as the person who dresses up on the weekend and goes to church? People's actions sometimes speak so loud that you cannot hear their words: they are saying "nice" words, with very mean actions. A favorite quote by Edgar A. Guest states, 'I'd rather see a sermon, than hear one any day; I'd rather one should walk with me than merely tell the way."

If you want to make friends for Christ, and win souls for His kingdom, you must first build genuine relationships that last. In time, God's time, people will want to know the Lord who inspires such a difference in your life.

Words of Love: Let no one seek his own, but each one the other's well-being. 1 Corinthians 10:24

DAY 95
SEVENTY TIMES SEVEN

Scripture: Then Peter came to Him and said, "Lord, how often shall my brother sin against me, and I forgive him? Up to seven times?" Jesus said to him, "I do not say to you, up to seven times, but up to seventy times seven." Matthew 18:21-22

Not again. Gina was very frustrated with the repeated bad behavior of her adult daughter. She was pretty fed up and was ready to throw her hands in the air and give up on her. Every time the young woman would mess up, she would come running to her mother with an apology, a cry for help and a promise to do better. This was repeated too many times to count, and Gina did not know how many more times she could bail her out of her escapades.

Then one morning, in her time with the Lord, she was led to the passage above. Daniel 9:9 says that the Lord our God is merciful and forgiving, even though we have rebelled against Him; and Colossians 1:13-14 tells us that the Father has rescued us from the dominion of darkness and brought us into the kingdom of the Son He loves; in whom we have redemption, and the forgiveness of sins. And, Ephesians 1:7 says that in Christ we have redemption through His blood, the forgiveness of sins, in accordance with the riches of God's grace.

Gina was convicted to try harder, and find new approaches to help her daughter, instead of giving up on her. Isn't that what the Father has done for us? How many times have you messed up? I have given up counting my mess-ups, but God has not given up on me. Forgiveness is a powerful thing, and our Father has forgiven us over and over again, giving us more than 'seventy times seven' of second chances. He is simply asking us to do the same for one another.

Words of Love: For if you forgive men their trespasses, your heavenly Father will also forgive you. But if you do not forgive men their trespasses, neither will your Father forgive your trespasses. Matthew 6:14-15

DAY 96
WORDS THAT HEAL

Scripture: Cast your burden on the Lord, and He shall sustain you; He shall never permit the righteous to be moved. Psalm 55:22

Jesus is our burden bearer and our problem solver. When we are aching from troubles without and within, He speaks words of love and comfort that heal our broken hearts.

Karen found this to be true when she was misjudged and maligned on her job. The Father of love sent her many healing words through caring friends who reminded her that she was special in God's eyes. Caring friends also directed her to positive and inspirational programing that uplifted her; gave or loaned her books with messages of encouragement; prayed with her, and invited her to church, where she heard the healing Word of God.

What were some of the words that provided a healing balm for Karen's heart? She says that the following are on her short list:

- "God made only one of you, and He doesn't want you changed; if He wants you improved, He reserves that task for Himself."
- The Lord is near to the brokenhearted and saves the crushed in spirit (Psalm 34:18).
- Fear not, for I am with you; be not dismayed, for I am your God; I will strengthen you, I will help you, I will uphold you with my righteous right hand. Isaiah 41:10
- "He heals the brokenhearted, and binds up their wounds." Psalm 147:3

Words of Love: And He said to me, "My grace is sufficient for you, for My strength is made perfect in weakness." Therefore, most gladly I will rather boast in my infirmities, that the power of Christ may rest upon me. 2 Corinthians 12:9

DAY 97
DON'T ROB ME OF MY BLESSING

Scripture: He has shown you, O man, what is good; And what does the Lord require of you, but to do justly, to love mercy, and to walk humbly with your God? Micah 6:8

Sometimes we become filled with pride in believing we have been blessed enough to bless others, but there is nothing that those being helped can do to bless us in return. I was in my mid-twenties when I learned that every one of God's children has something to give, and someone they can bless.

Sister Sanders was an elderly lady in my church. She was of very limited income, but exuded a love and a warmth that drew everyone to her. A group of us unofficially adopted Sister Sanders, and found joy in meeting some of her material needs. She was always grateful, but felt the need to show her gratitude with small tokens such as a couple pieces of fruits. Feeling that she was denying herself to extend those loving acts, we tried to discourage her actions.

One morning at church, Sister Sanders presented us with her usual little brown paper bag of goodies, for which we lovingly reprimanded her. The next words from her were a lesson I have never forgotten: "Do not rob me of my blessings." We sometimes develop pride in our ability to give. Receiving, on the other hand, humbles us. Let us be as grateful in receiving as we are gracious in giving.

Words of Love: Be kindly affectionate to one another with brotherly love, in honor giving preference to one another. Romans 12:10

DAY 98
SOMEDAY SYNDROME

Scripture: I must work the works of Him who sent Me while it is day; the night is coming when no one can work. John 9:4

It has been a childhood dream to be a published writer. I had written a few stories here and there, but never did anything with them. What I had was the "Someday Syndrome." "Someday" I would get to it, was my frequent comment. Pablo Picasso says, "Only put off until tomorrow what you are willing to die having left undone," and Charles Dickens said, "Procrastination is the thief of time, collar him." It took me many years for that "someday" to become today.

I have polled many of my friends about their dreams, and I am always delighted to see or hear of them moving forward with making those dreams a reality: One pursuing a dream to be a trader; another a vacation planner and travel agent; another to own a personal care home; and yet another's was to earn her doctorate degree.

What are your dreams? What are the hindrances to you accomplishing them? Are you suffering from the "someday syndrome" as well? Give your dreams to Jesus, and ask Him if they are according to His will. Ask Him to help you take steps to make "someday" become today, if your dreams are in His plans for you.

Words of Love: But seek first the kingdom of God and His righteousness, and all these things shall be added to you. Matthew 6:33

DAY 99
MAKING MY FATHER PROUD

Scripture: The Lord takes pleasure in those who fear Him, in those who hope in His mercy. Psalm 147:11

My dad was crazy about his girls. He was not very overt with his affections, but we knew how much he loved us. We were poor, but he was very kind and generous. I can still remember some of the practical things he bought me, especially at Christmas time. Every milestone was celebrated with his special smile of encouragement. I was an avid reader, and my father encouraged my reading habit. He would periodically look through the books I was reading, and discard those he thought inappropriate, but he never belittled my desire for books.

I graduated high school and went on to teachers' college. When I obtained my teachers' certification, you would have thought it was my dad who had graduated college. I spent the last week of my father's life at his hospital bedside. He was in a public ward, and could be heard telling everyone around him, "This is my daughter who is a teacher." The light in his eyes spoke of his pride as much as his words did.

Our Heavenly Father must be very proud, when we honor Him with our affection, our worship, our time, means, and talents. He has made an abundance of blessings available to us, and we can return thanks by doing acts of kindness that reflect His loving gifts to us. I want to live a life that makes my Heavenly Father as proud of me as my earthly dad was. Whether or not our earthly father was a reflection of our Father God, He has been so good to us that the least we can do is live to make Him proud.

Words of Love: Therefore, my beloved, as you have always obeyed, not as in my presence only, but now much more in my absence, work out your own salvation with fear and trembling; for it is God who works in you both to will and to do for His good pleasure. Philippians 2:12-13

DAY 100
OUR PERSONAL WITNESS

Scripture: Then behold, men brought on a bed a man who was paralyzed, whom they sought to bring in and lay before Him. And when they could not find how they might bring him in, because of the crowd, they went up on the housetop and let him down with his bed through the tiling into the midst before Jesus... Luke 5:18-25

At dawn, he appeared again in the temple courts, where all the people gathered around him, and he sat down to teach them. The teachers of the law and the Pharisees brought in a woman caught in adultery. They made her stand before the group and said to Jesus, "Teacher, this woman was caught in the act of adultery. In the Law Moses commanded us to stone such women. Now what do you say?" They were using this question as a trap, in order to have a basis for accusing him. John 8:2-6

These two stories speak to the motives behind our actions. In the story of the woman caught in adultery, for which the penalty was death by stoning, the action of those who brought her to Jesus was punitive instead of redemptive. Their witness was one of self-righteousness, trying to get rid of the "sawdust" in this woman's life, while neglecting the "boulder " that was threatening to their own lives.

In contrast, the paralyzed man needed the healing that only Jesus could give, and his friends were not concerned about appearances: either of taking him through the streets on his bed, if this was not a typical mode of transportation; or of gaining entrance through a roof when the door was impassable. Their goal was the healing and restoration of their friend. What great friends to have, and what a personal witness of God's love flowing through His children for one another.

What kind of witness are you displaying to the world and those with whom you interact on a personal basis? Do you aim to heal or to wound? Is the world seeing mere glimpses of Jesus in you, or do they know Him better from your interactions? The world is saying to us, "Show me Jesus in your actions, and I will believe the good things you tell me about Him."

Words of Love: But in your hearts revere Christ as Lord. Always be prepared to give an answer to everyone who asks you to give the reason for the hope that you have. But do this with gentleness and respect. 1 Peter 3:15

DAY 101
BEAUTY OUT OF ASHES

Scripture: To console those who mourn in Zion, to give them beauty for ashes, the oil of joy for mourning, the garment of praise for the spirit of heaviness; That they may be called trees of righteousness, the planting of the Lord, that He may be glorified. Isaiah 61:3

Jodie was an abused and abandoned child whom no one wanted. Life was very hard, as she was moved from one foster home after another. She was beyond the normal age of adoption, and felt very unloved. Although she was a beautiful girl, she had a sad and distrustful disposition.

Jodie had seen the biological children of one foster parent going off to college, and had dreams of becoming a social worker or a nurse. During her frequent moves from one foster home to another, the social worker was very kind to her; sympathetic to the pain of this forlorn child. A nurse had shown her love and care after an abusive incident landed her in the hospital. She ended up with an unplanned pregnancy, which threatened to derail any dreams of college.

Jesus Christ, the restorer of dreams, intervened in Jodie's life. When hope seemed gone, He provided a family who adopted Jodie and her unborn child. This Christian family poured so much love into Jodie that she became confident in who she was as a special daughter of God.

Today, Jodie is a Nurse Practitioner, working in a disadvantaged neighborhood, and pouring God's love and care into every hurting child that enters her practice. Christ promises that He will make beauty out of the ashes of our sin-plagued lives. He made something beautiful of Jodie's life, and He is eager to do it for you and me.

Words of Love: The Spirit of the Lord God is upon me, because the Lord has anointed me to preach good tidings to the poor; He has sent me to heal the brokenhearted, to proclaim liberty to the captives, and the opening of the prison to those who are bound. Isaiah 61:1

DAY 102
THE PAIN BEHIND THE ANGER

Scripture: And He said to me, "My grace is sufficient for you, for My strength is made perfect in weakness." Therefore, most gladly I will rather boast in my infirmities, that the power of Christ may rest upon me. 2 Corinthians 12:9

Sometimes, people who are outwardly angry and difficult to get along with are simply using their anger to mask their pain. James was one of those angry men who had lost the three women in his life whom he loved more than himself. One was his recently deceased wife of over thirty years; and the other two were twin daughters, with whom he had a broken relationship.

James' disdain for women became evident when he disrespected a group of women who were providing him needed services. Those women demonstrated the love of Christ in their acts of kindness, even though James hurled verbal insults at them. Their love broke his resistance, and he received the services he desperately needed. James found love again when he stopped blaming others for his pain, and when he opened himself to the warmth of friendship that others extended.

Are you angry about something or towards someone? Do you find it difficult to work, live, study, or play with others? Do you resist help, even when you desperately need it? Is there some painful experience eating at your core? I encourage you to take your heartaches to the Lord in prayer. He longs to soothe your pain. He is the healing balm of Gilead.

Words of Love: Many are the afflictions of the righteous, but the Lord delivers him out of them all. Psalm 34:19

DAY 103
PATIENCE TO BLOOM

Scripture: Then he waited seven days, according to the time set by Samuel. But Samuel did not come to Gilgal; and the people were scattered from him. So Saul said, "Bring a burnt offering and peace offerings here to me." And he offered the burnt offering. Now it happened, as soon as he had finished presenting the burnt offering, that Samuel came; and Saul went out to meet him, that he might greet him. 1 Samuel 13:8-10

On our prayer call one morning, one of my prayer partners shared the following story: She had bought some plants at a nursery, and the day following the purchase she called the nursery to report that the plants had not bloomed. Now, she is quite the jokester, which of course was not known to the store clerk who received the call. The lady was very professional, and proceeded to get some more details about the purchase, only to learn that it had not been twenty-four hours since the plants were bought. My friend's quick wit and sense of humor smoothed the conversation, and they both ended up having a good laugh.

During that same devotional time, my prayer partners and I learned of a desert plant which lies dormant for twenty-five years before blooming beautiful flowers. How is your patience? Are you one who wants to blossom the moment you are planted, or maybe even before your roots hit the soil? Can you wait for God to perform His perfect work in you? Do you feel like you have been waiting too long to see the manifestation of your dream?

Let patience have its perfect work in you. Do not force the petals open, or help the butterflies to fly. In patience, the true characteristics are being perfected: petals are formed, fragrance is developed and wings are strengthened. Be patient, and let God create the masterpiece that is His vision for you. Left to His timing, the outcome will have the look, feel, taste, and smell of all masterpieces from the Master's hand.

Words of Love: For we were saved in this hope, but hope that is seen is not hope... For we do not know what we should pray for as we ought, but the Spirit Himself makes intercession for us with groanings which cannot be uttered... Romans 8:24-26

DAY 104

CLOSE TO THE BROKEN-HEARTED

Scripture: The Lord is near to those who have a broken heart, and saves such as have a contrite spirit. Psalm 34:18

Father God, I believe, has a special place in His heart for the broken-hearted. During the time of writing this devotional, there were numerous news items of lives being lost to highway accidents. A few that stuck with me were: a father and two daughters, where two died on the scene, and one airlifted to a hospital but later died; a five-year-old killed by a hit and run driver, as he walked on a sidewalk close to his home with his grandmother; and a mother who was killed in a single car accident as she drove her children to school; which also left the oldest child in critical condition.

The hearts of every family represented in the incidents above were left broken. It is reported that one of the children in the last story voiced, as she wailed and tried to process her loss, "How am I going to take care of myself, I am only twelve years old?"

I picture Christ Jesus, drawing close to that little girl and wrapping His tender arms around her; shedding a tear for the evil wrought by sin, and comforting her with promises of bringing all suffering to an end one day. The Father has empathy for every hurting heart who has suffered a loss, because He knows the personal pain of separation and loss. Before you take your burdens to anyone else, take them to Jesus. He, more than anyone else, has the ability and the desire to heal the broken-hearted.

Words of Love: Fear not, for I am with you; Be not dismayed, for I am your God. I will strengthen you, yes, I will help you, I will uphold you with My righteous right hand. Isaiah 41:10

DAY 105
AN EXPERIENCE OF THE HEART

Scripture: In this is love, not that we loved God, but that He loved us and sent His Son to be the propitiation for our sins. Beloved, if God so loved us, we also ought to love one another. 1 John 4:10-11

It was Valentine's Day and I had just returned from a six-day trip to visit my sister. We had a wonderful time together, at times saying not a word; simply being in each other's presence. It was as if our hearts spoke a language that did not require words or actions.

I arrived at the airport and my husband was there to greet me. He did not bring flowers, as one husband had done for an arriving wife, but as he relieved me of my hand luggage and returned to retrieve my checked bag, my heart was touched. When we arrived home, I was greeted by the aroma of one of my favorite dishes. A quick trip into the kitchen confirmed what I had smelled. My beloved husband had made me a special dinner of some of my favorite foods, and there was a beautiful card with expressions of his love, to accompany the tasty fare.

What love languages speak to your needs, as you interact with those you love and those who love you? Mine is Acts of Service, and my husband's quiet acts of service that day spoke profoundly to my heart; much more than the generous gift of money that was tucked away in the card. Remember that some things cannot be expressed by words or actions, and must be experienced by the heart.

Prayer: Loving Father, the warmth and comfort of Your presence mean more to me than the generous gifts You lavish on me. Words cannot express it well enough for anyone else to grasp; each person must experience it with their own heart. Amen.

Words of Love: Light is sown for the righteous, and gladness for the upright in heart. Psalm 97:11

DAY 106
TAKING THE LESSER SEAT

Scripture: But when you are invited, go and sit down in the lowest place, so that when he who invited you comes he may say to you, 'Friend, go up higher.' Then you will have glory in the presence of those who sit at the table with you. For whoever exalts himself will be humbled, and he who humbles himself will be exalted. Luke 14:10-11

I was flying from West Palm Beach to Atlanta, and waited at the gate for the boarding announcement for zone one. The agent invited those needing assistance and traveling with small children to board first, followed by sky priority passengers. I saw another group moving quickly toward the jet bridge, and thinking I had missed something, I asked the lady ahead of me if the agent had made another announcement for zones one through four. The man with her said rather arrogantly, "No, this is only for priority passengers," and proceeded with the woman toward the agent. It was rather surprising, therefore, when the agent said to him, "Sir, please stand aside, it is not your turn as yet."

I was reminded of the scripture above. How unlike this haughty man, who was elevating himself above that which he was evidently entitled, was the seat mate I had on the second leg of my journey back home. This man was the owner of what appeared to be a successful company, and he was traveling to visit one of his prominent accounts. The conversation revealed that he travelled quite extensively, and he shared this information without pride or boast. Although he was a successful businessman, he was not traveling in first class, but in the second to last row of coach. Christ encourages us to humble ourselves, and allow Him to exalt us.

Words of Love: See how Ahab has humbled himself before Me? Because he has humbled himself before Me, I will not bring the calamity in his days...1 Kings 21:29

DAY 107
ONE DAY AT A TIME

Scripture: Rest in the Lord, and wait patiently for Him; Do not fret because of him who prospers in his way, because of the man who brings wicked schemes to pass. Psalm 37:7

Jessie was going through a rough spot in life, and was almost to the point of giving up. His life seemed without purpose, and he was drifting like a ship without a sail. Jessie's parents had material wealth. Externally they appeared grounded, but at home it was like shifting sands.

Jessie got mixed up with the wrong crowd, and had several encounters with the police, with his parents having to bail him out of jail. After this latest encounter, Jessie's parents sat him down, and told him that this would be the last time that they would intervene. They pledged to apply tough love to save their son.

At first Jessie thought this was just another of those lectures, and they would come running when he needed them again. Then he had a sense that something was different this time. His parents had been going through a transformation in their own lives, and had been praying for God to help them help Jessie.

That night Jessie had a dream. He had to cross a river, but there was no bridge; only some slippery moss-covered stones. To make matters worse, the water was turbulent. As he stood there pondering his fate, he saw a man with outstretched arms, standing on the first rock. He invited Jessie to take his hand, and follow Him. With the steady, yet gentle hand of his Guide, Jessie made it safely to the other side of the river. Just before the kind gentleman departed, He said to Jessie, "I am only a prayer away when you need Me."

That was the turning point in Jessie's life. The path was sometimes slippery like the riverbed stones in the dream, and sometimes the water was turbulent too; but Jessie learned to take it one step and one day at a time, with his hand firmly in the Savior's.

Words of Love: But those who wait on the Lord shall renew their strength; They shall mount up with wings like eagles, they shall run and not be weary, they shall walk and not faint. Isaiah 40:31

DAY 108
A FORETASTE OF HEAVEN

Scripture: And he showed me a pure river of water of life, clear as crystal, proceeding from the throne of God and of the Lamb... there shall be no night there: They need no lamp nor light of the sun, for the Lord God gives them light. And they shall reign forever and ever. Revelation 22:1-7

Konan and JoAnn were madly in love, and whenever they were together they were giddy and playful, and enjoyed each other's company. They were both deeply religious, and expressed that their love for each other was like a foretaste of heaven.

That comment left me with a "wow," and another of those moments of reflection. To experience the kind of love for another that feels like a foretaste of heaven is very powerful; and that is what our relationship with Jesus Christ offers. We need to long to spend time with Him, and to feel that excitement and giddiness in His presence.

Can you feel His loving arms holding you close as you snuggle with Him and open His Word? Hear Him speak kind and comforting words; watch and listen as He talks to you in nature: the gentle flowing brook; the chirping birds; the beautiful flowers.

See the sunrise and the sunset; hear the gentle falling rain; observe the unspoiled affection of a baby, as he smiles up at the face of a stranger, and melts the stoniest heart. Notice the kindness of a rough-looking teen that is extended toward a homeless beggar.

I can't wait for that glorious appearing of my Lord and Savior, and the beginning of forevermore in His presence. In the meantime, I welcome every occasion that gives me that 'foretaste of heaven' feeling.

Words of Love: Set your mind on things above, not on things on the earth. Colossians 3:2

DAY 109
LIVING A LIFE OF EXCELLENCE

Scripture: Finally, brethren, whatever things are true, whatever things are noble, whatever things are just, whatever things are pure, whatever things are lovely, whatever things are of good report, if there is any virtue and if there is anything praiseworthy—meditate on these things. Philippians 4:8

What does it mean to live a life of excellence? Does it mean to be always "at the top of the class"? Does it mean to have more than everyone else? No, what it means to me is to live a life of integrity, and to take "the high road."

Dave was doing quite well as a company team lead, but he saw an opportunity to become a foreman, and decided to go after it. The problem was that he would have had to do some things that bothered his conscience. He decided to work hard, and let God determine the course of his life.

Dave was well liked by his peers, and they had been quietly observing his actions. When he decided to let God lead in the affairs of his life, his fellow workers were even more impressed. This gave Dave an opportunity to share the love of Jesus with them, and he was blessed to lead several lives Christ.

In time, Dave's life of excellence was also observed by management, and he was promoted among the ranks. He exhibited humility and won even greater respect from the team. Today, Dave continues to advance in his organization, and he gives all credit to Jesus Christ.

Words of Love: But also for this very reason, giving all diligence, add to your faith virtue, to virtue knowledge. 2 Peter 1:5

DAY 110
MAKING DISCIPLES FOR JESUS

Scripture: Go therefore and make disciples of all the nations, baptizing them in the name of the Father and of the Son and of the Holy Spirit... and lo, I am with you always, even to the end of the age. Amen. Matthew 28:19-20

When I think of the Great Commission, I think of a train-the-trainer program. As each person is brought into the saving truth of God's Word, they are encouraged to tell someone else. Through this method of discipleship, God's truth is shared around the globe.

Many Christian denominations send members into the mission field, and they work tirelessly among the local people, so that when they leave the work of the gospel can continue. These faithful disciples live and work to win the confidence of the people among whom they are called to serve. As they immerse themselves in the culture, their goal is to achieve acceptance. Some of these missionaries endure great hardships, and some have even paid the ultimate price with their lives; but with pure motives, the seed is planted and a rich harvest will be reaped for God's kingdom.

The call to discipleship does not come with a tag saying "foreign missions only." God wants to use every believer to make other disciples for Him, and our call may be first to our family and friends, or to our neighbors around the corner. Each individual's approach may be different, but the goal should be the same: to win souls for Christ, and to make more disciples for Him. If we take this commission seriously, it should not be much longer before the whole world knows about the Savior.

If you have accepted Jesus as your Lord and Savior, you have accepted the call to discipleship. Let Matthew 28:19-20 resonate in your heart. We cannot allow the command to "go" fall on deaf ears. We have received our marching orders; now let us be about the business of our Commander-in-Chief.

Words of Love: Consecrate yourselves therefore, and be holy, for I am the Lord your God. Leviticus 20:7

DAY 111
AT THE NAME OF JESUS

Scripture: And it shall come to pass that whoever calls on the name of the Lord shall be saved. Acts 2:21

Gilliard lives in a country where Christianity is not embraced, and openly calling upon the name of Jesus often results in persecution. Everyone in the community knew that he worshipped "a different god," whom we know is the true God of heaven.

The part of the country where Gilliard lives was divided into multiple tribal groups that frequently fought against each other. Things were escalating, and the tribal leaders got word of a planned large-scale attack by two other tribes who had joined forces. Having seen firsthand the results of Gilliard's prayer in the past, the leader of his tribe asked him to pray.

Gilliard called the tribal leaders together. He thanked God for their brave leadership, but acknowledged that He, God, was the Leader over them all. He implored Him to save their community from utter destruction at the hands of those two tribes. They pledged to follow Him if He saved them, since their other gods had not provided the protection they sought.

Word came from the other tribal leaders requesting a meeting. As a result, a peace agreement was achieved and all the neighboring tribes lived in harmony. Gilliard had the opportunity to witness to the tribe about God's love for them, and many accepted Christ as their Savior. There is power in the name of Jesus, and we should call on Him often.

Words of Love: Nor is there salvation in any other, for there is no other name under heaven given among men by which we must be saved. Acts 4:12

DAY 112
TRUST HIM WITH ALL YOUR HEART

Scripture: Trust in the Lord with all your heart, and lean not on your own understanding; In all your ways acknowledge Him, and He shall direct your paths. Proverbs 3:5-6

Carmen accepted the Lord Jesus as her personal Savior when she was young. Things started out well in her home, as both her parents went to church and took the children. As she grew older, her parents' marriage began to fall apart and there was a great divide within the family. Her parents separated, divorced and remarried.

Although her faith was severely tested, Carmen trusted God and remained faithful to Him. When her siblings turned from the Lord, she drew closer. She found solace in her relationship with her best friend, Jesus. Carmen went through college, and pursued Marriage and Family Life Counseling. She has devoted her life to Christian counseling, and runs a busy clinic, helping families make it through difficult life circumstances.

Before every counseling session, Carmen prays and invites Christ to take center stage in the session and in the lives of the families who have sought help. She acknowledges to them that her trust is in Jesus, and all successful outcomes are credited to His divine intervention. Carmen has seen God work miracles in families: divorce plans aborted and marriages restored; court battles resolved with openness and humility among the parties; and custody battles resolved without the involvement of the legal system. She gives God all the praise for instilling in her, from an early age, a desire to trust Him. Carmen claims Proverbs 3:5-6 as one of the scriptures that helped to strengthen her walk with Christ. I pray that you will make it one of yours as well.

Words of Love: Fear not, for I am with you; Be not dismayed, for I am your God. I will strengthen you, yes, I will help you, I will uphold you with My righteous right hand. Isaiah 41:10

DAY 113
THE DEVIL IS ON THE PROWL

Scripture: Be sober, be vigilant; because your adversary the devil walks about like a roaring lion, seeking whom he may devour. 1 Peter 5:8

Angelique had made the decision for baptism. When her husband asked her why she was in a hurry to do so, she told him that it was time; she had put off making a public declaration of Jesus being the Lord of her life long enough, and she was ready. The day of the baptism was reportedly beautiful, with many family and friends present to witness her vows, and the symbolic dying to self and rising to walk in newness of life with Christ.

Satan was angry, and he went on a rampage. Angelique's husband became belligerent toward members of the church for no good reason. Then he did not want her to watch too many Christian programs, for fear she would become "too religious."

By God's grace, the trials that beset Angelique in those early days and weeks of her new birth experience drew her closer to Him. She studied the scriptures more deeply, and her prayer life was strengthened. As she shared her struggles, prayer warriors across the country prayed for her. From all accounts, Angelique is growing in her faith,

If you are new in your faith experience, and the attacks are mounting to discourage you, be encouraged, instead, and draw strength from the ever-present Jesus. The devil knows that he is a defeated foe, but he is fighting to the bitter end.

Words of Love: Therefore, submit to God. Resist the devil and he will flee from you. James 4:7

DAY 114
DOES GOD REALLY LOVE ME?

Scripture: For I am persuaded that neither death nor life, nor angels nor principalities nor powers, nor things present nor things to come, nor height nor depth, nor any other created thing, shall be able to separate us from the love of God which is in Christ Jesus our Lord. Romans 8:38-39

Mona was a happy child growing up, and her parents loved her dearly. Then in her preadolescent years, things changed. A trusted family friend abused her and she was crushed. She buried the pain deep inside, but it quietly raised its head repeatedly to destroy the relationships that were forged in adulthood.

Mona longed for peace. Could she trust anyone again? Did Jesus care about her pain? Did anyone truly love her? Where was everyone when she needed them? Mona built a wall around her that was almost impenetrable, and she kept the key locked tightly away in "a safe place;" a place where no one would retrieve it to hurt her again.

One day a friend shared Jesus with Mona. At first, she was hesitant to let Him in close. She felt that this would be like her other relationships, and soon she would be disappointed "again." The very wise friend told her that for healing to take place, she had to open up the wound and let the infection drain out. Mona took her friend's advice and began to open up about her past. Family and friends embraced her with love and understanding, and in their actions, she began to see the abounding love of Jesus Christ.

The scripture says, "Greater love hath no man than this, that a man would lay down his life for his friends." Mona learned that Christ went to the cross for her, and that, she agreed, was love at its highest.

Words of Love: But God demonstrates His own love toward us, in that while we were still sinners, Christ died for us. Romans 5:8

DAY 115
COMFORTED TO BE OF COMFORT

Scripture: Blessed be the God and Father of our Lord Jesus Christ, the Father of mercies and God of all comfort, who comforts us in all our tribulation, that we may be able to comfort those who are in any trouble, with the comfort with which we ourselves are comforted by God. 2 Corinthians 1:3-4

Do you have memories that cause you pain? Let them be the catalyst that helps you develop a heart and life of empathy for others. Where did you find comfort for your anguish? To whom did you turn? Did the person truly understand the depth of your pain? Did they cry with you and for you?

Petra could not understand the reason for the experiences she was having. There seemed to be no "rhyme or reason," and there was no relief in sight. She finally gave up her struggle for understanding, and said, "God, You must have a purpose in all of this, so show me, and I will be satisfied."

At first her heartfelt prayer for understanding seemed to fall on deaf ears, and her trials even intensified. Then God answered. A friend with whom she had not spoken in years called her in the middle of the night. The friend told Petra that she was impressed to call her. She felt that sharing some personal struggles she had experienced might help Petra in her life. Petra and her friend spent half the night sharing, crying, and praying together. At the end of the call, Petra finally found the comfort she had been seeking, and it came from one who herself had experienced God's comforting love extended to her.

As a child of God, there is purpose for your trials. When you find comfort from your heartaches, look for others who need to be comforted, and pass it on.

Words of Love: "Comfort, yes, comfort My people!" says your God. Isaiah 40:1

DAY 116
LIFE'S LAUGHABLE MOMENTS

Scripture: Then our mouth was filled with laughter, and our tongue with singing. Then they said among the nations, "The Lord has done great things for them." The Lord has done great things for us, and we are glad. Psalm 126:2-3

Laughter is good medicine. Life is too short, and we must learn to not take ourselves too seriously, or we run the risk of shortening it even more. Learning to laugh at yourself does not mean self-deprecation, but rather being confident in who and whose you are.

I had bought this pair of pants, and was as proud of how they fit as I was about the great price I paid for them. That is until I wore them the first and "last" time. I was almost at the end of my three-and-a-half-hour drive from my home to where I worked, when I stopped for gas. I finished pumping the gas, and turned to retrieve the receipt, when something felt unusual below my waistline.

Thankfully the gas pump and my car provided shelter, because my pants became unzipped and had succumbed to gravity. I "dived" into my car, looking around to ensure that no one had seen my moment of unintentional "flashing." I called a friend, and we had our "rib-cracking" laughter for the day. Or so we thought, until it happened again a few hours later, even though I took precautions to secure it with a safety pin. A large scarf saved the day, and formed a "fashion statement" of sorts.

Have you ever had one of those embarrassing moments when you want to bury your head in the sand and hope that the rest of you is not screaming for attention to every passerby? Have you allowed it to ruin your life, or have you been able to brush it off with laughter and move on?

We cannot change past events, so let us not allow them to determine our future. Learn to laugh at laughable situations, and let them be your teacher.

Prayer: Lord, help me learn to not take myself too seriously; to be able to laugh at myself, and to laugh with, but never at others. Amen.

Words of Love: A merry heart makes a cheerful countenance, but by sorrow of the heart the spirit is broken. Proverbs 15:13

DAY 117
YOUR BIGGEST DISAPPOINTMENT – YOUR BIGGEST BLESSING

Scripture: I called on the Lord in distress; The Lord answered me and set me in a broad place. Psalm 118:5

You may have heard the story of the sole survivor of a shipwreck, whose little hut on a lonely island went up in smoke, destroying everything he had. His hopes were dashed, and he questioned how God could put him through yet another agony. Wasn't the loss of everyone else on the ship enough? Wasn't it hard enough to try to survive the hardship of that island all by himself? Did God really even care?

I can understand the hurt and disappointment this man must have felt at best, and possibly even deep anger at the worst. Who could blame him, some may say. I am particularly grateful that we have a God with "thick skin." He understands our anger, which is often born of great pain. He doesn't say, "Okay, for having the nerves to be angry at me, I am going to withhold my blessings; and next time it would do you well to keep your mouth shut, and your emotions in check."

No, that is not my God. He is still working out His good purposes for us, even when we are upset with Him. The disaster of the fire that destroyed this man's hut was the smoke signal that drew the attention of a passing ship to his need. God, who is omnipresent, omnipotent, and omniscient, had orchestrated the events at the perfect time to bring about the needed rescue.

God's grace is wrapped up in every "burning hut" experience in our lives. We just have to trust Him that in the worst of circumstances, He has our best interest at heart.

Words of Love: Why are you cast down, O my soul? And why are you disquieted within me? Hope in God; For I shall yet praise Him, the help of my countenance and my God. Psalm 42:11

DAY 118
YOUR PIT OR MINE?

Scripture: The nations have sunk down in the pit which they made; In the net which they hid, their own foot is caught. Psalm 9:15

Angelina grew up with "friends" who were jealous of her. She worked hard and made good grades. She was respectful of, and respected by her teachers, and members of her community. Her parents were not wealthy, but they worked hard to expose Angelina and her brother to the best that their resources would allow. She excelled at everything to which she applied herself.

Angelina's family was committed to their Christian faith and they lived very upright lives in their community. As Angelina grew into the teen years her friends began to withdraw, because she did not join in most of their activities. These "friends" tried everything they could to entrap Angelina and get her into trouble. The protecting hands of God were upon her, however, and everything they plotted backfired on them.

Angelina studied law and went on to become a highly-respected judge, and an accomplished concert pianist. All the pits that were dug for her became pits that one after another of her childhood friends fell in themselves. Traps that were laid for her entrapped those who laid them, instead.

It was not long ago that Angelina had to recuse herself from the bench, when one who had attempted to do her great harm was brought before her for trial. The person got just punishment for the crime committed, and Angelina did not have to play any part in justice being meted out. The watchful eyes of the Lord are upon those who are faithful to Him, and He will not allow the enemy to destroy them.

Words of Love: But You have saved us from our enemies, and have put to shame those who hated us. Psalm 44:7

DAY 119
FRAGRANT PRAYERS

Scripture: Let my prayer be set before You as incense, the lifting up of my hands as the evening sacrifice. Psalm 141:2

Psalm 141 is a prayer of David for God to hear his cry for mercy and justice. He is pleading with God to accept his prayer as a sweet savor, and not let his enemy triumph over him. God loves when His children recognize His sovereignty, and bring their needs in penitence to Him. David was overlooked by his father, despised by his brothers, hated by Saul and feared by many. He was imperfect, as are all humanity since Adam and Eve's fall, and guilty of unfavorable acts, but he had a repentant heart.

In this Psalm, David asks God to make haste to him, and give ear to his cry. He was destitute and desperate. There is a quote which says that when all we have left is Jesus; we find that He is all we need. David did not have many in his corner, but he had the ever-present God, whose ears are always attuned to the prayers of His children.

The penitent cry of a contrite heart is fragrant to God; because He does not delight in our destruction, but rather in our salvation. The scripture says that the angels rejoice when a sinner turns his life over to Christ. In verses 8 and 9 of the same chapter, David tells God that his eyes are turned toward Him, and that he has implicit trust in Him; and then he begs God to not leave his soul destitute. He says, "Keep me from the snares which they have laid for me."

God is eagerly awaiting our prayers of repentance, praise and petition. He wants to hear it all; He just wants a conversation with us. Until the earth is restored and we can live in His presence, our prayers are the means of drawing close into His presence. Let us come often and fill His presence with fragrance.

Words of Love: Therefore, be imitators of God as dear children. And walk in love, as Christ also has loved us and given Himself for us, an offering and a sacrifice to God for a sweet-smelling aroma. Ephesians 5:1-2

DAY 120
KNOWING THAT GOD IS GOD

Scripture: Know that the Lord, He is God; It is He who has made us, and not we ourselves; We are His people and the sheep of His pasture. Psalm 100:3

A short reading which has floated around for years in many work places says, in effect, that God has our problems under control today and every day, and does not need our help in resolving them. What He does need is our cooperation to do things His way rather than ours.

I wake up each day, committing myself to God and asking Him to direct my path. So often along the way, however, my emotions kick into gear at some issue, such as an injustice, and I want to jump into action and do things my way. Thankfully, more often than not, the Holy Spirit gets to my "pause button" before I trip myself up, trying to run ahead of God.

It would make our lives a lot easier if we would recognize who is in charge; who the real boss is. God is in control, and He does fine multi-tasking, handling the controls of your life and mine all at the same time without any problems. It is when we try to help Him do His job that the controls get messed up. He often has to undo the damage we have done, before He can make things right again.

The problem is that we are either hard-headed, big-headed, or forgetful, because we make the same mistake over and over again. We would have more peace if we learned the lesson once for all: God's got this, and we just have to rest in that assurance.

Words of Love: Be still, and know that I am God; I will be exalted among the nations, I will be exalted in the earth! Psalm 46:10

DAY 121
JUST DO IT!

Scripture: His mother said to the servants, whatever He says to you, do it. John 2:5

Have you ever questioned a command given to you by someone else? Do you become resentful when someone says to you, "Just do it"? I listen to my friend interacting with her children, and it evidently frustrates her when they delay or question her instructions, so she clenches her teeth and says, "Just do it." They then quickly respond to her "marching orders."

How often we hesitate to respond to Christ's initial command. It would save us a lot of heartaches, and give us much more peace and joy, or we would see much quicker results if we would be obedient to Christ's instructions. Mary was confident in her Son's ability. Even though she had never before seen Him perform a miracle, she knew that her Son was no ordinary man, but the Son of God, and that all things were possible for Him.

Do you need a miracle in your life today? What is Christ asking you to do that seem so impossible? Are you questioning your ability or His? In your own strength, it may seem impossible; but remember that with God, all things are possible. So, go ahead, fill up those water pots, and borrow more containers to fill with oil. His ability is limited only by your faith, and your obedience. Today, whatever the Lord Jesus bids you, just do it, and watch Him work. You will be glad you did.

Words of Love: Now may the God of peace who brought up our Lord Jesus from the dead, that great Shepherd of the sheep, through the blood of the everlasting covenant, make you complete in every good work to do His will... Amen. Hebrews 13:20-21

DAY 122
TEAR DOWN THE WALL

Scripture: It shall come to pass, when they make a long blast with the ram's horn, and when you hear the sound of the trumpet, that all the people shall shout with a great shout; then the wall of the city will fall down flat. And the people shall go up every man straight before him. Joshua 6:5

I listened to a sermon recently on "Tearing Down the Wall." The speaker used Joshua chapter 6 as his scripture reference, and he gave me some "food for thought."

As I researched the chapter more intently, I found that Jesus' desire for all of us is that we live life more abundantly and free. He knows that abundant living will come when we remove barriers from our lives, and when we trust His work on our behalf.

The children of Israel were given a simple task: march around the city once a day for six days, and do nothing else. On the seventh day, march around the city seven times, and at the end of this march, blow the seven trumpets of ram's horns, carried by seven priests.

I, personally, do not believe that the power that brought the wall down was in the combined noise of seven trumpets, or the noise of all the people shouting; although that may have been possible. I believe the miracle of the fallen wall was in the Israelites' obedience. There was something behind that wall that God wanted to expose, and hopefully eradicate.

What is hiding behind your wall: Pride, guilt, resentment, hatred, unforgiveness, materialism, envy, jealousy? Isn't it time to get it out of your life and be free? Have you been trying, but not seeing any result? Jesus did not tell the children of Israel on which day the wall would come down. Don't give up marching around your "Jericho." It may be only a few steps from coming down. And go ahead, blow your horn of faith that God will do what He promises.

Words of Love: And the Lord said to Joshua: "See! I have given Jericho into your hand, its king, and the mighty men of valor." Joshua 6:2

DAY 123

NO BARRIERS

Scripture: Let us therefore come boldly to the throne of grace, that we may obtain mercy and find grace to help in time of need. Hebrews 4:16

Not many of us have direct access to people in "high places," such as presidents, monarchs, and the Pope. We would first have to go through the Secret Service, Scotland Yard, or Vatican Security, before we would be allowed into a meeting with them. We must have very good reason for wanting a personal audience with these people, before our request would even be considered. Then we must make the appointment, obtain multiple clearances, and be subjected to multiple levels of screening. The effort could be very daunting and exhausting.

The first time I went to a White House briefing, I got excited at the possibility of getting a glimpse of the sitting president, or at least have a tour of the White House. Neither happened, but the requirements to access the building on the grounds caused another reflective moment for me.

"How great... how great is our God? How great and awesome is He," yet there are no barriers to our access, whenever we desire. No appointments, no intermediary, no background checks or body scans; just a contrite heart bowing before Him in reverence and humility.

He beckons, "Come in the morning, at noon or evening time. Come in the midnight hour. Come now rather than later. Come often. Come with your joys as well as your sorrows. Come for yourself, and come for others too. The door is always open, the line is always clear. Come my beloved, there is room in my chair."

Words of Love: You will show me the path of life; In Your presence is fullness of joy; At Your right hand are pleasures forevermore. Psalm 16:11

DAY 124
WAITING WITH EXPECTANCY

Scripture: And behold, there was a man in Jerusalem whose name was Simeon, and this man was just and devout, waiting for the Consolation of Israel, and the Holy Spirit was upon him. It had been revealed to him by the Holy Spirit that he would not die before he had seen the Lord's Messiah. There was also a prophetess named Anna ... And coming in that instant she gave thanks to the Lord, and spoke of Him to all those who looked for redemption in Jerusalem. Luke 2:25-26 & 36-38

Simeon and Anna were both advanced in age. They were also both very devout, and spent much of their time in the temple, seeking God and interceding for Israel. Simeon, in particular, had the promise of God that he would live to see the Messiah. He lived with such expectancy that he recognized Him immediately when Jesus' parents entered the temple. Taking the Baby Jesus in his arms, he blessed Him, thanking God for fulfilling, not only the hope of Israel, but the desires of his heart. In his words, he said, "Lord, now let Your servant depart in peace, according to Your word: for mine eyes have seen Your salvation, which You have prepared before the face of all people; a light to lighten the Gentiles, and the glory of Your people Israel."

Anna interceded for Israel with fasting and prayers, in the temple, day and night. She came in at the time of Simeon's blessing, and she too gave thanks for Jesus and spoke of Him to all the people.

Are we waiting expectantly for the coming Messiah? This time He is not coming as a helpless baby who can be taken into one's arms and be blessed. He is coming as King of the universe to claim His subjects; as the Bridegroom for His faithful bride; and as our Savior to rescue us from a world He is about to destroy and make new.

Like Simeon, will we know Him in a personal way, and run to meet Him with eagerness, saying, "Lord, we have waited for you with confidence, knowing that You would come to save us"?

Like Anna, are we ready to tell everyone we encounter that the Messiah has come, and is coming back again to claim those who are faithful? Let us live as though we believe He is coming again; and let us help others to live with the same longing as well.

Words of Love: In My Father's house are many mansions; if it were not so, I would have told you. I go to prepare a place for you. And if I go and prepare a place for you, I will come again and receive you to Myself; that where I am, there you may be also. John 14:2-3

DAY 125
UNCONDITIONAL LOVE

Scripture: I will betroth you to Me forever; Yes, I will betroth you to Me in righteousness and justice, in lovingkindness and mercy; I will betroth you to Me in faithfulness, and you shall know the Lord. Hosea 2:19-20

The story of Hosea and Gomer is depictive of Christ's love for us. We have spurned His love, and caused Him much grief and pain; but He loves us so much that He is willing to purchase us from the grip of the world that holds us hostage. We have compromised our integrity, and have no credibility left. Our value has been diminished, because we have been thrown around from one "master" to another. Jesus watches with an aching heart. He has so much love to give, and wants to treat us like royalty.

I watched a television program of a woman who complained that she wanted to leave her husband because he was too "nice" to her. She said he told her that he loved her every day, and while she could tolerate hearing that once a week, daily was too much. He also made her breakfast and took it to her in bed, and gave her anything she wanted that his means could afford. But, she said, he was too "good" and she wanted out of the marriage.

It was the most absurd thing I had heard in regards to a relationship. Wait a minute, though, isn't that the story of Hosea and Gomer, as well as the story of Christ and us? Let us stop looking for love in all the wrong places, and realize the matchless love that God is waiting to bestow on us.

Words of Love: The Lord has appeared of old to me, saying: "Yes, I have loved you with an everlasting love; Therefore, with lovingkindness I have drawn you. Jeremiah 31:3

DAY 126
LITTLE DEEDS OF KINDNESS

Scripture: And be kind to one another, tenderhearted, forgiving one another, even as God in Christ forgave you. Ephesians 4:32

Life would be so much better if we were less selfish, and more thoughtful of each other. It would be like heaven on earth.

We have heard of the random acts of kindness that produce the "wow" factor, because they are unexpected and often outstanding. There are the little acts of kindness done daily, however, that make a world of difference to the recipient.

I live next door to two of the sweetest elderly ladies, and it gives me great pleasure to extend acts of loving kindness to them. They don't need the little things I do; their lives would be just fine without them. I believe my acts of love do more for me than they do for them. These ladies are equally kind to me. If they do not see my car moved when they know I am usually gone, or the paper taken up from my door, they ring my doorbell to check on me. Their kind gestures warm my heart.

The story is told of a blind beggar in whose extended can passersby dropped their coins. The man had a keen sense of hearing and knew people by their walk. One day a man stopped to talk to him and called him "brother." The next day as the kind gentleman drew near, the beggar's face lit up, and his usually drooped shoulders straightened. He shared with the man that his acknowledgement of him as a human being and a brother meant more than any material gift he could have given him.

Our deed of kindness does not have to be money or other tangible gifts. It may be the gift of the spoken word, or a smile, or a simple touch. It may be a listening ear and a sympathizing heart. Whatever you do, reach out and touch a life in a positive way today. Your deeds will not go unnoticed.

Words of Love: And the King will answer and say to them, 'Assuredly, I say to you, inasmuch as you did it to one of the least of these My brethren, you did it to Me.' Matthew 25:40

DAY 127
ABOVE ALL OTHER GODS

Scripture: For the Lord is the great God, and the great King above all gods. Psalm 95:3

Isn't it a great feeling to serve a God who is above all other gods? There have been many great men, but for me there is only one God. He is the Creator of the universe; by Him and for Him were all things made. Every other god has an origin, but my God is the Alpha and Omega; He has no beginning and no end; He always was and always will be. When I am sick, He can heal me; when I am sorrowful, He can comfort me. If I am lost, He can find me and safely bring me home. He is not daunted by the world's mighty armies, because the angelic host at His disposal is unnumbered.

Elijah invited the worshippers of Baal to call on their god to send fire and burn the sacrifice offered to him. As expected, their efforts failed miserably. After they had given up their futile attempts to attract the attention of their god, Elijah called upon the name of the one true God; God Almighty. He responded with fire, which consumed the sacrifice, the altar, and even the water in the trenches around the altar.

God proved Himself for Elijah, as He will do for us, to vindicate His name, and demonstrate His sovereignty. Call on Him with bold confidence, as did Elijah. He will not fail you.

Words of Love: I am the Lord, and there is no other; There is no God besides Me. I will gird you, though you have not known Me. Isaiah 45:5

DAY 128
GIVING MY BEST TO THIS MOMENT

Scripture: Brethren, I do not count myself to have apprehended; but one thing I do, forgetting those things which are behind and reaching forward to those things which are ahead. Philippians 3:13

I love moments of reflection. I was attending a health seminar, and the topic of the evening was "Outlook." On a display table were some sealed promise cards, so I selected one and proceeded to open it. On one side of the card was the confident assurance that I am loved; and on the other side was a quote which read, "I cannot change my past, but I can give my very best to this moment." This is a commitment I am making to myself.

This commitment is one of promise. It displays a positive attitude and outlook on my life, for this moment and going forward. What it says to me is that I will not accept failure, but instead, by God's grace, I will achieve success. Defeat is not an option, this attitude says; there is a goal to be accomplished and a vision of how to move forward.

God's children have an obligation to represent the Father with excellence, by doing the very best we can at every task, and in every circumstance. Anything less dishonors Him.

Yesterday is but a memory, tomorrow is only a dream, today, and in particular, this moment is all I have, and I will give it my very best.

Words of Love: And whatever you do, do it heartily, as to the Lord and not to men, knowing that from the Lord you will receive the reward of the inheritance; for you serve the Lord Christ. Colossians 3:23-24

DAY 129
ON THE HORIZON

Scripture: For as the lightning comes from the east and flashes to the west, so also will the coming of the Son of Man be. Matthew 24:27

I grew up by the beach, and was fascinated to look out on the horizon and wonder what was beyond that which the eye could see. I fantasized and dreamt of faraway lands. Whenever I saw ships passing on the horizon, I would have grand discussions with anyone around me about where they could be coming from, where they might be going, and what or who they might have on board. I was especially intrigued if it was at sunrise or sunset that these ships passed. I still have fond memories, which are accompanied by reminiscent smiles.

The term "on the horizon" had a double meaning for me, living on the beach. In those early days of my childhood, the beach was a popular thoroughfare for those living in the neighborhood. It took us to the town square, and as children, we would sit on the pristine white sands and wait to see our parents returning from "town." At the first glimpse of them on the "horizon," we would take off running down the beach to greet them, and see what goodies they had for us.

Those memories conjure up excitement when I think that Christ's coming is on the horizon. Are you living in expectancy, as it were, "scanning the eastern sky"? He will come, bursting through the clouds, with His angelic host, scripture tells us. He has great things in store for those who are awaiting His return. Will you be among that group?

Just as I waited for my Mama to burst on the horizon, on her return from town, or to see those ships burst on the horizon, from my beach-side vantage point, I cannot wait to see my blessed Lord and Savior appear on the horizon at His second advent. I know what He has in store for me: a place with Him in eternity. I cannot wait to occupy it with Him. How about you?

Words of Love: And behold, I am coming quickly, and My reward is with Me, to give to every one according to his work. Revelation 22:12

DAY 130
NEW BEGINNINGS

Scripture: Do not remember the former things, nor consider the things of old. Behold, I will do a new thing, now it shall spring forth... Isaiah 43:18-19

Personalized license plates intrigue me, and I work at deciphering them as diligently as some work at a crossword puzzle. For me, it is more than guessing what they are, but also what they mean. I recently saw one which read, "NU BGNS," and I determined it to be "New Beginnings." That was only the first part of the exercise. The second part was thinking about what it possibly meant to the owner, and what inspired it.

Was this person beginning a new life in a new country, starting a new career, getting over a bad relationship, starting a new business venture, or beginning a new life in Christ? Whatever it was, it was significant enough to make a public statement about it on their license plate.

Do you need a new beginning in your life? Are you longing to be rid of the stalemate and humdrum of your current existence and start afresh? Have you taken your need to the Giver of all good gifts, the One who says, "Behold, I make all things new"? He knows your need, but you have to rid yourself of the stuff that is occupying your space, and make room for what He wants to give you. His hands are not short, and His desire, as stated in John 10:10, is for you to live life to the fullest. So, go ahead, get ready to experience your new beginning.

Words of Love: The thief does not come except to steal, and to kill, and to destroy. I have come that they may have life, and that they may have it more abundantly. John 10:10

DAY 131
TRAPPED

Scripture: Put on the whole armor of God, that you may be able to stand against the wiles of the devil. Ephesians 6:11

One day I noticed a screw missing from the storm door at my apartment, and reported it to the management office as a low priority work request. The sequence of events that followed shows how God oversees the events of our lives, both great and small.

The following day, a friend who was visiting locked the storm door and the front door behind her. Neither of us thought anything unusual had taken place until the doorbell rang. It was the maintenance man, and I was pleased at their quick response to my work request.

I tried to open the storm door to show him the problem that needed to be fixed, and that was when we determined that we had a bigger problem on our hands. The storm door would not open. The missing screw had caused the door to fall out of alignment and when it was closed earlier, it malfunctioned and would not open. The entire door-jam had to be taken off to release the malfunctioning door.

We were trapped inside my apartment, unawares, and would have had no means of a quick escape had there been an emergency. The maintenance man, my friend and I all had a good laugh at our predicament.

A poignant reminder: Christ is our only hope of escape from this sinful world that entraps us. He will remove all barriers and give us true freedom.

Are you ready to be rescued? I did not have any need to panic, because help was present on the other side of the door. He was reassuring, stating frequently, as he laughed, "I am going to get you out." Thankfully, it was not long before he did just that.

Christ is even more reassuring than that kind maintenance man. He assures us that He is working moment by moment to unlock Satan's traps. Let us stand still and see the salvation of our God." He is standing by for the rescue.

Words of Love: But the Lord is faithful, who will establish you and guard you from the evil one. 2 Thessalonians 3:3

DAY 132
LIMITED POTENTIAL OR LIMITED EXPECTATION?

Scripture: Having then gifts differing according to the grace that is given to us, let us use them: if prophecy, let us prophesy in proportion to our faith; or ministry, let us use it in our ministering; he who teaches, in teaching; he who exhorts, in exhortation; he who gives, with liberality; he who leads, with diligence; he who shows mercy, with cheerfulness. Romans 12:6-8

I have a particular liking for quotes and witty sayings, and church signs provide some inspiring ones. Recently, one sign on a neighborhood marquee read, "Don't limit your potential based on other people's limited expectation."

What do you think of the child from the other side of the tracks who says, "I am going to be a doctor," or the one who says, "I will go to the moon some day"? Did you laugh and discourage them with words like, "Girl, be real, and learn to sew"? Yes, that young girl did learn to sew, but she became the best at her craft and went on to be a fashion designer to the rich and famous. That young man who wanted to be an astronaut, but was encouraged to learn to play sports, took the advice and honed his skills. He went to college on a sports scholarship and was very successful at the game. He used that opportunity to achieve great acclaim beyond the wildest dreams of his small town.

When others say, you can't, prove them wrong. When they say you can only attain to a certain level, supersede their limited expectation. Physical challenges don't have to hold you back. George Bernard Shaw, in the book titled Mrs. Warren's Profession, published in 1898, said this about overcoming obstacles, "`People are always blaming their circumstances for what they are. I don't believe in circumstances. The people who get ahead in this world are the people who get up and look for the circumstances they want, and if they can't find them, make them."

So, the next time someone says you can't do something, ask them if they know the capacity of your God. With His help, you can rise above any circumstances; overcome any obstacles, and your potential will not be limited by their limited expectation.

Words of Love: Therefore comfort each other and edify one another, just as you also are doing. 1 Thessalonians 5:11

DAY 133
BITTER TO THE CORE

Scripture: Let all bitterness, wrath, anger, clamor, and evil speaking be put away from you, with all malice. Ephesians 4:31

Have you ever met those people who are simply bitter at life? They are so unhappy with their own lives that they are bent on making life miserable for everyone else. It is difficult to be around these people. Life, in their opinion, has dealt them the most unfair blow. They are never content, and their "misery" is always someone else's fault. Someone always wrongs them, and life has always treated them unfairly. They have no "tickle bone," and it almost takes an "act of Congress," if not one of God, to make them "lighten up" and crack a smile. These people are not necessarily or intentionally trying to hurt anyone, but their bitterness with life can ruin it for those around them. They would do well to heed the words of the unknown author of the following quote, "If you continuously compete with others, you become bitter, but if you continuously compete with yourself, you become better."

On the other hand, there are some people who are so bitter at the core that they would think nothing of destroying the lives and livelihood of others at the drop of a hat. They scheme, plot, and lie, and are quite convincing, using whatever tactics that will accomplish their end. These are people who measure every success in life against the achievements of others. The neighbor got a riding lawn mower, just when they had bought the newest model Zero-turn, self-propelled push mower, so they become upset. A colleague bought a new car and jealousy filled them, so they made up stories that hurt this innocent person.

Bitterness destroys peace, especially that of the bitter person. Disappointment, if held on to, can cause the poisonous roots of bitterness to grow. So, if you have experienced disappointment in your life that has made you bitter, let the bitterness go. It has the potential of using you as an instrument to destroy others, but in the meantime, you are guaranteed to destroy yourself. Bitterness imprisons life, but the love of God releases it. Choose wisely.

Words of Love: And be kind to one another, tenderhearted, forgiving one another, even as God in Christ forgave you. Ephesians 4:32

DAY 134

FINDING JOY

Scripture: Though the fig tree may not blossom, nor fruit be on the vines; Though the labor of the olive may fail, and the fields yield no food; Though the flock may be cut off from the fold, and there be no herd in the stalls—Yet I will rejoice in the Lord, I will joy in the God of my salvation. Habakkuk 3:17-18

Joy comes from within oneself and is not determined by external circumstances. This certainly was the case in the life of the prophet Habakkuk. Although trouble assailed God's people on every side, and for a while it seemed as though the wicked were prospering; causing Habakkuk to wonder at God's strategy, yet he concluded that he would be joyful. He attested that he knew God would be his strength, and he would eventually walk upon high places.

This was also Cathleen's experience. She had to dig deep to endure the hardships of her life. She often cried out to God, and questioned Him regarding the strategy He was using to refine her and increase her trust. For a while it seemed as if her trials were not letting up, and she would never have peace. Things went from bad to worse. She prayed, fasted, sought counsel, and prayed some more. And then God answered. His answer was there from the time she first prayed, but her timing was not His. Cathleen found joy amidst the trials, as she resolved to let God have His way.

When the answer finally came, Cathleen realized that had she gotten the desired answer when she first prayed, she would not have been prepared for the blessings that God had in store for her. He had big plans for her life that, in her broken state, she would not have been able to be used fully by Him. Her time in the crucible of the fire was a time of preparation for what was to come; and when it did, her inner joy shone forth and lightened all the corners of her existence, bringing God much glory.

Are you being put through the fire? Don't despair. Present your needs to the Father, and wait on Him. Find joy even in the trials, and in time your joy will be complete.

Words of Love: Rejoicing in hope, patient in tribulation, continuing steadfastly in prayer. Romans 12:12

DAY 135
PARALYZING FEAR

Scripture: The fear of man brings a snare, but whoever trusts in the Lord shall be safe. Proverbs 29:25

Let's face it, we all have fears. Some may be irrational, but they are nonetheless real to us. I may have already shared my fear of precipitous roads, a fear which paralyzes my driving in certain areas. Because I never know when and where I will come upon such terrain, I do not rent a car to drive in areas where I am vacationing, and I don't seek after jobs that may require me to travel by car.

I was traveling alone to the funeral service of a colleague's family member, when I encountered slightly hilly terrain. There was not much of a drop-off, but there was no shoulder on this particular road. I came to a crawl, which was not a problem, until other vehicles came up behind me and could not pass because of the many corners. My heart raced, and I broke out in sweat. I had prayed at the beginning of my trip and I prayed again.

Christ tells us in His Word that He has not given us a spirit of fear, so where does mine come from? Fear, especially that which has no real basis, is of the devil. He is not our friend, regardless of how convincing his words may be. It is a game for him. He tries to get us to distrust a loving and caring Father.

I wish I could honestly say that all my irrational fears are gone. I am trusting God, however, that when I travel the winding and precipitous pathways of life, I will remember and be confident that He travels with me.

Are you struggling with fears that paralyze you? Are they standing in the way of your growth and success? Have you asked God for deliverance? What steps have you taken to deal with them? The scripture in John 10:10, where Christ says that He has come for us to live life to the fullest, applies to all areas of your life, including your fears. So, give that to Him as well, and watch Him give you deliverance.

Words of love: The thief does not come except to steal, and to kill, and to destroy. I have come that they may have life, and that they may have it more abundantly. John 10:10

DAY 136
ADVOCATE AND JUDGE

Scripture: Now as they were seeking to kill him, news came to the commander of the garrison that all Jerusalem was in an uproar.... So when he could not ascertain the truth because of the tumult, he commanded him to be taken into the barracks. Acts 21:31-34

Jesus Christ is the Christian's Defender and Judge. He serves this dual role in the throne room in heaven. No one else, nowhere else, can play such a role in our eternal salvation.

Jesus stands as our representative, with His shed blood offered as restitution for our sins. He sacrificed His life for us, yet He lives and intercedes daily for us at the right hand of God the Father. He says, "Through the power given Me by the Father, this son or daughter is forgiven, justified and sanctified." Satan hangs his head in defeat, angry that he has lost another soul to the loving and forgiving arms of Jesus.

I welcome my day of judgment, confident in the outcome; not because of my innocence, but because of His grace. He is a servant leader. He leads by example and encourages us to follow in His footsteps.

Words of Love: You shall not be afraid of the terror by night, nor of the arrow that flies by day... Because you have made the Lord, who is my refuge, even the Most High, your dwelling place. Psalm 91:5-9

DAY 137

STRETCH YOURSELF!

Scripture: For God has not given us a spirit of fear, but of power and of love and of a sound mind. 2 Timothy 1:7

I remember when I was considering the purchase of my first house, being very concerned how I would make ends meet on a limited state government salary. A dear friend knew how much I was questioning myself and told me: "Stretch yourself beyond where you feel comfortable, and you will be amazed at how much more you can do." He was right. I tightened the belt a bit here; went without a bit there; and found ways and means to do just that, "stretch myself." Of course, I committed it all to God, and He provided an additional part-time job. Once the doubts of my ability to accomplish this goal were released; and I had the willingness to step outside my comfort zone and trust God, ways began to open up.

What seems to be beyond your reach today? Is it a house, a car, a college degree or skill training program? Is it to start a new business or to save for retirement? Is it to do more mission projects or be a more generous giver? Ask God if that is what He wants you to do. If the answer is yes, He will make a way, and in partnership, He will help you to step out in faith, and stretch yourself to the limit of His limitless blessing.

Words of Love: Have I not commanded you? Be strong and of good courage; do not be afraid, nor be dismayed, for the Lord your God is with you wherever you go. Joshua 1:9

DAY 138
WILL THE REAL YOU PLEASE STAND UP!?

Scripture: And do not be conformed to this world, but be transformed by the renewing of your mind, that you may prove what is that good and acceptable and perfect will of God. Romans 12:2

There is an icebreaker game called two lies and a truth, that can be fun to play as it has the group guessing while learning about each other. There is another game where three people pretend to be the same person. The audience questions them and seeks clues to determine which one is the real person they all claim to be. At the end, the real person is asked to stand and be identified.

We sometimes put on a façade in public, but the real person generally comes out in private. There are many stories of dysfunctional families who pretend love and togetherness in public, but away from the eyes of the public there is abuse, and tremendous discord. The day often comes when the lies cannot be hidden any longer. The truth breaks out like wildfire, and efforts to contain it are futile.

When the mask is lifted, the disguise removed, and the real you is required to stand up and be recognized for who you truly are, you are unrecognizable to many. Those who know you well, however, saw you for who you really were in the shadows. You had lived a lie for so long, it was hard to face you when the facade was lifted. The layers of deception had to be peeled away like an onion.

There is hope, however. God is able to restore us when we give Him permission. Healing may be slow, but with honesty and openness, the necessary work of reshaping can take place. When family and friends see the changes being wrought in our lives by the love of Jesus Christ, they will be happy to identify with us.

Words of Love: But be doers of the word, and not hearers only, deceiving yourselves. James 1:22

DAY 139
CONTAMINATION AND PURIFICATION

Scripture: Depart! Depart! Go out from there, touch no unclean thing; Go out from the midst of her, be clean, you who bear the vessels of the Lord. Isaiah 52:11

We know the devastating statistics of clean water deprivation around the world. As a child growing up, our source of water was a spring about a quarter of a mile from my home. It was a large water hole, and you could literally watch the water come up from the spring head. The water was clean and cool, but had a brackish taste, which did not make it pleasant to use in sweetened beverages.

It wasn't until later in my childhood that the city water was piped to a spot half a mile away from my home. It was great to have a glass of lemonade without the salty taste of the spring water. It was an even greater joy to have clean water piped into our home in my early adult years. This water was tested and treated for contaminants, and we drank it with confidence that it would not make us sick.

Many peoples of the world are not as fortunate, and we should not take clean water for granted. There are countries where people trek long distances to fetch contaminated water, from which they and especially their small children become ill and often die.

Sin, like the polluted waters of the world, contaminates and defiles. The resulting illnesses of hate, jealousy, envy and others negative emotions cause debilitating illnesses that lead to death. What the world needs is the blood of Jesus Christ. It's the only thing that can purify us, and give us hope of a healthy life, now and throughout eternity.

Words of Love: Since you have purified your souls in obeying the truth through the Spirit in sincere love of the brethren, love one another fervently with a pure heart. 1 Peter 1:22

DAY 140
THE PEACE OF JESUS CHRIST

Scripture: Peace I leave with you, My peace I give to you; not as the world gives do I give to you. Let not your heart be troubled, neither let it be afraid. John 14:27

It is a wonderful feeling to be at peace with your life. My sister is one of the most contented persons I know. She is not bothered by what others have, where they go, or how they look. She is not a pushover, but she is calm and easygoing, ready to share, without expecting anything in return. She takes life in stride, not allowing a lot of what goes on around her to rattle her inner peace.

One year my sister decided to read the Bible through. She followed a reading plan, and accomplished her goal. I believe that effort taught her some lessons that brought her even greater peace, and early in the year following she made the decision to publicly declare Jesus as her personal Lord and Savior. Following her baptism, my sister seemed to be walking on cloud nine.

The Lord promises to give greater peace to those who love His Name, and my sister is a living testimony. How is your life? Are you caught up in the "rat race" of life, not satisfied with who you are, what you are, where you are? Are the how and why of daily existence causing you undue stress? Relinquish all your questionings to the One who longs to give you His peace. His is the peace that passes all understanding. It is a peace that quiets your anxious soul.

One line of the beautiful song, Wonderful Peace, by Warren D. Cornell (1889) says: "Peace, peace, wonderful peace, coming down from the Father above; Sweep over my spirit, forever, I pray, in fathomless billows of love." My prayer is that you will enjoy this kind of peace in Christ Jesus.

Words of Love: And let the peace of God rule in your hearts, to which also you were called in one body; and be thankful. Colossians 3:15

DAY 141
DEVOTION, NOT EMOTION

Scripture: So Samuel said: "Has the Lord as great delight in burnt offerings and sacrifices, as in obeying the voice of the Lord? Behold, to obey is better than sacrifice, and to heed than the fat of rams. 1 Samuel 15:22

On one of our morning prayer calls, we were reviewing the scripture of the twelve spies sent to check out the Promised Land. All twelve came back with news of the beautiful land, but ten discouraged entering, because of the so-called "giants" in the land. Caleb and Joshua were the only two dissenting voices. They stated in Numbers 14:8-9, that the Lord had removed His protection from that nation, and was with the Israelites, so they should not be afraid.

The level of ingratitude among the children of Israel caused Moses and Aaron to fall prostrate on their faces with grief. It was appalling to see how often they chose to overlook the goodness of God to them, and instead, grumbled and complained about one thing after another. Because of their lack of trust in God's continued care, they allowed the emotions of the masses to destroy their devotion to the Sovereign God, who had their best interest at heart.

Father God longs for us to take a step of faith into the eternal land He has gone to prepare for us. Sometimes the emotions of the moment may be positive rather than negative ones. We may be touched by a sermon, or the action of someone may inspire us to do what is right, but if that emotion is not followed by our devotion to live a changed life for Him, the emotions are for naught.

With the mind of Christ, let us assess every situation and ask ourselves what action would lead us into a closer and more trusting relationship with Jesus Christ. A life of devotion supersedes transient moments of emotion.

Words of Love: All Scripture is given by inspiration of God, and is profitable for doctrine, for reproof, for correction, for instruction in righteousness, that the man of God may be complete, thoroughly equipped for every good work. 2 Timothy 3:16-17

DAY 142
MAMA'S "SWEETS" CABINET

Scripture: But this I say: He who sows sparingly will also reap sparingly, and he who sows bountifully will also reap bountifully. 2 Corinthians 9:6

My mother was known for her baking: cornmeal pudding; sweet potato pudding; "toto"; and a favorite of the neighborhood kids: the cassava pone. She always had something sweet baked and stored in that little cabinet, sitting on top of a table in the outdoor kitchen. Visitors were assured of some baked goods from that cabinet before they said their farewells. As a child, I sometimes believed that the frequent visits of some were to secure a tasty treat from Mama's sweets cabinet.

My sister and I learned a lot about generosity and sharing from both our parents, and Mama, especially, taught us that the sharing of tasty food binds hearts in fellowship. Both of us find it hard to let anyone entering our door leave without an offer of something from our kitchen. In my young-adult years, I studied and taught food service. I baked a lot and blessed many with the sweet treats from my kitchen, but as we have gotten older, my sister is the one who carries on our mother's tradition.

Christ has storehouses "cabinets" of sweet treats that He is eager to share with us. Whenever we spend time in His presence, we are guaranteed to leave with all that we need, and always, plenty to satisfy our wants as well. Come often. His resources are not limited, and He won't feel that the only reason you've come is for the gifts He generously bestows, even if that is the case. The fellowship you will enjoy during the visit will hopefully keep you coming back.

Words of Love: If you then, being evil, know how to give good gifts to your children, how much more will your Father who is in heaven give good things to those who ask Him! Matthew 7:11

DAY 143
THE ROCK THAT IS HIGHER THAN I

Scripture: Lead me to the Rock that is higher than I. Psalm 61:2

The foolish man builds on shifting sands, but the wise man builds on the Rock, who is Jesus Christ. He is our solid foundation. We can also find shelter in the clefts from the raging storms of life.

Jasmyn enjoyed many successes in her life, and she was basking in the glories of the moment, not taking time to be grateful to the source of her success, Jesus Christ. Then everything began to crumble around her. She had grown up in a praying family, with parents who took all their needs to God, and who gave Him thanks and praise for all their blessings.

When Jasmyn was young, her parents recognized her God-given talents, and sacrificed to help her develop them and pursue a career in her field. The world also recognized her talents, and lured her with promises she felt she could not refuse. She had a good run showcasing her talents on the world stage, then things changed, and the unstable sand began to crumble as the angry waves began to pound on the fantasy house she had built.

Jasmyn went home for a visit, and intuitive parents noticed that something was wrong. She broke down and shared her struggles with them. Together, they turned to the Rock in earnest prayer, and He heard and answered the cry of their hearts. Today, Jasmyn has found refuge in the cleft of that Rock. She is leaning on Him, and using her talents for His glory. She loves to share her testimony, and sing the song, A Shelter in the Time of Storm, written by Vernon J. Charlesworth in 1880, and published in 1885 by Ira Sankey, which says: "Jesus is a Rock in a weary land, a shelter in the time of storm."

Yes, the foolish man builds on the shifting sands of temporary successes: career, beauty, wealth, and fame; but the wise man builds on the lasting foundation of Jesus Christ. He is our Solid Rock.

Words of Love: Therefore, whoever hears these sayings of Mine, and does them, I will liken him to a wise man who built his house on the rock... Matthew 7:24-27

DAY 144

I CHOOSE TO BLESS YOU

Scripture: And my God shall supply all your need according to His riches in glory by Christ Jesus. Philippians 4:19

Taste and see that the Lord is good. Blessed is the one who takes refuge in Him.

Marcie's life had its ups and downs, its highs and lows; not unlike many single mothers who were struggling to feed, clothe, shelter and educate three small children. She was committed to working hard and setting an example for the children to follow, breaking the generational cycle of total government dependency. She was very bright and gifted, but she was being challenged with managing the needs of her gifted children, and working two jobs to make ends meet.

Several months earlier, Marcie had entered a competition with a proposal for a home-based project, but she had not received any feedback. She took it to the Lord in prayer, and decided to let Him handle it if it was His will. Several more weeks went by, and then she got a call asking why she had not responded to the letter they sent her more than a month earlier. Marcie explained that she had not received any correspondence, but she would be delighted to meet with them at their convenience.

Marcie met with the group the following day, with her portfolio in hand. They were even more impressed as she shared greater details with them, and they were eager to enter into a partnership with her. Marcie had applied for a patent for her product. She wanted to ensure that she would retain a majority share of her business, while having the financial backing and expertise of this entrepreneurial group.

Marcie gives honor and praise to God for His abundant blessings. Her success has made her more faithful to Him, and He continues to bless her faithfulness.

God has blessings in store for you today. Trust Him, and do not give up on your dreams. Your "letter" may have been lost in the mail, but prayer can activate the call that will bring you the opportunity of a lifetime. Are you ready for the blessings?

Words of Love: For I know the thoughts that I think toward you, says the Lord, thoughts of peace and not of evil, to give you a future and a hope. Jeremiah 29:11

DAY 145
CONFUSED, SHOCKED, AND FURIOUS

Scripture: Immediately many gathered together, so that there was no longer room to receive them, not even near the door. And He preached the word to them. Then they came to Him, bringing a paralytic who was carried by four men. And when they could not come near Him because of the crowd, they uncovered the roof where He was. So when they had broken through, they let down the bed on which the paralytic was lying. Mark 2:2-4

In the story of the paralytic, told in Mark chapter 2, three distinct emotions emerge:

(1). The paralytic was so desperate for healing that when the crowd posed a barrier to his goal, his friends raised the roof of the house where Jesus was speaking, and let him down into the presence of the Great Healer. Imagine the man's confusion, therefore, when instead of addressing his perceived need of healing and restoration of his legs, Jesus addressed his spiritual need. Jesus read the deep longing of the paralytic's heart, and so before He granted him physical healing, which He eventually did, He offered him spiritual healing, with the words, "Your sins be forgiven you."

(2). The crowd, I believe, was shocked that Jesus gave something, in this case forgiveness of sins, to someone who did not verbally express a need for it. The beauty of our Savior is that He sees the needs and deep longings of our hearts, even before we know we need and want these things. And, in addition to knowing, He is eager to give good gifts to us.

(3). The third emotion which emerged in that gathering was outrage. The religious leaders were furious that Jesus made such a claim of being able to forgive sins. We know that only God has the power to forgive sins, therefore, Christ had to be claiming to be God. These religious haters were convinced that such blasphemy had to be punished, and it was punishable by death. Jesus had signed His own death warrant.

A very gifted speaker once said that in order for Jesus to give the paralyzed man legs to walk, "spiritual legs, so to speak," He had to subject His own legs to be nailed to a tree. For Him to enable us to dance, that glorious dance of redemption, He had to die. And, for Him to ensure our resurrection from the grave to eternal life, He had to be buried and Himself be raised. Thanks be to God that the cross shows Him lifted up, and the empty grave shows Him raised up. This gives us hope.

Words of Love: When Jesus saw their faith, He said to the paralytic, "Son, your sins are forgiven you." Mark 2:5

DAY 146
THE ALL-WISE GOD

Scripture: The fear of the Lord is the beginning of wisdom; A good understanding have all those who do His commandments. His praise endures forever. Psalm 111:10

Priscilla was convinced that Jerome was the guy for her. She had not known him long, but he had "swept her off her feet" with his good looks and his smooth talk. Jerome spoke little of himself but Priscilla, nevertheless, became deeply involved. She was blind to the many signs that were evident to her family and close friends.

Priscilla was successful, in her thirties, and desperate to marry and begin a family. When she began to pressure Jerome, he began to withdraw, while still professing his love for her. Priscilla then did what she should have done months earlier: she sought God's guidance. Even though she had not been faithful in serving Him, He was there for her when she called on Him.

Priscilla uncovered some things about Jerome that would not make for a good and lasting life together. She was heartbroken, but thankful to God who was watching over her, and looking out for her eternal welfare. She recommitted herself to the Christian values she once believed in, and trusted God to provide the right companion for her, in His time and according to His will. In time, God did, and she and her beautiful family served God faithfully together. One line of the song Trust and Obey by John H. Sammis, written in 1887, says it well, "Trust and obey, for there is no other way; to be happy in Jesus, but to trust and obey." Let us trust our all-wise God. He always knows what is best for us.

Words of Love: But this is what I commanded them, saying, 'Obey My voice, and I will be your God, and you shall be My people...' Jeremiah 7:23

DAY 147
STRENGTH ENOUGH FOR TODAY

Scripture: He gives power to the weak, and to those who have no might He increases strength.... Isaiah 40: 28-31

The opposition was very strong against Lisbeth, and there were days when she did not think she would be able to endure. She loved her work and was passionate about the opportunity to serve the people, but the mission field was tough, and life was difficult for her every day.

Personal and corporate prayers kept Lisbeth sane in her hostile work environment. Every morning she began her day with the same prayer: "Lord, please give me enough strength for today." The Lord was faithful, and He answered the cries of her broken heart. Each day Lisbeth received just enough strength to endure that day's hardship, but her energy and her emotions were spent in the process. She began to get sick as a result.

A friend shared the scripture above with her, along with the following thought: "If God brings you to it, He will bring you through it." The barriers did come down, and Lisbeth continued to work among the people; making service to their community her lifework.

When asked about her years of struggle, she had this to say: "Looking back, I thank God for drawing me closer to Him through the struggles. I became a better person as a result, and those very struggles enhanced my service for His glory."

Words of Love: Be strong and of good courage, do not fear nor be afraid of them; for the Lord your God, He is the One who goes with you. He will not leave you nor forsake you. Deuteronomy 31:6

DAY 148
COURAGE FOR THE JOURNEY

Scripture: Have I not commanded you? Be strong and of good courage; do not be afraid, nor be dismayed, for the Lord your God is with you wherever you go. Joshua 1:9

Today is a continuation of the individual and very personal journey that each of us is on. It may just be one of those days of special challenges. Sometimes we go up mountainous slopes, and sometimes we barrel downhill; sometimes we navigate deep curves, and sometimes there are mirages straight ahead. Sometimes we swim wide channels, and sometimes we cross on shaky bridges. Whatever the circumstances of today's journey, I believe most of us can use some encouragement to carry on.

"Where do I find this courage," you may be asking, "because my road ahead is not very promising?" The answer is in Jesus. In the scripture above, God assured Joshua that His presence would be with him wherever he went. God offers you and me the same assurance for our journey today.

I took a stand on an issue that could have caused me to lose a lucrative opportunity. It was not a difficult decision, because God promises to stand beside us when we stand for right. He brings good out of even bad situations for His children's benefit.

Words of Love: Therefore, my beloved brethren, be steadfast, immovable, always abounding in the work of the Lord, knowing that your labor is not in vain in the Lord. 1 Corinthians 15:58

DAY 149

MY NEEDS ARE SUPPLIED

Scripture: And my God shall supply all your need according to His riches in glory by Christ Jesus. Philippians 4:19

Linda was working in a country far from home and her family. It was a sacrifice to be away from her three boys, but she was doing it for their future. Although she originally entered the country legally, she had overstayed her time, and could not travel freely. She had missed many milestones and special events in her boys' lives, and she was eager for change. Because her employers knew of her visa status, they took advantage of her, paying her less than they agreed to, and sometimes not paying her at all.

A friend introduced me to Linda by phone and asked me to pray for her. During our short conversation, she frequently praised God with the words, "My needs have been supplied. I have been able to educate my boys, and now I am planning to go home." Interestingly, a few days after this telephone encounter with Linda, I read a devotion entitled, "Abundant Supply." God's supply has not been limited for Linda, and neither has He run out of supply to meet your needs or mine.

I can say, with joy and thankfulness, that no need of mine has gone unmet. Sometimes I have selfishly wanted things that God saw were not good for me to have, and in His wisdom, He did not let me have them, but He has lovingly supplied every need. Have you brought your needs to the altar? He says in Psalm 84:11 that He will not withhold any good thing from His children. He is waiting to hear from you.

Words of Love: For He satisfies the longing soul, and fills the hungry soul with goodness. Psalm 107:9

DAY 150
ROSLYN'S CLOSE CALL

Scripture: Call upon Me in the day of trouble; I will deliver you, and you shall glorify Me. Psalm 50:15

The passage from which the above scripture is taken says that we will honor God for His deliverance, and that is what Roslyn lives for. She was only fourteen years old when she had her close call, and she knew it was God who protected her. It was spring break, and the family was vacationing by the beach. They were having so much fun, and then it happened. "Shark," someone called, and in a flash Roslyn felt the bite. She began to go under water as the shark circled again. Strong, brave swimmers who saw what happened were not willing to let her go without a fight. They rushed to her aid, and with determination, rescued her from the jaws of death.

Roslyn was rushed to the nearby hospital, and it was hard to believe that she did not lose a limb, or worse yet, her life. Some said she was lucky, but Roslyn was quick to correct them with the fact that her guardian angel saved her. She said she saw the shark just in time to say: "Jesus, save me." The Father heard the desperate cry of a young girl, and dispatched an angel to shield her from the worst. She healed from the bite, and shares her testimony every opportunity she has.

Many of us have faced close calls in our lives. There are occasions when all we have time to say is "Jesus." Thankfully, God reads our hearts, and hears our cry for help. While the outcome may not always be what we hope for, we must never fail to call on Him, and thank Him regardless of His response.

Words of Love: It shall come to pass that before they call, I will answer; And while they are still speaking, I will hear. Isaiah 65:24

DAY 151
BOYCE'S FRIEND ROSS

Scripture: Make no friendship with an angry man, and with a furious man do not go, lest you learn his ways and set a snare for your soul. Proverbs 22:24-25

Boyce's friend Ross was known for "losing his temper" at the slightest agitation. It did not take much for him to "fly off the handle," as the saying goes. Boyce was a good Christian young man, and he was warned about keeping company with Ross, who was always getting into fights. Boyce's mom often said to him: "Be careful, you are known by the company you keep."

One day, Boyce and Ross were driving along. Ross was doing the driving, when someone cut them off in traffic. Ross' temper boiled, and no counsel from Boyce could prevent what happened next. Ross caught up with the other driver at a stop light, got out of his truck, walked up to the man's car and smashed his windshield. He was arrested; and Boyce was also detained for questioning, before being released.

Boyce loved his childhood friend, and was not willing to give up on him. He had begun praying for his salvation before this incident. He had also told Ross that unless he was willing to get help, they would not be able to hang out together anymore, as people were beginning to associate him with Ross' bad behavior.

That incident was a blessing in disguise. Because of the injury that the other driver sustained from the broken windshield, Ross served some time in jail. He had time, and help from the religious books that Boyce provided him, to reflect on the path his life was heading. On his release from jail, he attended church with Boyce, and eventually gave his heart to Jesus.

The stories do not always end so well. Often the "bad apple" spoils the good ones. So, the counsel in Proverbs is wise, and young and old alike would do well to heed it.

Words of Love: Open rebuke is better than love carefully concealed. Faithful are the wounds of a friend, but the kisses of an enemy are deceitful. Proverbs 27:5-6

DAY 152
HIS PLANS ARE BETTER THAN MINE

Scripture: Commit your works to the Lord, and your thoughts will be established. Proverbs 16:3

"Lord, that is not what I asked you for, and neither did I sign on for this." These were Claire's words when the doctor shared with her and her husband the results of some tests that had been recommended during her pregnancy. They had been married for quite a while and she had not gotten pregnant by normal means. Then they tried other methods, and were delighted when she became pregnant.

Midway during the pregnancy, Claire's doctor had suspicions that things were not going well, so, tests were ordered, and her fears were confirmed. There was some deformity that would make for a very challenging life for both the child and the family. Counseling was provided, but the couple decided that this child was God's gift to them, and they would honor Him by raising her to His glory.

At birth, Claire and her husband were ecstatic that Angel was not as severely impacted as she was expected to be. She brought the family much joy. Her smile lighted any room she entered, and she never met a stranger. A local support group, family, and friends provided much support. Angel lived a full life and benefited from advances in research on her condition.

Claire and her husband frequently reflect on the options that were opened to them during those first difficult days after the test results. This is what they share: "If we could have seen the end of the journey, we would have chosen no other path than Christ has led us." What a testimony of faith and trust. Truly, His plans are better than ours.

Words of Love: Trust in the Lord with all your heart, and lean not on your own understanding; In all your ways acknowledge Him, and He shall direct your paths. Proverbs 3:5-6

DAY 153

A NEW BEGINNING

Scripture: That you put off, concerning your former conduct, the old man which grows corrupt according to the deceitful lusts, and be renewed in the spirit of your mind, and that you put on the new man which was created according to God, in true righteousness and holiness. Ephesians 4:22-24

January 1st is only one new beginning, which comes around every year. Sometimes people seem to wait for that time to start some new thing; but every day we have the opportunity for a new beginning. In my field as a dietitian, I have seen many people who have been given second chances at life after a serious diagnosis, and they are often told that they must change their eating habits. Many of them come with the attitude, "Just fix it so that the changes I have to make are minimal."

Christ promises to do a new thing in our lives, but He needs our cooperation. He wants to work in concert with our behavior changes. We have to give Him our will, and ask Him to make His will ours. It certainly takes God's will to overcome old habits, and to incorporate new ones, but with Him, all things are possible.

In the same way that we have to embrace God's strength to make changes regarding our physical health, we have to ask Him to do a new thing in our hearts for the improvement of our spiritual health. More than anything, Jesus wants to restore us spiritually. He wants us to be spiritually healthy. He wants to make a way in the wilderness of our hearts, and create rivers of living water in us. Then our spirits will be revived, and life in Him will be made new.

Words of Love: Therefore, if anyone is in Christ, he is a new creation; old things have passed away; behold, all things have become new. 2 Corinthians 5:17

DAY 154
QUICKSAND

Scripture: The Lord is my strength and my shield; My heart trusted in Him, and I am helped; Therefore, my heart greatly rejoices, and with my song I will praise Him. Psalm 28:7

Stop resisting the struggles of life, and rest in God's abiding love. This is good advice, when we stop to think of it. Wrestling with life's struggles serves us little good, because the battle is not ours in the first place. When we fall into "quicksand," it serves us better to lie down and relax, rather than trying to fight our way out. The movements only cause us to sink deeper.

As a child, I remember crossing the shallow riverbed close to my aunt's house, where the river met the sea. It was notorious for having quicksand. I was always afraid, so I would never cross it alone. My mother would always tell us: "If you ever encounter quicksand, don't try to fight your way out of it, as the movement only makes it worse; just keep still and call for help." I later learned that lying flat is even better.

As an adult, I realize that the quicksand of life still entraps us when we try to go it alone, or when we engage in a struggle to extricate ourselves. Our loving Savior's watchful eyes see every move we make. He knows where we are, hears our desperate cry for help, and has a plan in place to save us. He knows His plans for us at the end of the experience, and He whispers gently, "Lie back and rest in My everlasting arms of love."

Words of Love: For by grace you have been saved through faith, and that not of yourselves; it is the gift of God, not of works, lest anyone should boast. Ephesians 2:8-9

DAY 155
SURPRISED?

Scripture: I marvel that you are turning away so soon from Him who called you in the grace of Christ, to a different gospel. Galatians 1:6

When someone does something nice and unexpected for us, we often say, "I was pleasantly surprised." I have shared with you about a friend who came to have dinner with me, and brought me the most beautiful bunch of yellow roses. Her thoughtfulness was such a surprise and delight, that the memory still brings a warm smile to my face.

Well, not all surprises are pleasant and bring a warm feeling. Deception and betrayal by those you trust often leave you not just deeply hurt, but also surprised as to their motive. Sometimes you are left at a loss for words.

It is interesting to note that Christ was not surprised by Judas' betrayal or Peter's denial; hurt and disappointed yes, but not surprised. I believe that Peter was more surprised at his own action, because he had sworn allegiance to his Lord and Savior, stating that he would die for Him.

Thankfully, Christ loves us so much that even when our actions break His heart, He knows that it the enemy who causes us to act contrary to His love, and He does not hold it to our account when we repent. That which we would, we don't do; and that which we would not, that is what we do.

Words of Love: But God demonstrates His own love toward us, in that while we were still sinners, Christ died for us. Romans 5:8

DAY 156
A BOLD MOVE

Scripture: Trust in the Lord with all your heart, and lean not on your own understanding; In all your ways acknowledge Him, and He shall direct your paths. Proverbs 3:5-6

After teachers' college, I worked in education for eleven years in my home country, then decided to advance my personal education. I left the security of family and a stable career, to pursue a new life in America.

I relate to the story of Abraham, who left his home and friends to go to a land he knew nothing about, because God had directed him to do so. Like Abraham, who did not know what to expect in this new country, this whole experience was a journey of faith for me, especially because my finances were unsure. It is with gratitude that I look back over the years in school, remembering how I depended on God totally for my sustenance. Although it was a struggle, through His mercies, I fulfilled the goals I had set out to accomplish. Some called it a bold move; others may call it reckless; I just say, "Thanks be to God for His leading."

In the words of the beautiful hymn, "He's Never Failed Me Yet," everywhere I go I want the world to know, Jesus Christ has never failed me. We can make bold moves when we walk in His steps.

Words of Love: Fear not, for I am with you; Be not dismayed, for I am your God. Isaiah 41:10

DAY 157
SURRENDERING ALL TO CHRIST

Scripture: I have been crucified with Christ; and it is no longer I who live, but Christ lives in me... Galatians 2:20

Evangelist J. W. Van DeVenter wrote a beautiful song in 1896 entitled, "I Surrender All." The first verse says: "All to Jesus I surrender, All to Him I freely give; I will ever love and trust Him, In His presence daily live."

If we have been crucified with Jesus Christ, then there is no question that we must surrender all to Him as well. We must surrender our pride, our self-interest, our ego. We must freely give God our time, our talents, and our treasures to be used for His glory.

There is much we can all do in regards to surrendering to Jesus Christ. Some of us have the talent, but do not have the treasure. Give what you have. Others have the treasure, but are limited in time. Give those treasures, so those with the time can do the work. Those of us with time should use it joyfully in God's work.

I believe that more than anything else, however, God wants us to surrender ourselves totally to Him. He does not want ninety-nine percent of us. That would not be good enough. He wants and deserves all of us; because He has given His all for us.

So what about our pride, ego and self-interest? We must learn to let go of hurt, anger, and grudges. We must look out for the interests of others as much as for ourselves. We must learn forgiveness, and give others the benefit of the doubt, recognizing that we often misjudge intentions. We often accuse others wrongfully, and assume the worst in many circumstances.

Surrendering all means giving Christ everything and every part of our lives. Only then can we be used fully for His glory.

Words of Love: Rest in the Lord, and wait patiently for Him... Psalm 37:7

DAY 158
LIVING HARMONIOUSLY

Scripture: Behold, how good and how pleasant it is for brethren to dwell together in unity. Psalm 133:1

I love to look at old photos and reminisce on the occasions surrounding them. They bring back wonderful memories, and make you want to have those experiences again. That is why many people have, and look forward to, frequent family reunions; or why classmates have class reunions.

In my church, we were always looking for reasons to celebrate. We had sweetheart banquets for Valentines; spring festivals; fall hayrides; couples' retreats; women's retreats and breakfasts; prayer summits; weekends and summer camps for children, teens and families; and anything in between.

What are your family memories, and your experiences within the family of God? Do you look forward to the weekly reunions, when you get together to worship? Is there much fellowship, or are you among the first to get out the door, into your car, and out the parking lot? What is your anticipation of heaven? Do you look forward to your biological family and church family being there, or are you praying that if they are, they stay far from you?

If we are not able to resolve conflicts here on earth, and live harmoniously with each other, chances are we would be very uncomfortable in heaven, where we would be required to be in their presence throughout eternity. The passage in Psalm 133:1-3 continues by saying that harmonious living is like the dew of Hermon, and as the dew that descended upon the mountains of Zion, for there the Lord commanded the blessing, even life for evermore. Harmonious living here on earth is part of that eternal life we want, and look for, in Jesus Christ. When we love our neighbors as ourselves, one of the two great commandments, it is much easier to live harmoniously with them.

Words of Love: If it is possible, as much as depends on you, live peaceably with all men. Romans 12:18

DAY 159

JESUS CARES

Scripture: What is man that You are mindful of him, and the son of man that You visit him? Psalm 8:4

God's goodness and His gracious kindness amaze me constantly. I feel so undeserving of His blessings, especially the awesome gift of Himself on Calvary. As we approach the Easter season, we are reminded of Jesus Christ taking away the darkness of sin from us and giving us His marvelous light. This is not a gift to be spurned; but rather, one to grab hold of tightly and never let go. It makes me want to shout the words of the beautiful song by the title, "No One Ever Cared for Me Like Jesus," written by Dr. Charles Frederick Weigle, in 1932, during a time of much sadness.

I came to know Jesus early in my life, but took Him for granted many times through the years. It is with much gratitude that I look back over the journey so far, and realize God's faithfulness as He has stood by my side through my many failures. Today I acknowledge His great love and care, and place my hands firmly in His, entrusting the remainder of the journey to Him. I feel compelled to invite you to do the same, knowing that He lovingly cares for you as much as He does for me.

John 10:13 says of the hireling caring for the sheep: he flees in times of danger, because he is a hired hand and is more concerned for his own safety than he is about the safety of the sheep, but with Jesus it is different. He puts our safety before His own. He lays His life on the line for us. He truly cares.

Words of Love: I am the good shepherd; and I know My sheep, and am known by My own. John 10:14

DAY 160
STANDING UP AND STANDING OUT

Scripture: Watch, stand fast in the faith, be brave, be strong. 1 Corinthians 16:13

What a sad epithet, if at the pinnacle of our success, we take all the credit for ourselves, we project ourselves as being self-made, and we discredit the Giver of all good gifts. On the other hand, what happens when you stand up for Jesus and stand out in the crowd, to the ridicule of everyone?

How do you feel about praying over your food in the presence of others? Are you afraid to acknowledge the goodness of God in your life, to tell others what He has done for you? Do you live up to the values you have learned in Christ? Is standing up for right and justice making you stand out too much? Do you feel uncomfortable living a life dedicated to Jesus in an environment of secularism?

Christ has not promised that being different would be popular or comfortable, but He does admonish us to be a peculiar people. It is not hard to live right around others of like belief, but it is quite another story to practice your faith among others who do not share your beliefs.

Kirstie's strong Christian life influenced Erin for Christ. Then to Erin's disappointment, Kirstie changed and began to walk away from the Lord whom she had loved so much. Through prayer and love, Erin reintroduced Kirstie to her first love: Jesus Christ. Today, they are both standing strong for Him.

Words of Love: Remember therefore from where you have fallen; repent and do the first works, or else I will come to you quickly and remove your lampstand from its place—unless you repent. Revelation 2:5

DAY 161
LIMITLESS POSSIBILITIES

Scripture: But Jesus looked at them and said, "With men it is impossible, but not with God; for with God all things are possible." Mark 10:27.

What are some of the things you perceived impossible in your life, in the lives of your family, in your community, or maybe in your lifetime? Did you think it possible to travel to the moon, or live in outer space for months and years? Were your "impossibilities" that of achieving a college education or owning a home?

Was your "impossibility" seeing a loved one, for whom you have been praying, come to know Jesus Christ as Lord and Savior? Were you struggling with unresolved issues, or broken relationships, and never thought forgiveness and restoration possible?

Father God is a God of limitless possibilities. Whatever the issue you thought impossible, great or small, God delights in showing you that all things are possible for Him. Today may be the day He wants to enlarge your territory. It may be the day when He wants to show you unmerited favor. It may be the day that He wants to show you what forgiveness and restoration look like. It may be the day when He wants you to see your prayers answered, or your dreams fulfilled.

Whatever you do, never place limits on God. He cannot be contained by our limited perspective. Since He is the Creator of everything, He is greater than all of His creation. He is bigger than our thoughts. Our limited thinking is no match for His limitless abilities. After all, He is God, and He desires to do great things for us.

Words of Love: Jesus said to him, "If you can believe, all things are possible to him who believes." Mark 9:23

DAY 162
YES, YOU CAN!

Scripture: I can do all things through Christ who strengthens me. Philippians 4:13

I ran home crying, after my second attempt at the scholarship program for grammar school returned unfavorable results. For the second time, I had only gotten a partial scholarship. At the young age of twelve years old, I felt like a failure.

My mom, though herself disappointed for me, consoled and encouraged me. How wonderful to be affirmed, especially when we doubt ourselves.

Do you need encouragement today? Pour out your heart to our loving Father, and ask Him to send someone or something to lift your spirit and help you move forward. My mother would not let me give up after a couple failed attempts. She did not allow me to have a pity party; instead she helped me to get up and dust myself off, and prepare for the next opportunity.

If you do not need encouragement, who can you encourage along this bumpy and winding road of life? Someone needs to hear kind words today such as, "I know you can." "Is there something I can do to help you?" Communities, like chains, are only as strong as their weakest links. Let us work to strengthen our communities today, by strengthening those who need an encouraging word or a helping hand. Together we can make the lives of others better. We will all be stronger for it.

Words of Love: Be anxious for nothing, but in everything by prayer and supplication, with thanksgiving, let your requests be made known to God... Philippians 4:6-7

DAY 163

NOT BEYOND REACH

Scripture: Where can I go from Your Spirit? Or where can I flee from Your presence? If I ascend into heaven, You are there; If I make my bed in hell, behold, You are there... Psalm 139:7-12

Are you striving for some goal that seem unattainable; beyond your reach? Do you feel that you have done something so wrong that you are beyond God's reach? The following stories provide perspectives:

Toni grew up in a large family where none of the girls went to school, and the boys only had a few years of grade school education. She was labeled as rebellious when she shared her dreams for not only a high school education, but a college degree. "That is beyond your reach," everyone told her, but Toni, who had been quietly reading God's Word, learned that through faith, anything in His will was within reach. She was confident that He would make a way, and He did.

Montel was heading down a wrong path. He felt that he had strayed so far from the values he was taught as a young boy, that he was beyond God's redemption. One night when he was at rock bottom, and close to taking his own life, he cried out to God for help. God in His love stretched out His arm of mercy and saved him. A repentant heart is always within God's reach.

Whatever your circumstances today, remember that no one and nothing is beyond the reach of the Almighty. Cry out to Him, whether it is to fulfill a dream, if it is in His will, or a heart cry for salvation. He longs to show Himself faithful on your behalf.

Words of Love: No man shall be able to stand before you all the days of your life; as I was with Moses, so I will be with you. I will not leave you nor forsake you. Joshua 1:5

DAY 164
WE PRAYED FOR YOU TODAY

Scripture: Again, I say to you that if two of you agree on earth concerning anything that they ask, it will be done for them by My Father in heaven. Matthew 18:19

Whether we pray individually or corporately, hearts of prayer warriors are lifted up daily for God's children everywhere. We pray for your physical maladies to be healed; we pray for your emotional turmoil to be eased; we pray that your relationship issues be resolved; we pray for your financial woes to be settled. We pray for those in school, that your studies are successful; and we pray for you in business or on the job, to have successful careers and businesses.

For those of you in government: city, county, state, and federal, we pray for you to be servant leaders. For those in healthcare and other service industries, we pray for you to recognize that those you serve are created in the image of God, and deserve the best you have to offer. We pray for the oppressed, and for the oppressors. We pray for all colors, races, ethnicities, languages, cultures, classes, castes, genders, and religious persuasions.

Our hearts were lifted up to God on your behalf today. We should pray for one another, so, as you pray today, I ask that you lift up God's children everywhere. That will include my prayer partners and me as well, and for that I thank you.

Words of Love: And this I pray, that your love may abound still more and more in knowledge and all discernment. Philippians 1:9

DAY 165
OUR OMNIPOTENT LORD

Scripture: You alone are the Lord; You have made heaven, the heaven of heavens, with all their host, the earth and everything on it, the seas and all that is in them, and You preserve them all. The host of heaven worships You. Nehemiah 9:6

Gracious God, You are majestic in all the earth. You show Your might in the wind, which one moment is forceful enough to unsettle the elements; yet, gentle enough the next to rock us to sleep with the beautiful sound of nature surrounding us.

Merciful Savior, I love how You are powerful, yet restrained. You told the angels to hold back the wind of strife, until You give the command. Help us to recognize Your power and majesty, and to stand in awe in Your presence. You are powerful enough to heal the woman who by faith touched the hem of Your garment; powerful enough to raise Jairus' daughter, and Lazarus from the dead; and powerful enough to heal the servant of the centurion when he trusted You to simply speak the word, and it would be accomplished.

Your matchless power has been used throughout centuries to save, rescue and bless humanity, yet You chose not to use it for Your own benefit. You could have called legions of angels to rescue You in Gethsemane or whisk You from the cruel cross; yet with all Your might and power, You subjected Yourself to death at Calvary for me.

Words of Love: Therefore, know that the Lord your God, He is God, the faithful God who keeps covenant and mercy for a thousand generations with those who love Him and keep His commandments. Deuteronomy 7:9

DAY 166

"JUST CHILL!"

Scripture: Be still and know that I am God... Psalm 46:10

"Mommy, just chill," the son said to his mother. "You have to learn to relax. You are too uptight about everything." My friend wanted to be mad over what she saw as a scolding from her child, but she smiled instead, knowing he was right.

The family was expecting company for a large reception. There were still a few details to come together for the occasion, and the mother was driving herself and everyone around her absolutely crazy. The event was several days off and the family had hired an event coordinator, but she would not allow herself to relax.

Jesus invited His disciples to come away from the hustle and bustle of all that was happening around them. He knew the importance of being still, and allowing oneself to catch a breath. There is a beautiful song which says it in those very words, "Just breathe."

In a world where so many things scream for our attention at the same time, it is often very difficult to relax. Jesus extends the same invitation to you and me, however. He bids us: put down the cell phone; turn off the computer; leave the dishes, the laundry, the vacuuming and the cooking for a while. Go sit in a swing in the backyard; listen to the birds; enjoy the flowers. Take a prayer walk, and be rejuvenated. "Just spend some time with Me," He entreats us; "It will make the tasks lighter when you resume them, or at least you can put them in their right perspectives."

Words of Love: I am the vine, you are the branches. He who abides in Me, and I in him, bears much fruit; for without Me you can do nothing. John 15:5

DAY 167
YOU SHOULD HAVE TOLD ME

Scripture: These things I have spoken to you, that in Me you may have peace. In the world you will have tribulation; but be of good cheer, I have overcome the world. John 16:33

"Mom," the teenage daughter cried, "you should have told me." She had just learned that her mother was suffering from a rare and aggressive form of cancer. The shock was too much for her to bear, as the prognosis was not good. The daughter was at the end of her senior year of high school, and the mother wanted nothing to interfere with her focus on her studies.

Exams were now over, and senior trip was a blast. There were two months before this young lady would go off to college. There was a summer of freedom to enjoy family and friends; and now this news. The family came together for a meeting, and the daughter insisted on delaying college for a year to spend time with her mother. The college she had selected was very understanding, and she would not lose her scholarship.

It was a year of immense bonding for the entire family, but especially for mother and daughter. The mother helped her daughter secure a firmer grip on her Lord and Savior, which might not have happened under different circumstances. They were inseparable, and both developed a closer relationship with Jesus.

Today, Jessie does not have her mother; but she has her best friend, Jesus. She thanks our loving and gracious Father for the gift of that special year that she and her mother were blessed to spend together.

Words of Love: And He said, "My Presence will go with you, and I will give you rest." Exodus 33:14

DAY 168

CREATED FOR A SPECIAL PURPOSE

Scripture: But indeed, for this purpose I have raised you up, that I may show My power in you, and that My name may be declared in all the earth. Exodus 9:16.

Mark Twain said that the two most important days in your life are the day you were born, and the day you find out why. The first, you have no control over; the second, you should diligently seek to discover.

We are all created for a purpose, one that no other person can rightly fulfill. Have you found out yet for what purpose you were created? Ask God to show you. What are your natural inclinations? What do you enjoy doing? How does it benefit humanity and bring glory to God?

When you find your purpose, dedicate yourself to pursuing it. That does not mean you won't have to work at developing and mastering it. What it does mean is that it will bring you inner satisfaction when you see others being blessed by it, and know that it pleases your Father above. I can just imagine the smile on His face, when He sees us fulfilling His plan for our lives.

I read of a physician who was very unhappy practicing medicine, but he loved to play music. So, he left his practice and joined a music band. When I read the story, he was not making a lot of money playing in the band, but he was very happy and fulfilled. I also knew a nurse who left nursing to pursue a career as a financial planner, and had no regrets. Many have left lucrative careers to follow their heart in ministries serving others, and have found inner peace.

So, what has God laid on your heart? Do you feel called to serve in a specific capacity, but you are questioning that calling? You will be happiest when you are doing what you feel called to do. If you yield to your calling, but lack the skills, be encouraged; remember, God equips those He calls.

Words of Love: There are many plans in a man's heart, nevertheless the Lord's counsel—that will stand. Proverbs 19:21.

DAY 169
SHARING IN YOUR SORROWS

Scripture: Bear one another's burdens, and so fulfill the law of Christ. Galatians 6:2

Isn't it amazing to know that when you are sorrowful, the God of the universe shares your sorrows? So often, our "friends" are only there for us in the good times, but when things get bad, they are nowhere to be found. That was the case of the prodigal son. I believe we call those people "fair weather friends." When you are on top of the world, they are beside you, singing, "Let the good times roll." But don't fall on hard times, because they are likely to step over you in their haste to get away.

God, on the other hand, runs towards you in times of sorrow. He is there to pick you up, dust you off, and offer you His shoulder to lean on. If you are too weak from the pain and anguish of your circumstances, He gently lifts you in His arms, and carries you to a place of safety. He then stays with you through the difficulties, and even offers to stay with you always. You don't have to worry about Him being intrusive; He does as much as you allow Him to.

What a wonderful Savior is Jesus, God's Only Begotten Son. What a wonderful Savior is Jesus my Lord.

Words of Love: For His anger is but for a moment, His favor is for life; Weeping may endure for a night, but joy comes in the morning. Psalm 30:5

DAY 170
TRAVELING COMPANION

Scripture: That which we have seen and heard we declare to you, that you also may have fellowship with us; and truly our fellowship is with the Father and with His Son Jesus Christ. 1 John 1:3

I am retired and I do some consulting in the capital city of the state where I live. I have an apartment in the city and travel between my home and this apartment for a few days of work each month. The long commute provides a wonderful time to commune with God through prayer and the Word. Our conversations are a special treat. They are open, honest and very "raw," and sometimes they leave me in tears. At other times, I burst into songs of praise and thanksgiving.

Whenever I get sleepy along my commute, as I sometimes do, He uses different strategies to keep me awake. I am so thankful for His watchful eyes over me, and over the road on which I travel. In Luke 24:13-35 is the story of Jesus with two of His disciples on the road to Emmaus. As much as they enjoyed the conversation and marveled at the teachings He provided them, they lost sight of who He was. They were blinded by their own lack of faith.

Because life is a journey, we don't have to be on road trips to have the companionship of the Good Shepherd. He delights in walking beside us every day. What an awesome privilege to have the Omnipotent and Omniscient Father as our Omnipresent Companion. It is the opportunity of a lifetime.

Words of Love: Stay with me; do not fear. For he who seeks my life seeks your life, but with me you shall be safe. 1 Samuel 22:23

DAY 171
FOREVER AND FOR ALWAYS

Scripture: Therefore, a man shall leave his father and mother and be joined to his wife, and they shall become one flesh. Genesis 2:24

It was our eighteenth wedding anniversary and my husband came home with a lovely card, a dozen beautiful red roses, and an invitation to dinner. I reflected on our first meeting, and a short three-month courtship, followed by a wedding attended by many family and friends.

There were moments of sheer panic during the planning of the wedding, when I questioned if we were being too hasty to take those vows. After all, they were "forever and for always." There have been bumps in the road, but here we were eighteen years later; feeling very blessed, and looking forward for another eighteen years.

When God united Adam and Eve in the first marriage in the Garden of Eden, He no doubt intended theirs and every married couple after them to commit to lives of togetherness separated only by death. He said a man should leave mother and father, and cleave to his wife, and together they should become one flesh.

Sin has destroyed the value and sacredness of marriage, but God desires to restore it. He likens His relationship with His bride, the church, to a marriage union. He promises to come back for His beloved, with the assurance that there will be no more separation. We will live and reign with Him through the ceaseless ages of eternity, forever and for always.

Words of Love: Nevertheless, let each one of you in particular so love his own wife as himself, and let the wife see that she respects her husband. Ephesians 5:33

DAY 172
OMNIPRESENT

Scripture: "Am I a God near at hand," says the Lord, "And not a God afar off? Can anyone hide himself in secret places, so I shall not see him?" says the Lord; "Do I not fill heaven and earth?" says the Lord. Jeremiah 23:23-24

"Where was He when I needed Him?" Julian cried. "Why did He not protect her from danger, when she had always been so faithful to Him? Why did He let my Mama die such a horrible death?"

These are not unfamiliar questions from people who are emotional with grief at the loss of someone they love, especially when the death is unexpected, and horrific. And then, I have heard the answer: "The same place He was when His Only Son hung on Calvary's cross."

Yes, God is everywhere, and at all times. He is not absent from our sufferings, even if He does not rescue us from them. The three Hebrew boys were not spared the fire, and neither was Daniel spared the lions' den, but God was there with them.

Our God is a God in the bad times as well as the good times. He agonizes in our suffering, just as much as He celebrates in our joys. We must trust Him that there is a divine purpose for every event in the lives of His children, even when the fog of despair rolls over our hearts. In due season, He will make all wrongs right.

Words of Love: I will instruct you and teach you in the way you should go; I will guide you with My eye. Psalm 32:8

DAY 173

LET GO OF THE DOOR

Scripture: May the Lord answer you in the day of trouble; May the name of the God of Jacob defend you. Psalm 20:1

A friend told the story of a loving dad and his young son who were about to enter a building. Both the little boy and his dad reached for the door handle at the same time. Knowing that the door was too heavy for the little fellow, and realizing that his little hands would be squeezed if he grabbed the handle while the boy was still holding it, the father said gently, but firmly: "Son, let go of the door." He had to repeat himself more than once before he got the little boy's attention.

How many times has our loving Father told us to let go of the door we have been holding on to? Sometimes we are bent on charging ahead at full speed, while grabbing for the door to enter into an experience that will only cause us pain. We think we can handle the door, as well as what is beyond the door, but our loving Father knows best, and He tries to restrain us.

He is saying to us, "Let Me get the door, and let Me make sure that what is beyond it is okay for you, before you charge into it." He is trying to restrain us out of love. He wants only what is best for us, and implores us to heed His gentle chidings.

Words of Love: God is our refuge and strength, a very present help in trouble. Psalm 46:1

DAY 174
PRAY FIRST

Scripture: Praying always with all prayer and supplication in the Spirit, being watchful to this end with all perseverance and supplication for all the saints— Ephesians 6:18

We are admonished to "come boldly to the throne of grace." Not with arrogance, as though we are God's equal, or as if He owes us something, but rather, we should approach the Father with confidence, knowing that He longs to hear from us. When should we make prayer the first thing? Before everything we do. And why? Because He is the Creator and we are His created beings. We need Him for our very existence.

With acknowledgment of God's sovereignty, we should always pray when we come into His presence. Then we should thank Him for the privilege of bringing our needs or the needs of others to Him. Ask Him for the humility and willingness to listen to Him, and when He tells us that some things are not for us to know, let us ask Him to help us trust His divine wisdom. Then let us thank Him for how He will work things out, according to His great plan for us.

Words of Love: Be anxious for nothing, but in everything by prayer and supplication, with thanksgiving, let your requests be made known to God; and the peace of God, which surpasses all understanding, will guard your hearts and minds through Christ Jesus. Philippians 4:6-7

DAY 175

GETHSEMANE

Scripture: What! Could you not watch with Me one hour? Matthew 26:40

Have you ever gone through some rough experiences and desperately needed someone to talk to, pray with, or just cry on their shoulder? Someone to provide some consolation: that human touch. Have you always had that person you needed, when you need them? Jesus experienced that human need the night He contended with the forces of the evil one, and struggled with the weight of our sins. How our Savior longed for human solace, as He sought His Father's intervention.

I can only imagine, but not truly fathom, the agony He was enduring as He prayed for another way to save humanity other than the way of the cross. His agony was so intense that the scripture says His sweat was as drops of blood. His humanity desired a way out because He knew the suffering He faced. It was a journey He had to conclude alone, but He wanted His closest friends to buoy Him up and for the final phase. How my Savior needed His friends' support, yet they failed Him when He needed them most.

Before we judge those three beloved disciples too harshly for denying our blessed Lord the simple request to "watch with Him" while He prayed, think: How often have we denied Him the simple request of spending time with Him in prayer? Gethsemane reminds me of deep, agonizing prayers. Today, let us meet Jesus in "Gethsemane," with the assurance that He will tarry with us in our agony, and provide the answers we need to whatever struggles we are experiencing.

Words of Love: Continue earnestly in prayer, being vigilant in it with thanksgiving. Colossians 4:2

DAY 176
A FORGIVING GOD

Scripture: If we confess our sins, He is faithful and just to forgive us our sins and to cleanse us from all unrighteousness. 1 John 1:9

"No ifs, ands, or buts; our God is a forgiving God." This was an emphatic statement from one member of the touring music team to the other team members. "You speak as one with experience," another team member ribbed. "I bet, if we think about it honestly, every born-again Christian can make that statement emphatically," the first student responded.

One of the chaperones decided to join the conversation for some mature perspective, and what followed was a deep, heart-searching discussion on why Jesus was so forgiving. When God created man, He desired to have an intimate relationship with him. He spent time communing with him in the garden daily. Sin entered and short-circuited the relationship, causing the disobedient pair to hide from God when He came for His usual visit with them.

God knew the likelihood of this happening, because of the power of choice He gave to mankind at creation. He wanted us to love Him with hearts overflowing with a desire for intimacy with Him, not from a sense of obligation or programmed response. He already had a plan in place to save the crowning jewel of His creation, should he choose to disobey. Because of His forgiving spirit, He did not annihilate humanity and start over. He certainly had the power.

Sin causes separation from the Father, but Jesus is the bridge of forgiveness and restoration. He is not about to give up on us, though sin often widens the chasm. He wants to reestablish this special bond with us. He is pursuing us and wooing us back to Himself. How long will we turn our backs on Him?

Words of Love: If you confess with your mouth the Lord Jesus and believe in your heart that God has raised Him from the dead, you will be saved. Romans 10:9

DAY 177
ALIVE FOR EVERMORE

Scripture: Now if we died with Christ, we believe that we shall also live with Him… Romans 6:8-9

How profound is that knowledge? Jesus Christ, whom Satan thought he had conquered that Friday, when He was nailed to a cruel cross, conquered death on Sunday morning, and rose from the grave. Christ had gained the victory, and in essence had the last laugh.

Before Mary and the other women knew He had risen, they were heartbroken. Their sorrow, I believe, was not that He had not fulfilled the expectation to establish an earthly kingdom, where they might have some position of honor or power. It was the loss of their precious Lord and Master. Their heart was in the right place, which is why, I believe, Jesus appeared to them first.

What a difference it makes when the risen Christ lives in our hearts. That was the purpose of His ultimate sacrifice. The scripture says that heaven rejoices when one sinner gives his heart to Jesus; when He, the risen Savior is invited to take up permanent residence in his heart. The fact that Jesus lives forevermore at the right hand of the Father would be meaningless if we reject the intercession He is making for each of us.

Christ left heaven in the first place to assure us a place there. The road to our restoration cost Him His life. Let us be thankful that the grave could not contain Him. He broke the chains of Sheol, and is alive forevermore, and because He lives, there is hope for all humanity.

Words of Love: The last enemy that will be destroyed is death. 1 Corinthians 15:26

DAY 178
GOD'S AMAZING GRACE

Scripture: But may the God of all grace, who called us to His eternal glory by Christ Jesus, after you have suffered a while, perfect, establish, strengthen, and settle you... 1 Peter 5:10-11

Jenny sat in the back of the meetings each night. Something drew her to the seminars, and the subject matter touched her heart, but she felt undeserving of God's love that the speaker spoke about. He was not a dynamic, hellfire preacher, but rather a deliberate and systematic teacher, who opened the Word of God and made it clear and simple.

Jenny's heart softened a little more each session. There was usually a thoughtful song to begin the meetings; one which generally went along with the subject matter for that session. The singers glorified God with their selections, which were very inspirational. After each song, Jenny's heart was ready to receive God's message from the speaker.

For the session dealing with God's grace, the song "Grace Greater Than Our Sin" was sung. Jenny was so moved by the rendition of the song and presentation that she broke into tears. She wanted to run to the front and cry out to God, "I yield, I yield," but she contained herself. Then it happened: the speaker asked the singer to sing the opening song one more time, as he thanked God for His amazing grace extended to all of humanity.

As the chorus was being sung one last time, the audience was invited to join in the singing. Singing those words was the "one drop" that overflowed Jenny's cup, and she yielded her heart to Christ, never to look back to the world of sin anymore. Jenny is still firmly grounded in her relationship with Christ, and not surprisingly, her favorite topic of discussion is God's amazing grace.

Words of Love: The grace of the Lord Jesus Christ, and the love of God, and the communion of the Holy Spirit be with you all. Amen. 2 Corinthians 13:14

DAY 179

THE PRICELESS VALUE OF TRUE FRIENDSHIP

Scripture: By this we know love, because He laid down His life for us. And we also ought to lay down our lives for the brethren. 1 John 3:16

Here I was, sitting in a restaurant for two hours, waiting for this ethnic dish to be ready, because my friend wanted it. Getting to the restaurant in the first place was somewhat treacherous, as it was storming, and we were under a tornado watch.

My friend is acutely aware of my fear of driving in bad weather, and she assured me that my safety was more valuable than the food, but I also knew how long she had been wanting this particular dish. I had the time, and our friendship was worth the effort expended. While I waited on the dish which was being prepared to order, she sent me a text which said, "Thanks for loving me enough to do it."

The beauty of our friendship is that my friend would have done the same thing for me. She makes sacrifices to do things for me that only those who place great value on friendship would consider doing. We don't take each other for granted, and we give thanks to God for being in each other's life.

It was the Thursday before Good Friday, and I reflected on how much Jesus loves us, to go to Calvary for something we desperately needed: salvation. I was only paying a few dollars for this meal for my friend, but Christ paid the ultimate price: His life, to secure a place at the King's table for you and me. Now that is true friendship!

Words of Love: But God demonstrates His own love toward us, in that while we were still sinners, Christ died for us. Romans 5:8

DAY 180
DIAMOND IN THE ROUGH

Scripture: They shall be Mine," says the Lord of hosts, "On the day that I make them My jewels. And I will spare them as a man spares his own son who serves him." Malachi 3:17

A former colleague of mine and her family love to spend their vacations mining for jewels. She tells stories of occasionally having a great find. I am intrigued, watching her tell of the excitement at finding a stone that ends up being very beautiful, once cut and polished.

Her stories remind me of television shows about mining for diamonds, and the investment people and companies make in areas they believe are rich with minerals. They often show small stones that they find, but rarely do you see them display any stone of significant size.

To my untrained eye, the stones are simply dirty rocks of insignificant value. However, to the trained eye of the miner/prospector, he sees diamonds just waiting to be cleaned up, and cut to shape and size.

In the same way I would overlook an uncut diamond, because it resembles any old dirty stone, we often overlook God's children, writing them off as useless, having little or no potential. Thankfully, God views us with eyes of love, and He sees our potential in His hands. When our Savior picks us up from the pile or the pit, we may be diamonds in the rough, but when His skillful hands clean us up and cut us in the most beautiful shapes to highlight our best qualities, we will be priceless jewels.

Words of Love: Since you were precious in My sight, you have been honored, and I have loved you; Therefore, I will give men for you, and people for your life. Isaiah 43:4

DAY 181
A WAY OUT OF NO WAY

Scripture: Thus says the Lord, who makes a way in the sea, and a path through the mighty waters... Behold, I will do a new thing, now it shall spring forth; Shall you not know it? I will even make a road in the wilderness, and rivers in the desert. Isaiah 43:16-19

Have you ever been in a situation where you thought, "This is it, there is no way out of this unscathed"? Most of us have been there.

Zany knows the feeling only too well. She was a teenager when her mother died, and her father walked away. Her siblings who were younger were adopted quickly, but no one wanted a teenager with an attitude. So, Zany went from one foster home to another. She did not trust anyone, because she had been abused too many times by those she trusted.

Then, what seemed to be the worst thing happened: Zany was raped and became pregnant. She was sent to a home for unwed mothers, and there, of all places it seemed, she found love, acceptance, and best of all, she found Jesus. Zany flourished in this unlikely environment. With newfound confidence, her attitude changed, and in her mid-teens, Zany and her baby girl were adopted by a loving Christian family.

Zany excelled in school, catching up and surpassing many of her classmates with stable homes all their lives. She graduated at the top of her class and was offered scholarships to several prestigious universities. She chose one close to home, where she could be close to her family. Today, she is an expert in her field, and respected by her colleagues. She makes her parents proud.

When Zany thought that there was no way out of her unfortunate childhood circumstances, God made a way for her. That same God knows our individual circumstances, and says to us, "Let Me work out your situation for you."

Don't tell a child of God what she can't do, because she will simply tell you what her God can do. Don't tell him that there is no way. He will tell you that Jesus is both the way-maker, and the Way.

Words of Love: Jesus said to him, "I am the way, the truth, and the life. No one comes to the Father except through Me. John 14:6

DAY 182
ONE PINT VS EVERY DROP

Scripture: For He shall give His angels charge over you, to keep you in all your ways. Psalm 91:11

It was a lovely day and my church was sponsoring a blood drive in honor of a member who had a bone marrow transplant. The service began with the children leading out in beautiful praise music. I slipped out to the blood mobile to donate blood, with hopes of returning in time for the sermon. There were quite a few people in line, which was a positive sign for a successful drive.

One elderly lady ahead of me passed out after donating, and we commented that maybe she should not have given blood. The paramedics came and she was taken to the hospital for follow-up. When it was my turn, I joked with the nurse, to relax, and in seven minutes had given my pint of blood.

During the fellowship meal which followed, I told the person sitting next to me that I felt light-headed. That was the last thing I remembered before I lost consciousness. The experience reminded me of the sacrifice Christ made to give me eternal life. My gift of one unit of blood may have helped somebody in a crisis, temporarily. Christ's gift of His life provides us with eternal life, if we accept it. I am not letting Him shed His precious blood in vain. You have access to that life-saving blood as well. Don't allow His sacrifice for you to be worth nothing.

Words of Love: For even the Son of Man did not come to be served, but to serve, and to give His life a ransom for many. Mark 10:45

DAY 183
LOVE WITHOUT MEASURE

Scripture: Therefore, as the elect of God, holy and beloved, put on tender mercies, kindness, humility, meekness, longsuffering. Colossians 3:12

Bernard of Clairvaux said the true measure of God's love is that He loves without measure. It is a long shot to find any earthly comparison which comes close to the love of God and Jesus Christ for humanity.

It is one thing to love someone who shows us love and affection; but to love a stranger or someone who hates us to the point of endangering our life to save theirs is quite another.

I was hurrying to a meeting when I observed something beautiful. A woman with evident physical challenges was struggling to get her motorized wheelchair over a curb. A man was driving up a side street, saw her struggle, stopped his van and jumped out to help her. He placed himself in possible danger to save a stranger in greater danger. From my rearview mirror, I could see her back in her chair on level ground, and on her way down the sidewalk.

I did not hear her say, "Thank You," even though I want to believe she did, but I believe gratitude was the last thing on that gentleman's mind. He saw a need and, with the love of God flowing from his heart, he rushed to meet it.

Need knows no color and neither does love. Christians must love as Jesus loves.

Words of Love: And just as you want men to do to you, you also do to them likewise. Luke 6:31

DAY 184
LIFE'S DIFFICULT MOMENTS: OPPORTUNITIES FOR GROWTH

Scripture: And not only that, but we also glory in tribulations, knowing that tribulation produces perseverance; and perseverance, character; and character, hope... Romans 5:3-5

There are many Bible stories of people who shone like bright stars in moments of great difficulty. There are the stories of Daniel and the three Hebrew boys, Ruth, Esther, Job, Joseph and many others. The common thread in all of these stories is the challenge each person faced: challenges that would have caused many to give up and lose their faith. These believers became more grounded in their faith, however, and they grew spiritually by leaps and bounds.

What is it that made these men and women of God stronger when the road was rough, and the challenges hard to endure? What made them soar, as though on the wings of eagles, when others would have given up? What made them grow in their walk with the Lord? The answer, I believe, was their faith. Job said it best in Job 13:15, "Though He slay me, still I will trust Him."

What difficult period of life are you experiencing presently? Is it wearing you down? Are you giving up and folding under the pressure? Have you wondered why it is lasting so long? My question to you is: "Have you grown any in and through this trial; have you profited any from it; are you learning anything to help you better prepare for the next one?"

Job learned that God could restore his losses multifold. Esther became a praying queen who sought and obtained God's deliverance for her people. Joseph suffered years of imprisonment for his faithfulness, but God restored him. He grew in his relationship with his Lord and Savior.

God wants to teach and establish us in our suffering. The scripture says, 'Whom the Lord loves He chastens.' Life's difficulties are for our grooming and growth. Let us subject ourselves to the Master Teacher; we will be better for it.

Words of Love: You are of God, little children, and have overcome them, because He who is in you is greater than he who is in the world. 1 John 4:4

DAY 185

THE BEST WAY TO HEAL IS TO SERVE

Scripture: Our hearts ache, but we always have joy. We are poor, but we give spiritual riches to others. We own nothing, and yet we have everything. 2 Corinthians 6:10 (NLT)

Howie served in a nursing home ministry, after the death of his father who spent the last years of his life a resident at the home. His father was very happy there; and was well cared for by the staff, who were very dedicated to their work of caring for the residents. Howie visited his father on Sundays, and enjoyed sharing the worship time with him. They listened intently to the group that ministered to the residents every Sunday for over twenty years.

Howie was so impressed by the spiritual blessing of the ministry to the residents and staff, that at the passing of his father he joined the ministry. In his grief, Howie found healing in service. I was privileged to see him in action, and what a blessing he and his fellow ministry members were to those they served. It was evident that Howie and the other ministry leaders enjoyed preparing for and spending time with the residents every week.

If you are suffering from the pain and anguish of loss, find an avenue for service. As you minister to the needs of others, your pain will become more bearable. That is how God works. He says to give and it will be given back to you in full measure, pressed down and running over. The hand that plucks a rose petal and shares it with another is left with the lingering fragrance himself. May any anguish you bear today be minimized or alleviated as you serve a world that needs to see the love of God through the lives of His children.

Words of Love: Therefore, you now have sorrow; but I will see you again and your heart will rejoice, and your joy no one will take from you. John 16:22

DAY 186
"SON-BEAM"

Scripture: For it is the God who commanded light to shine out of darkness, who has shone in our hearts to give the light of the knowledge of the glory of God in the face of Jesus Christ. 2 Corinthians 4:6

Watching the sunset from the cliffs at the lighthouse is a sight to behold. As the rays of the setting sun hit the water, it radiates a warm glow and generates excitement from the crowd lining the cliffs at the nearby cafe. If sunbeams can generate so much excitement, it baffles me that people cannot get excited about the "Son-beams" radiating from the faces and through the Christ-inspired actions of love from Christ's followers. Christians are the eyes, ears, hands and feet of the Savior. They radiate His love; they are like Christ in action.

When the Holy Spirit lives, loves, and serves through us, there will be nothing but Son-beams shining in the morning, at noonday, and at the setting sun. I want His character to radiate from me every day.

The story is told of a village where the people set out to find the one who reflected the life of Christ more than any other. They looked everywhere and at everyone: princes, nobles, religious leaders, and dignitaries. No one emanated the radiance they expected. Then one day a kind but quiet and unassuming man's face became radiant. It was what the community was looking for, but not expecting to find in one of such low estate. The poor man himself was astonished.

Jesus wants to shine His beams of love from each of us: from humble hearts totally surrendered to Him. What a surprise to many, when those from whom they least expect it shine bright rays of sunshine, demonstrating that the Son dwells within.

Words of Love: Let your light so shine before men, that they may see your good works and glorify your Father in heaven. Matthew 5:16

DAY 187

PROVE ME NOW

Scripture: "Bring all the tithes into the storehouse, that there may be food in My house, and try Me now in this," says the Lord of hosts, "If I will not open for you the windows of heaven and pour out for you such blessing, that there will not be room enough to receive it." Malachi 3:10

Peter was a new believer with limited income, so he balked at the notion of tithing. "I cannot afford to give one tenth of my meager income to God," Peter reasoned. Week after week he felt impressed to return a tithe as the Word of God admonished, but Peter resisted, as the needs of the family increased.

This son of God, who was a fisherman like Peter of the Bible, struggled within his heart, but eventually decided to trust God. He fished with a rod and reel, and decided to test God with his trade. He pledged to give every tenth fish he caught to the Lord. Something strange happened: every tenth fish was bigger than the other nine. No one knew Peter had made this pact with God. The first day he thought it was just a fluke, but every day thereafter the same thing happened.

Peter was tempted to cheat and take the fish that were larger for himself, but he decided to honor his commitment. As Peter was proving God, God was testing him. In essence, they both lived up to each other's expectations. Peter found that God could be trusted to honor our faithfulness. Peter's fishing began to return greater profitability, and as his family's needs were met, Peter poured more and more of the blessings he received into God's work.

The community was amazed at Peter's success and his generosity, and he was not abashed to share the story of God's blessings with anyone who asked. Many have been drawn to Christ through Peter's story. Not everyone in Peter's community experienced the same degree of financial success, but the entire community saw improvements in many aspects of their lives, thanks to one person who took God at His word and proved that He is faithful to His promises.

Words of Love: Do not withhold good from those to whom it is due, when it is in the power of your hand to do so. Proverbs 3:27

DAY 188
CONVICTED ON FALSE EVIDENCE

Scripture: Then she spoke to him with words like these, saying, "The Hebrew servant whom you brought to us came in to me to mock me; so it happened, as I lifted my voice and cried out, that he left his garment with me and fled outside." Genesis 39:17-18

Have you ever been falsely accused, or do you know someone who has? Many people have gone to prison, and many have lost their lives on false evidence. We have heard of mistaken identity, and that is hard, but what is even harder to comprehend is when someone knowingly misrepresents the truth, and some innocent person suffers the consequences.

The story of Joseph is one of those heart-wrenching stories, because the evidence that seemed so conclusive was a complete misrepresentation of the facts. Potiphar's wife did not get what she wanted, and the very thing from which Joseph ran, with the words, "How can I do this evil and sin against my God?" is what she accused him of. Joseph spent several years in prison for a crime he did not commit.

It has been centuries since Joseph's story, but evil practices continue. Innocent people are still victimized, and suffer because of evidence which is so convincing, yet untrue. Joseph remained faithful to God, and in time his faithfulness was rewarded. The story does not tell us that Potiphar's wife ever confessed to lying. I believe that Potiphar knew the truth, but acted cowardly. He probably knew his wife's tendencies, but may have perceived the evidence too strong to disregard. God knew the truth, however, and that was all that mattered to Joseph.

When you face challenges in life, and the cards seem stacked against you; when the evidence, though false, is very convincing, let God take up your case. The people of the world, who lie and plot evil like Potiphar's wife, may appear to be victorious in the short run, but in His time, God will vindicate and restore you. Be faithful to the end.

Words of Love: And Moses said to the people, "Do not be afraid. Stand still, and see the salvation of the Lord, which He will accomplish for you today. For the Egyptians whom you see today, you shall see again no more forever." Exodus 14:13

DAY 189
THE CASE HAS BEEN SETTLED

Scripture: My little children, these things I write to you, so that you may not sin. And if anyone sins, we have an Advocate with the Father, Jesus Christ the righteous. 1 John 2:1

Have you ever been summoned for jury duty, and instructed to call the night before for instructions regarding your participation? This is one time when serving is not convenient. Try as you may, however, you cannot find any good reason to request an excuse.

The evening before the big day arrives, and you call the number on the summons for instructions. Imagine the joy when the recorded message states: "If you are calling in response to a jury summons, the case has been settled." You throw up your hands in the air and shout, "Alleluia."

If you thought you were happy, let me tell you about real joy. The case being tried was mine. Representatives from both the prosecution and the defense had met for pre-trial consultations. The accuser appeared, and it was evident that the case against me was very strong. Sin abounded in my life, but I have repented and have exhibited great sorrow for my wrongs. Jesus steps up to the Father and says, "I died for this one, and she is mine; I have paid her debt, and this case is settled."

I fully deserved the sentence I would have received, had the case gone to a jury trial, but thank God for arbitration. Christ worked hard on my behalf, and now praise God, I am free. Your case might be next. How confident are you in your defense team? I recommend Jesus. He is simply the best.

Words of Love: Deliver those who are drawn toward death, and hold back those stumbling to the slaughter. Proverbs 24:11

DAY 190
GETTING TO THE HEART OF THE MATTER

Scripture: The heart is deceitful above all things, and desperately wicked; Who can know it? Jeremiah 17:9

Selfishness is one reason for societal breakdown, and the problems that plague humanity. When we drill down we find that a lack of love for each other is to blame, and when we dig even deeper, we find that our sinful nature is the root cause. Yes, sin is at the root of our problems.

Joslyn tells a story that spotlights this sin problem, and begins with the "I" problem. She is from a family where personal needs and wants became each person's all-encompassing focus, regardless of how much harm it brought to the others. At an early age, the children were left to fend for themselves as the parents engaged in self-appeasing and destructive behaviors. With little or no resources, it was every man for himself.

When social services became aware of the family dynamics and got involved, the pattern of self-centeredness had already been deeply ingrained, learned as a survival mechanism. Little by little, however, the love shown by others began to take effect. Like a patient gardener, it required much digging to unearth the problem. The root had to be cleared of the briars choking it, and then it had to be fertilized with kindness, and watered with acceptance. Gradually, there was evidence of an improved root system.

By God's amazing grace and the unfailing love of His children through whom He works to accomplish His purpose, Joslyn's life rebounded and sprouted new growth. Her siblings began to recover as well. To God be the glory, great things He has done.

Words of Love: Sing to the Lord, for He has done excellent things; This is known in all the earth. Isaiah 12:5

DAY 191
THE TERRIBLE PRICE OF DISOBEDIENCE

Scripture: But the children of Israel committed a trespass regarding the accursed things, for Achan the son of Carmi, the son of Zabdi, the son of Zerah, of the tribe of Judah, took of the accursed things; so the anger of the Lord burned against the children of Israel... Joshua 7:1-26

We have heard many horror stories of people who did not take advice, and suffered the consequences. Such was the heart-wrenching story of the mother who left her children at home under the supervision of the older sibling, with the instruction to remain at home until she returned from work mid-afternoon. She promised to take them to the park before dinner that evening. The two younger children were excited about the afternoon prospect of a trip to the park, but Cosmo felt he was big enough to do his own thing.

Shortly after the mother left for work, Cosmo gathered his two siblings and laid out his alternate plans. They would finish their chores early, and then they would accompany other neighborhood kids down to the river for a quick swim. They would be back before their mother returned from work, big brother assured them, and she would be none the wiser for their disobedience.

The scripture says beware your sins find you out. This intended fun trip that mother was not supposed to know about turned into a disaster. The mother received an urgent call of a near-drowning accident at the river involving several children, including one of hers.

God granted Cosmo's family favor, but his best friend paid the price, trying to save his sister. He suffered a brain injury from which he never recovered, and the guilt was almost more than Cosmo could bear.

The Bible admonishes us to honor our parents and respect their godly instructions. This was a very costly lesson for Cosmo. He learned skills beneficial to his friend's medical care, and devoted his life to helping him. Always at the forefront of his mind was his friend's selfless act to save his sister, and his disobedience that necessitated it. Christ admonishes us to listen to wise counsel, and live.

Words of Love: I spoke to you in your prosperity, but you said, 'I will not hear.' This has been your manner from your youth, that you did not obey My voice. Jeremiah 22:21

DAY 192

BROKEN

Scripture: For thus says the High and Lofty One who inhabits eternity, whose name is Holy: "I dwell in the high and holy place, with him who has a contrite and humble spirit, to revive the spirit of the humble, and to revive the heart of the contrite ones." Isaiah 57:15

The Women's Ministries Department of my local church sponsored a tea party and asked us to wear hats and gloves, and bring a favorite tea cup. I brought a beautiful tea cup, purchased in Amsterdam, with picturesque scenes of the Netherlands. As I exited my car at the church, I dropped the bag and shattered the cup. This treasured memento was now worthless, and fit only for the trash bin. My friend Mary took the bag of broken china home with her, and a year later she presented me with this delicately wrapped gift at a Christmas party I was hosting.

Imagine my surprise and delight to see my tea cup restored to a thing of beauty. She had painstakingly put all the pieces back together. At a cursory glance, it looked perfect, but she was quick to point out what the rest of us already knew: it would never again serve its original purpose for drinking tea. It now serves as a reminder of the love and sacrifice of a friend to put the broken pieces back together with such care. The biggest reminder and lesson from that experience, however, is that we are all broken vessels, and that nothing we can do will be sufficient to restore us to wholeness again.

There is One, however, who is skilled in restoring broken pieces. He relishes the challenge of restoring those whose lives are so shattered, it is hard to find the pieces. He says that those who have been forgiven much love Him more.

Come with your brokenness. Christ wants to make you whole again. Unlike the work of my beloved friend, when He finishes His work in you, you will be better than before. Lay your broken pieces at the foot of the cross. He is the only one capable of such restorative work.

Words of Love: He heals the brokenhearted and binds up their wounds. Psalm 147:3

DAY 193
ONE DAY CLOSER

Scripture: Who also said, "Men of Galilee, why do you stand gazing up into heaven? This same Jesus, who was taken up from you into heaven, will so come in like manner as you saw Him go into heaven." Acts 1:11

At devotion number fifty, I had self-doubts about the project I had undertaken. Friends and loved ones encouraged me, however, and now I see the proverbial glass being more than half full, and every devotion takes me one step closer to the goal.

Christ has not revealed to us the date or the time of His return, but today we are closer to His coming than we were yesterday. Skeptics say that since the beginning of time, it has been touted that Jesus is coming again. In their opinion, nothing has changed and life progresses as it always has. Is that the truth, though? What about the signs that the scripture tells us would be fulfilled before His return? The truth is that they have almost all been fulfilled.

What does it matter, however, if His return is tomorrow, next year, or the next thousand years? Christ told us that He was going to prepare a place for us in His Father's kingdom, and that He would come again and restore us to Himself, so we can live with Him throughout eternity. None of us will live to be a thousand years in this life, as it is. No one else before us has. But with Jesus' promise, we all have something to beyond this life to look forward to, if we accept the gift He offers us today. There is one thing which is certain: Christ's return is one day closer than it was yesterday.

Words of Love: Watch therefore, for you do not know what hour your Lord is coming. Matthew 24:42

DAY 194
IT'S NOT OVER YET

Scripture: The Lord your God in your midst, The Mighty One, will save; He will rejoice over you with gladness, He will quiet you with His love, He will rejoice over you with singing. Zephaniah 3:17

There seemed no end to the struggles. Two weeks had passed, and little Johnny was still in the hospital PICU. Some days there was a glimmer of hope, and on others everyone had more questions than answers. Then just when the family was the tempted to ask, "Why us, why our beautiful and active child?" our attention was drawn to another family who was losing their baby.

Sin and its devastating results on God's perfect creation are not over yet. Satan seeks every opportunity to cause us to doubt the goodness of the Almighty. The earth is marred, but there is still evidence of a loving and gracious God. We never learned the outcome of the other baby in the hospital with Johnny, but we kept praying for that child and all children around the world who, in their innocence, endure immeasurable pain and suffering.

True, the trials and hardships are not over yet, but deliverance is just around the corner. Just a little while, and Jesus will come. The night is still dark, but I can see the dawn breaking in the distance, and with it I have a resurgence of faith. "Hold on," is the encouragement to the faithful. The future is known to the One who created times: past, present, and future, and He is trustworthy

Words of Love: For I know the thoughts that I think toward you, says the Lord, thoughts of peace and not of evil, to give you a future and a hope. Jeremiah 29:11

DAY 195
VIGILANCE

Scripture: Watch therefore, for you do not know when the master of the house is coming. Mark 13:35

I have been very open about my passion for shopping: bargain shopping in particular. I cut coupons, search weekly advertisements, and price match at participating stores. In addition, I download apps that allow me to compare prices within a specified distance, and look for in-store promotions. It is not unusual to find items with marked-down prices in stores, but at the cash register, the item rings up at the original price. That happened in a store that I patronized only occasionally.

I only needed bananas on this particular day, but being the shopper that I am, I checked the beautiful displays to see if there was anything on sale that I wanted. I spotted some packages of multi-colored bell peppers on sale for under three dollars. I did not have any at home, and the price was reasonable, so I picked up a pack and proceeded to the cashier with my two items. I was surprised when the cashier said the total was almost six dollars for the three peppers and three bananas. I advised her of the display price which she checked, verified, and corrected, with an apology.

This was another moment of reflection for me. I wondered about our vigilance regarding issues of salvation, as well as human suffering. Do we watch the times and the signs as much as we watch the things of this world that hold our interest? Among other things, we are vigilant about our sports, our politics, and our entertainment. Also, what a difference it would make if we were as quick to spot the agony and immense suffering of those around us, rush to be the hands and feet of Jesus, and with the love and compassion of Christ, bind up the wounds of the broken. This kind of vigilance would send ripples of love around the world. People would not only hear the gospel, but they would see the gospel in action. Hearts would be drawn to the Savior, and Jesus would come. What a day of rejoicing that would be.

Words of Love: And what I say to you, I say to all: Watch! Mark 13:37

DAY 196
THE TRIP OF A LIFETIME

Scripture: For the Lord Himself will descend from heaven with a shout..., and with the trumpet of God. And the dead in Christ will rise first. Then we who are alive and remain shall be caught up together with them in the clouds to meet the Lord in the air. And thus we shall always be with the Lord. 1 Thessalonians 4:16-17

What great trip is on your bucket list? Is it a trip to the mountains or to the sea? Is it to see one of the seven great wonders of the world, the site of the former Twin Towers, the Grand Canyon, or the great Sequoias? One of my prayer partners anticipated her daughter's school trip to the United States East Coast. She was going along as a chaperone.

I imagined their excitement and anticipation to visit historical sites and tour the museums in New York, Virginia, Maryland and Washington, DC. A Broadway play was also in the plans for these teenagers and their chaperones. That trip might very well have been the trip of a lifetime for many of them.

Within a couple days of that school trip, another group was planning a European trip to include Berlin and Rome. This was also a historic trip: to walk, as it were, in the footsteps of Martin Luther, the Great Christian Reformer. I was to be a part of this tour, and more than a week before departure, I was packed and ready to go. My passport had been checked and rechecked; and the itinerary and e-ticket were printed.

I could not help but think about the trip the redeemed will make with our Lord and Savior, when He comes back at the second advent. What preparation have we been making? Is our "passport" ready? We won't have to pack a suitcase for this trip. Begin your preparation today. It will be here before you know it, and like the five wise virgins, we want to be ready to accompany the Bridegroom through those pearly gates.

Words of Love: And if I go and prepare a place for you, I will come again and receive you to Myself; that where I am, there you may be also. John 14:3

DAY 197
YOU'VE BEEN CHOSEN

Scripture: For many are called, but few are chosen. Matthew 22:14

The setting of this comment was the parable of the wedding feast prepared by a king for his son. He sent his servants to inform the invited guests that the preparation was complete, and they should come to the marriage supper. These invited guests, who knew the time because they had received an invitation, made excuses, and chose not to attend. In the context of modern society, they must have returned the RSVP, accepting the invitation with delight; but now that all the food was prepared, they were declining to attend.

What a waste of resources that might have been. I can imagine the king saying to himself, "There are many who would gladly enjoy the great spread I have prepared. Those who have made excuses about attending will be missing out on this festive occasion. My table will be full, and we will all have a good time." Before he could sit down to enjoy the occasion, however, he had some business he had to attend to. Those who made light of his invitation, and even harmed his servants, paid for their callous behavior with their lives. The party then went on as planned.

Jesus has prepared a banquet feast for His children. It is the marriage of the Lamb, and we are all invited. Have we cleared our calendars, and accepted the offer of the wedding garment; the white linen raiment of Christ's righteousness? Don't take the invitation for granted. Christ has His faithful children everywhere, and He will gather them together for the big day. I don't want to be simply among those who were called, who heard the word of God, and responded to the invitation, only to grow cold and walk away. I want to be among those who are awaiting the day with great anticipation. I like to dress up, and that white robe is going to look regal against the beautiful glow of my recreated body. What a day of rejoicing that will be.

Words of Love: For the Son of Man will come in the glory of His Father with His angels, and then He will reward each according to his works. Matthew 16:27

DAY 198
ONLY BELIEVE

Scripture: But when Jesus heard it, He answered him, saying, "Do not be afraid; only believe, and she will be made well." Luke 8:50

Jairus, ruler of the synagogue, came to Jesus and fell down at His feet, and besought Him to come to his house. You see, his only daughter, about twelve years old, whom he loved dearly, lay dying. His faith was strong, and he trusted that if Jesus came and prayed for her, she would be restored to health. Jesus agreed to Jairus' request, and proceeded toward his home, but the needs of the community were great, and the crowd was thick, as people sought healing. Jesus was therefore delayed. Then the sad news reached Jairus, "Your daughter is dead, trouble not the Master."

Imagine how distraught Jairus must have been, at the news that his beloved daughter had died. I can only imagine the thoughts that possibly crossed his mind: "If only Jesus had gotten there in time. If only He had not been delayed, my daughter would still be alive." Luke 8:50 is a verse that speaks of the confidence of our beloved Savior, and the encouragement He gives us, to trust Him. The passage says that when Jesus heard it, He spoke the words in the passage above to the bewildered father. He then went to the home, where He laid hands on the little girl and restored her to life.

What seemingly impossible challenges are you facing today? God offers you the same assurance He gave to Jairus: "If you will only believe, I will make this situation right for you. If you only believe, the answer you have been waiting for, and hoping for, is on its way." In anticipation of a victorious outcome, go ahead and thank the Father for His gracious resolution; for making a way out of no way; for granting victory in the face of defeat.

Prayer: Father, You are magnificent and gracious, the Great Healer and Restorer. I thank You for what You have already done in my life, and for what You are doing in this particular situation; and now I patiently wait to see the manifestation of Your great power. I believe in You, Father, and I honor You with faithful trust. In Jesus' precious Name... Amen.

Words of Love: But He said, "Do not weep; she is not dead, but sleeping... Little girl, arise." Luke 8:52, 54

DAY 199
TAKING THE PLEDGE

Scripture: If a man makes a vow to the Lord, or swears an oath to bind himself by some agreement, he shall not break his word; he shall do according to all that proceeds out of his mouth. Numbers 30:2

People take all kind of pledges, though they may be called by many different names; i.e., Pledge of Allegiance; Chastity Pledge; and marriage vows. Many pledges are mere formalities, and may be broken within moments of being made. You may have heard the term, "It is not written in blood or on stone." How poignant that Christ's pledge to us was written with His blood, and the response He expects from us was written on two tablets of stone.

As much as I love my country, and pledge allegiance to upholding the tenets of its foundation, my first allegiance is pledged to the One who sacrificed His blood for me. I am taking the pledge to give Him first place in my life. In so doing, I will honor all of His precepts, wrapped up in two big bundles: to love Him with all of my heart; and to love my neighbor as myself.

When I love God, I will be obedient to all that He commands. I will not shortchange Him with any of the gifts and talents that He has given me, but will use them for His glory, and for blessing others. I will not try to usurp His position of being number one, but will always be delighted to decrease as John said, so that He can increase. I will pledge to yield first place to Him, and to let Him lead in all the affairs of my life. This is a pledge I will take without hesitation. How about you? Take the pledge... it's worth it.

Words of Love: You shall not pervert justice due the stranger or the fatherless, nor take a widow's garment as a pledge. Deuteronomy 24:17

DAY 200
PACK YOUR BAGS

Scripture: Being confident of this very thing, that He who has begun a good work in you will complete it until the day of Jesus Christ. Philippians 1:6

The conference announcement read: "Pack your bags," and was accompanied by the following checklist of things to include:
- Comfortable business casual clothing
- Denim and pearls for the moonlight market
- Cash to shop local farmers
- Walking shoes
- Exercise outfit
- Business cards for networking

I received similar guidance as we got closer to the time for our European group tour. These helpful instructions caused me to contemplate on how I am packing for the trip to my eternal home. I thought it would be fun to see what the Internet had to offer, so I googled "packing for heaven," and found a link to "Packing Grandma's China: A Journey to Heaven." I did not register to get the book online, so I have not determined its content. However, I do believe that all my earthly possessions will be left behind, and everything I will need will be provided for me there. Then, why do I need to pack a bag, and what would I put in it?

I believe the fruit of the Spirit may be all I need for that heavenly trip. A humble and repentant heart: one that seeks forgiveness for all known and unknown sins; one that acknowledges Jesus Christ as Lord and Savior; and one which seeks to do good for His children, and build up His kingdom. I know He longs for my companionship, and I cannot wait for Him to show me the sights of heaven. I don't want anything to encumber me. What are you packing for your journey? Check to see what will travel well, and plan to travel light.

Words of Love: And we know that all things work together for good to those who love God, to those who are the called according to His purpose. Romans 8:28

DAY 201
FOR EVERY "YES" A "NO" IS REQUIRED SOMEWHERE

Scripture: For the grace of God that brings salvation has appeared to all men, teaching us that, denying ungodliness and worldly lusts, we should live soberly, righteously, and godly in the present age. Titus 2:11-12

What are some of the things for which you want a "yes" answer in life? What happens when you don't get the answer you seek? Are you mad at the world, yourself or God? What strategies have you applied to obtain the desired outcome? Take a look at some practical applications:
- You want to buy a home, but although your income is good, you cannot save enough for the deposit. Have you considered saying no to dining out five to six days per week, and taking a mini vacation every three months?
- You want to lose weight but your weekly weigh-ins are not showing any progress. Have you considered eliminating some comfort foods; reducing the portion sizes of others; and making others only "sometime foods" rather than "everyday staples"?

Discipline is the name of the game. We want success in life, but we want it on our terms and it must not cost us anything. "I don't want to have to make any changes or modify my lifestyle," we say. "I want to be bright-eyed and alert for that 'make or break' business meeting, but I want to stay up late the night before, and have a good time with my friends." We must invest in, give up, or say "no" to some things, if we want to achieve a "yes" answer to others.

The same is true for our spiritual lives. If we want a closer walk with God, we must say no to running with the devil. Remember, we cannot serve two masters; we cannot say yes to both God and Satan at the same time, and when we say yes to Satan, we are inevitably saying no to God.

Let us be strong and courageous. Let us say a firm no to the devil, and experience the victories that Christ will begin to orchestrate on our behalf.

Words of Love: knowing that the testing of your faith produces patience. But let patience have its perfect work, that you may be perfect and complete, lacking nothing... James 1:3-5

DAY 202
PARALYZED BY FEAR

Scripture: I sought the Lord, and He heard me, and delivered me from all my fears. Psalm 34:4

It happened on a Thursday night in March. My church began a series of meetings that evening, and because the weather was bad a friend offered to pick me up for the opening session.

My friend, who lives in the opposite direction of the meeting site, and has a busy schedule, had a couple over for dinner before the meeting. Time did not permit her to clean up her kitchen after dinner, and she planned to spend the night at my house, to give us a jump start on a six-hour road trip we had planned for the next day. I accompanied her home to clean up her kitchen, and get back to my house before it got too late.

My friend has a large pit bull, which she feeds inside the house. She gave me fair warning that she was bringing the dog in for a few minutes. I went into panic mode, and barricaded myself in the farthest corner of the dining room, with a high-back chair placed before me for security.

Christ says He does not give us a spirit of fear, but of a sound mind. Yes, it is true that God wants us to use good judgment to live life to the fullest, but He also wants us to trust Him and not be paralyzed by fears, many of which are irrational. If fear is hampering your progress, personal, professional, social or spiritual, it is time you release it to the Father. He longs to give you victory, so you can reach your optimum potential in His service.

Words of Love: Fear not, for I have redeemed you; I have called you by your name; You are Mine. Isaiah 43:1

DAY 203
THE ANOINTING

Scripture: The Spirit of the Lord is upon Me, because He has anointed Me to preach the gospel to the poor... Luke 4:18

One Sunday morning, I was privileged to be part of something very special. A group of prayer warriors from our weekly prayer call were delegates to our church's constituency meeting. They gathered in the room where the nominating committee was to conduct business, to pray for each participant. Several of us who were not in attendance at the meeting joined the group by conference line.

The room and all its furnishings were anointed and prayed over: that the Spirit of Christ would symbolically rain down, and reign in the heart of each person sitting in those chairs, and writing at those tables. We prayed for them to have the mind of Christ, and promote His agenda instead of their own. We prayed that business would be conducted with love and humility, decency and order. We prayed that at the conclusion of the sessions, delegates would know that Christ was present in all the affairs, and that each nominee, elected or not, would leave with their dignity intact, conscious that the Father was in control.

I felt the anointing of the Holy Spirit on me during that season of prayer, and I asked Jesus to re-consecrate me for His work. I also prayed that each person who reads this devotion will feel the same anointing of the Holy Spirit on your life, and that you will go forth as a mighty warrior for Christ, and draw others to Him.

Words of Love: Now He who establishes us with you in Christ and has anointed us is God, who also has sealed us and given us the Spirit in our hearts as a guarantee. 2 Corinthians 1:21-22

DAY 204
DEFEATED

Scripture: Be sober, be vigilant; because your adversary the devil walks about like a roaring lion, seeking whom he may devour. 1 Peter 5:8

The constituency meeting was called to order as the delegation took its seat. A prayer was said and the rules were read. Now it was time for the business of the day, and there were many items. The agenda was opened and the process began. Some delegates were veterans at the process; others were new, unsure of themselves and the proceedings, and looking to the more seasoned members for guidance.

Many prayers had been lifted up over the weeks and months leading up to the meeting, and while some were at ease, others did not quite know what to expect. The college gymnasium and adjoining rooms had been anointed and prayed over, and the watchful eyes of prayer warriors scanned the gathering to offer silent prayers for anyone who appeared uncomfortable. That was not the case, however, because the presence of the Holy Spirit, as prayed for earlier, had taken full control.

Business was conducted in a spirit of love and kindness, with respect and empathy for those nominees who were not elected. Those nominees, in turn, conceded graciously to the winners, and offered support for the leadership moving forward. The devil expected hand-to-hand combat, but God defeated him with heart-to-heart contact. All praise and glory to the King of kings, and Lord of lords. Victory was won for His kingdom and the devil was a defeated foe.

Words of Love: Therefore, submit to God. Resist the devil and he will flee from you. James 4:7

DAY 205
GRAFTED INTO THE VINE

Scripture: And if some of the branches were broken off, and you, being a wild olive tree, were grafted in among them, and with them became a partaker of the root and fatness of the olive tree, do not boast against the branches. But if you do boast, remember that you do not support the root, but the root supports you. Romans 11:17-18

It was late at night and I needed to have been asleep. Many thoughts were flooding my mind, however, so I tried to write some more. That was not the therapy for the hour, though. My spirit was needing to be "poured into." I turned on the television to one of my favorite Christian channels, and the subject was about the Life and Ministry of Christ.

One of the discussion points used the imagery of a grafted fruit tree. The speaker referenced an apple tree with four or five varieties grafted as branches to the main trunk. They all feed from the same source of nutrients, he pointed out; but when they develop and produce fruit, each grafted branch bears fruit unique to the variety grafted.

What a picture of how God works in believers' lives. By His great love, we are grafted into Him. He nourishes us from His wellspring of living water, and His Son, Jesus Christ, provides the rays of spiritual sunshine necessary for photosynthesis to take place. If we stay connected to Him, we will be nourished to full maturity and fruition.

Christ wants us to retain our God-given individuality and uniqueness. Each of us is given divine attributes for a particular purpose and work. Each variety of fruit appeals to different taste buds: some like juicy and sweet, others like crisp and tart, while others have a preference for a combination of both. When we function according to our unique qualities, we are happier and find our walk with Christ more fulfilling. His one request is that we stay connected to the Vine.

Words of Love: Yes, I have loved you with an everlasting love; Therefore, with lovingkindness I have drawn you. Jeremiah 31:3

DAY 206
THINGS TO DO, PLACES TO GO, AND PEOPLE TO SEE

Scripture: There are many plans in a man's heart, nevertheless the Lord's counsel—that will stand. Proverbs 19:21

"What is on your agenda today?" my sister asked, two days before my European trip. My suitcase was packed, but there were a few last-minute things to do, like going to the hairdresser and getting some inflatable neck pillows. I was getting dressed as we talked on the phone, and I was eager to get moving, so I said to her, "Sis, I've got to hang up as I have things to do, places to go, and people to see." We both chuckled at that comment, but it left me with some questions.

When we make our plans, do we consult with Christ first? Do we involve Him every step of the way, or do we finalize them, and then expect Him to give us His stamp of approval? Sometimes we think things are too simple or mundane to talk to the Father about, but God wants to be intimately involved in every aspect of our lives. Let us commit our ways and all our plans to Him. We will then be led to the right places; our eyes will see suffering humanity, and determine where we can lend a hand, and we will meet people whom we can bless or who can be a blessing to us. So, first on our knees, with hearts lifted heavenward, and then about the Master's business. Let's commit to making His agenda ours, and His will our own.

Words of Love: Listen to counsel and receive instruction, that you may be wise in your latter days... Proverbs 19:20

DAY 207
LURED INTO SIN

Scripture: You will be accepted if you do what is right. But if you refuse, then watch out. Sin is crouching at the door, eager to control you. But you must subdue it and be its master. Genesis 4:7

Jonathan was a talented young musician, who was gifted in playing several instruments. He also wrote beautiful lyrics, and had the voice of an angel. He was handsome and charming, and served his church in many capacities with his musical abilities. There was an older group of influential members, however, who refused to embrace anything modern or contemporary. They constantly complained, and threatened to withhold their financial support, if their wishes were not heeded.

In the meantime, several popular and successful music groups enticed Jonathan with the lure of lucrative contracts, and the promise of an amazing career. The temptation was very strong, especially because of the lack of appreciation and constant complaining from "Christians" who should have been uplifting and encouraging.

Jonathan auditioned with one group that he thought might be a good fit. Praise God, because of much prayer, his first tour convinced him that he was in the wrong place. The struggle was intense, though, and Jonathan sank into depression. God used this time to woo His searching child, and He won Johnathan's heart.

Another career path opened up and Jonathan pursued it. Today he uses both his professional skill and his musical abilities to the Father's glory. He credits the love of God, and a caring and supportive family, for drawing him back from the pits of darkness. Are you an encourager of young talents in your church, or are you so stuck on your brand of worship that you discourage their walk with Christ?

Words of Love: But beware lest somehow this liberty of yours become a stumbling block to those who are weak. 1 Corinthians 8:9

DAY 208
THE WAY

Scripture: Jesus said to him, "I am the way, the truth, and the life. No one comes to the Father except through Me." John 14:6

It was in the days before GPS, and I was traveling with directions from one of those roadside assistance companies. The trip had gone very well until I hit some detours and became disoriented. I was making the twelve-hour trip alone, and planned to overnight with friends at the eight-hour mark. It was late afternoon, and I had not been to this city before. I was hesitant to ask just anyone for help, so I stopped and called my friend. I gave her my location, and she got me back on track. I made it to her home just before nightfall.

I believe that we are in the twilight of this earth's existence. Jesus is not far from coming back for those who are fervently watching and waiting for Him. The adversary has roadblocks and detours all along the way. His goal is to throw us off course, and make us disoriented so that we lose our way. The navigation devices have been scrambled and it is becoming harder to navigate the journey.

Hope is not lost, however. Jesus is on the main line. He is eager to provide us with directions for a safe passage home. This phone line is still open and working just fine. No efforts of our foe can scramble or disconnect it. What a privilege to have our calls go directly to the Creator of the universe.

When I am in distress, I pour out my heart to Jesus about getting off course and losing my sense of direction. I panic when I am disoriented, but Christ assures me of His longing to guide me safely home. GPS may take us off course, but with Jesus, we never have to be lost eternally.

Words of Love: For thus says the High and Lofty One who inhabits eternity, whose name is Holy: "I dwell in the high and holy place, with him who has a contrite and humble spirit..." Isaiah 57:15

DAY 209
LOVE ME BACK

Scripture: Indeed, He would have brought you out of dire distress, into a broad place where there is no restraint; And what is set on your table would be full of richness. Job 36:16

What a sad picture of one person giving all the love that is in his or her heart to give, and desperate for that love to be reciprocated. With tears of sadness they plead, "Love me back, that is all I ask." The picture breaks your heart to watch the other person walk away, without as much as a backward glance.

Now take another look. That person begging to be loved in return is the Creator of the universe. He is saying to us, "I have loved you with an everlasting love; with loving kindness have I drawn you." So why are we walking away from such everlasting love? Christ is eagerly waiting to enter our hearts. He has so much love to give, He wants to shower you and me with all the goodness of His unlimited resources. What is it that your heart desires? If it is good for you, and the timing is in your best interest, He will not withhold it from you. He even bestows His goodness on us when we turn our backs on Him. But the ultimate jewel that He is eager to give us can only be obtained when we love Him back. This priceless gift is eternal life with Him. What an offer, and yet so many of us simply walk away from it.

This invitation is a very personal one. It is offered to, and must be accepted by, each of us individually. Will you turn and walk away or will you run into His outstretched arms? The decision to love Christ back is one that none of us will ever regret. We have nothing to lose, but everything to gain by reciprocating to a love like no other. Today, I am shouting out to Him: yes, Lord, if You will still have me, filthy and spent, I do love You back. I see the tears of joy in His eyes, and see the warm look of acceptance. There is no greater feeling than to love and be loved in return.

Words of Love: Jesus said to him, "'You shall love the Lord your God with all your heart, with all your soul, and with all your mind." Matthew 22:37

DAY 210
EACH LIFE HAS MEANING

Scripture: **T**herefore, if anyone is in Christ, he is a new creation; old things have passed away; behold, all things have become new. 2 Corinthians 5:17

*N*o life is worthless. We were all born with a purpose. It is our responsibility to determine what that purpose is, and pursue it.

During my long transatlantic flight from Rome to Atlanta, I decided to watch a movie. The story was about an elderly woman with an amazing gift, but she had an illness that made her an outcast in many societies. Her gift helped a struggling young man improve his business, until word got out about her disease.

This woman, who was childless, took a special interest in this young man, and a young girl she had met in his business. Not only did she teach them the skill she possessed, but at her death, she left them the tools that had helped her hone her skills over the decades.

I was reminded of the lepers who discovered that an entire community, rich with resources, including food, had been abandoned by an army. Instead of selfishly enjoying the spoils by themselves, they risked their lives, and broke strict protocol so that they could share the good news with those inside the city. It also reminded me of Rahab, who, although a harlot, risked her safety to help the Israelite spies.

What is your purpose? For what were you created that no one else can accomplish? Have you been challenged by some unfortunate circumstance in life, and now feel that there is no meaning to your existence? Do you need a Rahab, a Ruth, an Esther, or a little boy with five loaves and two fish to remind you that there is a purpose for your life as well?

We cannot all be Michelangelo, who painted the ceiling of the Sistine Chapel. Although others who helped are nameless, they certainly facilitated the process of him accomplishing such great work. Sometimes the people who plant the seed of faith are not known or acknowledged, only those who bring the fruits to harvest. However, in heaven everyone who fulfilled the purpose intended for them will be rewarded. So, shake off those feelings of despair, begin with something in your comfort zone, and ask God to expand your horizons.

Words of Love: For we are His workmanship, created in Christ Jesus for good works, which God prepared beforehand that we should walk in them. Ephesians 2:10

DAY 211
THE APPIAN WAY

Scripture: Now it happened as they journeyed on the road, that someone said to Him, "Lord, I will follow You wherever You go." Luke 9:57

The part of the Appian Way in Rome, once traveled by the Apostle Paul, is a beautiful cobblestone path. As I walked a short distance of the road, I pictured the apostle walking alone or with his traveling companions along this dusty road, and finally arriving at their purposed destination.

Once a fierce objector of Christ and those who followed Him, Paul was now as fierce and determined to proclaim Him, and to suffer and die for Him. I can imagine this once hardened face, bent on destroying the Savior's Name and those who were called by the name Christians, now softened and tender from the heart transformation he experienced on the Damascus Road. I can only imagine how tired his body must have been from the long journey of sailing and walking, but how energized his spirit must have been to proclaim the truth of the Risen Savior.

The song, "I Want Jesus to Walk with Me," came to mind as I wrote this devotion, and I pictured Paul telling Jesus that now that He had changed his heart, and given him a new focus, He would have to walk with him. The people who knew him as Saul would recoil from him, unless Jesus opened their hearts to his changed life, and the message of salvation that he now brought.

What about us? Are we willing to walk the "Appian Way" to spread the good news of Jesus, and can people see the change in us? Are our faces now softened by the glow of God's love, and are our words kind and gentle, yet firm and true? Have we made this long walk only for show, or are we willing to pay the price of fellowship with the King of kings, and Lord of lords? It could be a very costly decision. But then, Jesus paid the ultimate price. The scripture says to count it all joy when we fall into diverse places for our faith in the Gentle Lamb who is also the Lion of Judah. He will eventually break every chain, and give us the victory in His name.

Words of Love: And whoever does not bear his cross and come after Me cannot be My disciple... Luke 14:27-33

DAY 212
LET HOPE, NOT HURT...

Scripture: As the deer pants for the water brooks, so pants my soul for You, O God. Psalm 42:11

"My hope is built on nothing less than Jesus' blood and righteousness. I dare not trust the sweetest frame, but wholly lean on Jesus' name," are words from the most famous of Edward Mote's song, My Hope is Built on Nothing Less, written in 1834. What is the foundation of your hope? How is hope defining your tomorrow?

I saw an interesting quote on a church marquee which read, "Let hope, not hurt ..." The traffic was moving at a fairly fast pace, and I had missed the concluding line of the quote, so I decided to add my own conclusion. The following are some of the thoughts that came to my mind:
- Let hope, not hurt determine your destiny
- Let hope, not hurt propel your success
- Let hope, not hurt determine how you treat others
- Let hope, not hurt define and strengthen your walk with Christ
- Let hope, not hurt foster a spirit of forgiveness in you

Christ wants to take your hurts and replace them with hope in Him. He knows that life is not a bed of roses; He is the Creator of the universe, and it wasn't smooth sailing for Him when He walked this earth, So, He counsels, "stop dwelling on your past, and the injustices that you perceive were done to you. Let hope for what I have in store for your future replace any hurt you might have endured. Trust in My all-wise providence. There was a divine purpose in the process, even though you could not see or understand My plan."

Time does heal hurts, and by trusting the wisdom of a loving Father, you finally exchange the hurt for the great hope. When you do, the fog lifts and the way ahead becomes clear. Although the experience is not one you relish, in the big scheme of God's plan you realize that you would not change much, if anything at all. You can then conclude, "It will be worth it all, when I see Jesus." Life's trials will be very small, for the relationship you develop with Him.

Words of Love: My brethren, count it all joy when you fall into various trials. James 1:2

DAY 213
BRING ME YOUR BROKENNESS

Scripture: Come to Me, all you who labor and are heavy laden, and I will give you rest... Matthew 11:28-29

In Rome, Italy, I had the privilege to walk the "Holy Stairs" and to witness others climbing them on their knees. This, I imagined, was symbolic of their contrite heart and repentant spirit. The imagery stayed in my mind and in my heart, and then the words of the popular song, "If You're Honest," began playing in my head. At 3:30 a.m. I had to put these words on paper.

My Precious Savior is standing, not necessarily at the top of the "Holy Stairs," but certainly at the foot of the cross. He is saying to you and me, "I died on this cross for your sins. You do not have to do penance any more, however well-intentioned and genuine you may be. All I require is that you come with your brokenness, and give Me your heart."

That is easy enough. My Loving Lord has already done the hard work for me. It is work that I could not do for myself, because His salvation cannot be earned; it is a gift, but what a price He paid. If you and I value the immense sacrifice He made to provide us with this gift, we would run to the cross, and lay all our burdens before Him. He is eager to lighten our load, and restore our broken spirits.

The song lyrics say to bring our brokenness, because mercy is waiting on the other side. Let's be honest: we desperately need God's mercy, and He is so gracious that He cannot wait to bestow it on us. Take a mental picture of those pilgrims climbing the Holy Stairs, in search of a heart transformation, and then listen to the invitation of the Savior. He says it does not require a long pilgrimage, just a lonely heart that longs for the companionship of the Creator. You may give Him your heart from the privacy of your home, your hospital bed or your prison cell. You may be driving your car, working at your trade or sitting in your recliner. Wherever the Spirit pricks at your heartstrings, yield. You will find that to be made whole, you must first come to the Restorer, broken.

Words of Love: Fear not, for I am with you; Be not dismayed, for I am your God. I will strengthen you, yes, I will help you, I will uphold you with My righteous right hand. Isaiah 41:10

DAY 214
FOR THE PLEASURE OF YOUR COMPANY

Scripture: The steps of a *good* man are ordered by the Lord, and He delights in his way. Psalm 37:23

You have heard the saying, "I am a born romantic," and have probably used it yourself. Well, I can remember a gentleman, in my young adult years saying, "For the pure pleasure of your company, my dear." I believed he must have just read the line somewhere, and was trying to impress me, rather than having a genuine love interest. God, on the other hand, longs for the pleasure of our company out of genuine love. He sought Adam and Eve daily in the Garden of Eden, to spend time with them, for nothing more than the pure pleasure of their company. As a matter of fact, He created mankind for the sole purpose of an intimate relationship with Him.

Do you view God's effort as desperation for love, or do you see it as an effort on the part of the One True God, who has so much love to give, that He would create people on whom to shower this love? If someone you know desires to take you on a world tour for the simple pleasure of your company, you might be inclined to say yes, if you determine them reputable and genuine.

Jesus Christ has a stellar reputation: He is the Creator of the universe; He is King of kings and Lord of lords; He is the Friend of all friends. His words are true, and never change; His promises are sure and they stand forever. He says He has gone to prepare a place for you and He is coming back for you. He is going to take you across galaxies to live with Him for a thousand years, and then He is going to restore you to a recreated "Eden," where He can spend time with you forever, for the pure pleasure of your company. Wow, an invitation like that should not be refused.

Words of Love: For the Lord takes pleasure in His people; He will beautify the humble with salvation. Psalm 149:4

DAY 215
WHO'S WATCHING YOU?

Scripture: The eyes of the Lord are on the righteous, and His ears are open to their cry. Psalm 34:15

There is a story of a builder, whose friend gave him the contract to build a house. He was asked to spare no expense, and if he needed more money, it would be made available, with proper receipts. The builder used cheap materials to construct the house, and was able to pocket a sizable amount of money from the savings. He was known for his deception and poor building practices, but his friend had to prove it for himself.

The builder provided his friend, who was now his client, with frequent reports; but questioned why he never came by to check on the progress. His friend responded that he trusted him to do a good job. This should have touched the conscience of the builder, to improve on the work he was doing, but he was "rotten to the core," and nothing moved him to change his evil ways.

Upon completion of the house, which was beautiful on the outside, he called the client to do a walk through, and to hand over the keys. Imagine his surprise and utter dismay, when his friend said to him, "The house is yours, under one condition, you must live in it." He went on to say, "My family and I have decided to stay in the house we currently occupy." The contractor was dumfounded, not because of the generosity of his friend, but because he had just built his shoddiest dream house.

God is watching you, even when no one else is. What if the poor-quality job you have turned out, under the disguise of a beautiful exterior, is your ticket to success or failure; a promotion or dismissal; heaven or hell? What would be your fate? A wise recommendation would be, "Do right, because it is the right thing to do."

Words of Love: Learn to do good; Seek justice, rebuke the oppressor; Defend the fatherless, plead for the widow. Isaiah 1:17

DAY 216
HIDDEN TREASURE

Scripture: I will give you the treasures of darkness and hidden riches of secret places, that you may know that I, the Lord, who call you by your name, Am the God of Israel. Isaiah 45:3

I have heard many stories of people making a profit of hundreds, thousands, and occasionally even millions of dollars on articles they purchased at some junk yard or garage sale. You have heard the saying, "One man's trash is another man's treasure." One example of this was a news report I heard of a jacket that was once worn by a famous sports figure, and purchased for seventy-five cents at a Salvation Army store. It turned out to be worth thousands of dollars. Imagine the elation of the person who now owned this treasure.

The scripture tells us of a man who discovered some great treasure on a piece of land. He knew he could not claim "finders' keepers" on someone else's property, so he sold his possessions and invested all his resources in this property. Only then could he rightfully claim the treasure as his own.

There are many hidden treasures waiting to be discovered in the Word of God. There are people in countries where access to a Bible is restricted. Owning and reading one publicly could mean death. Yet there are many people who have risked it all to have access to this treasure. What sacrifices are we making for this great treasure chest? Is it sitting in plain view on our coffee tables, holding a place of prominence in our homes, but not being opened and read to enrich our lives? If we are not "drinking from the rich fountain of truths" in the Holy Bible, it might as well be "trash" to us.

Let us commit to digging deep in the scripture for the buried treasures placed therein. There are nuggets of truth on every page, and rich gems just waiting to be mined by searching hearts. The "gold rush" is on, and there is enough for every seeker, so let us not waste another minute. Start digging.

Words of Love: You search the Scriptures, for in them you think you have eternal life; and these are they which testify of Me. John 5:39

DAY 217
REPURPOSING ME

Scripture: Yet indeed I also count all things loss for the excellence of the knowledge of Christ Jesus my Lord, for whom I have suffered the loss of all things, and count them as rubbish, that I may gain Christ. Philippians 3:8

I believe one of the buzz words of the twenty-first century is "repurpose." There was not a dictionary definition for the word repurpose, but from the meaning of the word purpose, it is apparent that to repurpose is to resolve to do something other than the original purpose for which it was intended. To make, or do something new or different.

I thought about all the discarded materials one sees laying around almost everywhere you turn, and how many of them are being transformed into new and useful things. I prayed a prayer right then: "Father God, please repurpose my life into something new and useful for Your service. I have no idea what that would look like; but I trust You, the Great Restorer, to fashion me into something meaningful."

I read a story of a privileged young man who, with his friends, wreaked havoc in the community in which they lived. One night an encounter with a past acquaintance turned his life around and gave him a new sense of purpose. He amended his ways and became a valuable contributor to the community he once menaced.

How is it in your life? Do you feel like you have maximized your potential or served a useful purpose? Could your natural gifts and abilities be used to fulfill a new mission? Do you have resources at your disposal that could be used to satisfy a need? Do you have idle time to give to a worthy cause?

I have a retired neighbor who takes the sick and elderly residents of her "fifty-five and older community" to their doctors' appointments. She feels useful and they are tremendously blessed by the generous gift of her time. There is work for every child of God to do. None need feel useless. Commit your ways to Him, and He will direct your path.

Words of Love: For even the Son of Man did not come to be served, but to serve, and to give His life a ransom for many. Mark 10:45

DAY 218
HIS EYES ARE ON YOU

Scripture: The eyes of the Lord are in every place, keeping watch on the evil and the good. Proverbs 15:3

In one of the galleries leading to the Sistine Chapel in Rome, there is a very special painting of Christ on the cross. As you walk toward the picture, Christ appears to be making direct eye contact with you, and when you pass the painting and look back, His gaze appears to be still fixed on you, and your eyes seem locked with His eyes.

There is a song that says His eyes are on the sparrow, and I know He watches me. Christ's gaze is not intrusive, as though He is waiting to catch us in some wrongdoing, and it is not one to be afraid of. No, it is a tender longing gaze; one which seems to say, "Don't pass me by. I did this all for you, because I want to spend time with you."

There are some beautiful words in the song, "I Hear the Savior Say." He says He knows our strength indeed is small, so we should watch and pray, and find in Him our all in all. Jesus knows the battles we fight, and the struggles being waged inside of us. His longing gaze attracts us, and draws us to Him, but the world also calls out to us in loud and angry tones, saying, "Don't pause, you don't have time for this. There is too much to see and do." Sadly, we often listen to the noise of the world, instead of the gentle whisper of the Savior. Look back... His eyes are still beckoning you.

Words of Love: For He looks to the ends of the earth, and sees under the whole heavens. Job 28:24

DAY 219

COMFORTED TO BE OF COMFORT

Scripture: Blessed be the God and Father of our Lord Jesus Christ, the Father of mercies and God of all comfort, who comforts us in all our tribulation, that we may be able to comfort those who are in any trouble, with the comfort with which we ourselves are comforted by God. 2 Corinthians 1:3-4

I went through a very difficult time in my life, and sometimes asked God, "Why?" He did not answer me, except to say, "Just trust Me." He assured me that He knew what He was doing. Intellectually, I knew there was a purpose for the trials, but emotionally, it took everything I could muster, to make it from one day to the next. I purposed in my heart that I would come through the trials with my dignity intact, even though Satan, working through his agents, were bent on breaking me.

Through the dark days of those trials, God provided comfort through Christians who were strategically placed in my life. He provided glimpses of Himself in nature that lifted my spirit. He also provided places of refuge where my soul could hide, and my spirit revived, and then He came through the person of the Holy Spirit, and cradled me in His loving arms.

Gradually, God revealed the purpose of my agony. He said in His word that as we are strengthened and comforted, we should comfort and strengthen others. In less than a year after my time of great pain, a friend began to go through a similar situation. It is one thing to sympathize with someone, and it can sometimes even seem patronizing; but it is quite another story when your life experiences line up with the struggles of others.

God allows us to go through experiences, from which He either rescues us later, or comforts us in them, so that we can, in turn, use those experiences to be a blessing to someone else. So, let us stop being self-centered and self-pitying. Let us see the bigger purpose in all of our encounters and experiences. We have gone through our fire. Now let us be of comfort to someone else as they go through theirs.

Words of Love: A new commandment I give to you, that you love one another; as I have loved you, that you also love one another. John 13:34

DAY 220
IT IS ALL MINE

Scripture: So, let each one give as he purposes in his heart, not grudgingly or of necessity; for God loves a cheerful giver. 2 Corinthians 9:7

A humorous, yet poignant story is told of a twenty-dollar bill and a one-dollar bill that were being retired from circulation. As the bills lay side by side, they engaged in a conversation. The one-dollar bill asked the twenty-dollar bill if it had travelled much, and what were some of the places it had visited.

The twenty-dollar bill was glad to have been asked, and was delighted to share its exciting travel escapades. "Oh, I have been to Las Vegas, Nevada and Atlantic City, New Jersey. I have been to many restaurants and places of amusement. I have also gone into many stores and other places of business."

Then the twenty-dollar bill turned to the one-dollar bill and asked, "How about you? Tell me some of the places to which your travels have taken you." The one-dollar bill smiled and answered, "I have been mainly to churches: the Baptist Church, the Methodist Church, the Episcopalian Church, the Seventh-day Adventist Church, and the Catholic Church, among others." The twenty-dollar bill turned to the one dollar bill, with a serious and searching look, and asked, "What is a church? I have never been in one."

All that we have are gifts from God, and He expects us to return to Him with the same generosity that He has given to us. He does not ask us for twenty dollars when He only blesses us with enough to return one dollar; but let us not give Him only a dollar when He has blessed us abundantly with more than we could ask for. Remember that we can never out-give God.

Words of Love: Give, and it will be given to you: good measure, pressed down, shaken together, and running over will be put into your bosom. Luke 6:38

DAY 221
OUR SOVEREIGN GOD

Scripture: The secret things belong to the Lord our God, but those things which are revealed belong to us and to our children forever, that we may do all the words of this law. Deuteronomy 29:29

Sometimes we are of the very haughty opinion that God should let us in on everything that He does, and we become "righteously indignant" when He does not. So, who do we think we are, anyway? It is true that He says He calls us friends, because He has shared things with us that one does not usually share with a servant. Let us be grateful for what He shares with us. It is enough to draw us into a close relationship with our Creator and Savior.

Our questions of the God of the universe should be ones for instructions on how He wants us to live, and move, and have our beings, and how He wants us to serve Him and others.

The next time you consider challenging God over the way He operates, just remember who He is, and who you are. I am reminded of a child who asks a parent why, and receives the answer, "Because I said so." It is often followed by words such as, "And by the way, I am the parent, and I don't owe you an explanation." Whether you agree with this response or not, it is simply saying, "stop questioning my authority." If a parent deserves and sometimes demands this level of respect, imagine the deference and reverence we owe to our Sovereign God. He is our Savior and Lord, Redeemer and Friend, but not our equal.

Words of Love: Therefore, know this day, and consider it in your heart, that the Lord Himself is God in heaven above and on the earth beneath; there is no other. Deuteronomy 4:39

DAY 222

HE'S ABLE

Scripture: Therefore, He is also able to save to the uttermost those who come to God through Him, since He always lives to make intercession for them. Hebrews 7:25

Have you ever hoped for some miracle, and wondered why Jesus was not providing the answers you were not just hoping for, but desperately longing for? Have you questioned God as to why He answered a similar request for someone else with a profound "yes," but was denying your request? What kind of battle waged inside of you, as you pondered this apparent unfairness?

God's "no" is not an inability on His part to perform miracles, nor is it a lack of care for your sorrow. Being God, He does not always explain His ways, or give us reasons for what He does. Just know that He is able, and that He has our best interest at heart. The Son has a wise purpose for every circumstance under the sun. Job did not see that at the beginning of his trials, and he wondered what he had done to deserve the troubles he was undergoing. God had to stop him in his track with the counter question. "Where were you when I created the heavens, and did all the other things that I, as God did?"

What God was, in essence, saying to Job is, "It is not your place to question Me. You simply need to trust Me." That same God, who is able to do all things, restored to Job more blessings than he had before. He is also the same God who operates in our lives today, and He is just as able now as He was in the days of old, to do great and awesome things in our lives of us, as we learn to trust and depend on Him.

Words of Love: Be strong and of good courage, do not fear nor be afraid of them; for the Lord your God, He is the One who goes with you. He will not leave you nor forsake you. Deuteronomy 31:6

DAY 223
RELEASE ME

Scripture: Now to Him who is able to do exceedingly abundantly above all that we ask or think, according to the power that works in us, to Him be glory in the church by Christ Jesus to all generations, forever and ever. Amen. Ephesians 3:20-21

There was a popular song in my youth with lyrics that stated, "Release me, and let me love again." Steffon and Carlie had been "madly in love." For a while they were inseparable, and had big plans for their future together. Then something happened. Steffon was introduced to Jesus, and fell deeply in love with Him. Carlie did not share in his experience, and made it clear that she wanted no part of this love triangle. However, she was reluctant to let Steffon go. She wanted him to give up his new-found Love.

It became a real battle. Steffon still loved Carlie, and wished that she could enjoy what he had found in Christ, but he was not prepared to let go of Jesus to maintain their relationship. This love was real, like nothing he had ever experienced before. He was committed to pursuing this relationship like his life depended on it, which it did: his eternal life, that is.

The battle that ensued was so strong that Steffon had to ask his family of faith to intercede on his behalf. He met with Carlie to share what his love for Christ could mean for them as a couple. He told her that his love for Christ would make him be a better husband and lover to her. He told her that this love triangle was beneficial to all relationships; as they needed Christ at the center to succeed.

When Steffon saw that Carlie's heart was not for Christ, and that to continue a relationship with her would interfere with his relationship with his new Best Friend, Jesus, he told her lovingly but firmly: "Release me and let me go. Eternity with Christ is of far greater value than anything this world has to offer." Two years later, Carlie's heart, too, was touched by the love of Christ. Then she understood Steffon's abiding love for Him. If there is anything standing in the way of your relationship with Christ, it is time to pray for release.

Words of Love: He who loves father or mother more than Me is not worthy of Me. And he who loves son or daughter more than Me is not worthy of Me. Matthew 10:37

DAY 224
GOD KNOWS BEST

Scripture: O Lord, You have searched me and known me. You know my sitting down and my rising up; You understand my thought afar off... Psalm 139:1-3

I turned my heart heavenward with many questions for my God. We often have these periods of questioning and strong debates. One thing for sure is that at the end, I never feel defeated or a loser. It is more like a win/ win situation. God shows me the flaws in my thinking or my actions, and I leave with a renewed sense of trust and confidence in His abiding love for me, and His willingness to be my guide on the perilous waters of life's sea.

My "why" questions, as well as my "how, what/who, when and where" are all met with the response: "In My time I will reveal it you. For now you see darkly as through a glass, but then you will see face to face." God showed me that if He was to reveal the future to me now, there would be no reason for me to have faith in Him. He told me that some things are not even known to Him, but to the Father only, such as the time of His return.

Every one of us has the same opportunity to be saved. God does not have a clique amongst His children, a group of favorites who has more "inside information" than others. We are all pointed to the Word of God. The responsibility then becomes ours to walk hand-in-hand with Christ, who knows the way. Job 23:10 says, "But He knows the way that I take; when He has tested me, I will come out as pure gold."

Whatever unpleasant situation I am going through in my life, it is but a test. I can question or debate it with the Master all I want, but in the end, I must yield to His divine plan, if I am to pass the test. It is not intended to break me; simply to strengthen me. God wants jewels in His kingdom. If the streets are to be made of pure gold, and the gates of pearls, imagine the character and characteristic of its occupants. I have purposed in my heart to allow the Potter to mold and reshape me, so that I can come through the testing fires as the purest of gold, fit for eternity.

Words of Love: He reveals deep and secret things; He knows what is in the darkness, and light dwells with Him. Daniel 2:22

DAY 225
MY MOTHER AND ME

Scripture: Honor your father and your mother, that your days may be long upon the land which the Lord your God is giving you. Exodus 20:12

Two friends and I spent one Mothers' Day at a nursing home where they had become part of an ongoing ministry, operational for over twenty years. It was a joyous time of sharing with the residents and honoring the mothers with cards, flowers, and cookies. We sang songs of faith, shared poetry and readings, and the Word of God was lifted up.

As I listened to residents share their memories of their mother, it brought back fond memories of my own mother. One person told how her mother taught her and her siblings to be respectful. Another shared the sacrifices his mother made for him and his siblings, and yet another stated how her mother worked in unison with her dad to raise their family. She said her mother would not make any important decision without the involvement of her father: she would always say to them as children, "Now we have to wait and discuss that with dad." They were a team.

My mother was the disciplinarian in our family. She never subscribed to the notion of "sparing the rod and spoiling the child," and I believe I brought that philosophy of hers to bear more than any other of my siblings. I also believe I was her favorite child, only because I was the "baby." My siblings did not take that very well, and used it to their advantage to cause me more grief, since she had to let me "have it" to try to prove them wrong. The scripture says, "whom the Lord loves, He chastens;" so I accepted that my mother's discipline, though sometimes harsh, was intended to bring out the best in me. Well-intentioned discipline, administered with love, fits us not only for this life, but for eternity with the Father above.

Words of Love: When Jesus therefore saw His mother, and the disciple whom He loved standing by, He said to His mother, "Woman, behold your son!" Then He said to the disciple, "Behold your mother!" John 19:26-27

DAY 226
A ROOM FULL OF STUFF

Scripture: Do not lay up for yourselves treasures on earth... for where your treasure is, there your heart will be also. Matthew 6:19-21

Have you ever been to an estate, garage or yard sale, to a flea market or thrift store? All you see around you is a room full of stuff. Sometimes you are so overwhelmed that you don't know where to begin to look. I love to frequent these places, and I inevitably leave with even one more piece of that "stuff." If I would listen, there is usually a little voice saying something to the effect, "You know you don't need to add one thing more to the already overcrowded closets and cupboards at your home." I bet you know the response: "But it is such a good bargain, I cannot pass it up." The problem is that all the other "good bargains" have caused a dilemma of space.

The question that begs for an honest answer is: Why do we keep accumulating? It is one that you may want to answer for yourself. I am ashamed to answer, because I would have to say that for me it is greed. It is one more of this, or one more of that, depending on our interest, but it is one more than we need. It is certainly more than I need. So, go ahead, get an accountability partner if necessary, and let us commit to uncluttering our lives and those rooms which are just full of stuff. If we don't master the problem, it will certainly master us.

Words of Love: No one can serve two masters; for either he will hate the one and love the other, or else he will be loyal to the one and despise the other. You cannot serve God and mammon. Matthew 6:24

DAY 227
PREPARING FOR THE BATTLE

Scripture: Put on the whole armor of God, that you may be able to stand against the wiles of the devil. Ephesians 6:11

How do you prepare for battle? If you know you are about to face some challenges, do you walk into it unprepared, with the attitude, "I am going to wing it," or do you prepare, with strategies and defensive gear that give you a 'fighting chance'?

Let us just for a moment say that the battle is with food, and you are going to a Thanksgiving or Christmas gathering. What do you do? You can prepare some lighter options of your favorite dish for the Thanksgiving meal, or have a healthy snack before going to the Christmas party.

I attended a couple of celebratory gatherings in Denmark during Rotary International's Centennial Year. I do not drink alcohol, and had listed that information on my dietary preference card, prior to the trip. A bottle of non-alcoholic wine was strategically positioned by my place card on the table at both gatherings. I would have been happy to drink water; but they were very gracious hosts, and were not satisfied to have me raise a toast with water. In planning for that trip, I was proactive and prepared for occurrences I knew I would likely encounter.

If we prepare with such diligence for the day-to-day "battles" that we face in life -- taking a stick on our neighborhood walk; shopping on a full stomach; wearing a life vest when boating -- how much more important that we prepare with the Word of God, to fight inevitable spiritual battles? The Holy Spirit will recall to our memories those things that we have studied and placed in our memory banks, but we cannot expect to withdraw what we have not deposited.

May God help us to prepare for the battles in which the devil is waiting to engage us. In our strength alone, we are no match for Satan, but with Christ, victory is guaranteed.

Words of Love: The Lord will fight for you, and you shall hold your peace. Exodus 14:14

DAY 228
EMPTIED AND WAITING TO BE FILLED

Scripture: O God, You are my God; Early will I seek You; My soul thirsts for You; My flesh longs for You in a dry and thirsty land where there is no water. Psalm 63:1

Somebody once told a children's story at my church, using an illustration that was beautiful and poignant. Props included a large glass bowl filled with sand, stone, and toys, among other things. She emptied the large glass bowl of all the items in it, then she proceeded to refill it with the items she had just removed from it. She began with the sand, which took up half the bowl, and the remaining items could no longer fit.

The story teller tried different configurations, without any success. Then she reconfigured in a specific order, pouring in the sand last, and it all fit perfectly. She guided the thoughts of the children, and the adults as well, to the fact that when we accept Jesus Christ into our life, we must be emptied of all the stuff in us, and allow Christ to fill us in a manner that puts things in the right order.

We need to make Christ the foundation of our lives, and begin each day with Him. He will then order our steps in ways that bring Him glory and give us the best opportunity to succeed at whatever tasks we pursue. We must be emptied of hatred, malice, anger and strife, so that we can be filled with love, forgiveness, peace and unity. We must be emptied of the desire to receive, so we can give more; emptied of the desire to be served, so we can be of service; and emptied of pride, so we can be filled with humility.

Words of Love: Now may the God of hope fill you with all joy and peace in believing, that you may abound in hope by the power of the Holy Spirit. Romans 15:13

DAY 229
THE GOOD YOU DO FOLLOWS YOU, AS DOES THE EVIL

Scripture: Do not be overcome by evil, but overcome evil with good. Romans 12:21

I was very saddened to learn of the termination of a very skilled professional, because of practices that were against her company's policies. Saddened though I was, because this lady had so much to offer, I was reminded of the saying that the good you do will follow after you, and the evil you do will also catch up with you.

As I processed the report of her fall from grace, I was reminded of how devoted David was to Saul, but Saul pursued him with a jealous rage, bent on destroying him. He was the one, however, who met a very sad end. This lady had been a part of a fellow professional being unjustly terminated, and now she had reaped what she sowed. The hole she had dug for her colleague was not closed, and she herself had now fallen into it. A very sad ending, indeed.

No one should rejoice, however, because the cycle could be repeated. Instead, let us pray for those with evil in their hearts, lest they meet a similar fate. We should allow stories like David and Jonathan, in 1 Samuel chapters 18 & 20, guide our actions. Jonathan was very kind to David when his father, Saul, tried to kill David. He did not begrudge David the succession to the throne, even though, had God not chosen David, Jonathan would have been the successor. He was a friend indeed, and David did not forget his friend's kindness. After both Saul and Jonathan's deaths, when David became king, he sought out their heirs to do something good for them. He found Mephibosheth, the crippled son of Jonathan, and treated him with kindness.

Jonathan's good to David did, indeed, live after him. Unfortunately, Saul's evil, as did this lady's, caught up with them. Since it is a sure thing that you will reap what you sow, how about planting fields of good deeds, to ensure a harvest of blessings?

Words of Love: But do not forget to do good and to share, for with such sacrifices God is well pleased. Hebrews 13:16

DAY 230
HIS PERFECT TIMING

Scripture: But those who wait on the Lord shall renew their strength; They shall mount up with wings like eagles, they shall run and not be weary, they shall walk and not faint. Isaiah 40:31

You probably have heard the saying, "God may not come when you want Him to, but He is always on time." So, stop trying to move ahead of God. His timing is perfect. This counsel was as much for me as it was for my friend in this story.

My dear friend was dating this precious gentleman, who I believe God had brought into her life after the death of her beloved husband. In her eyes, appropriate time had passed, and this gentleman was not making the move she expected and desired. I, too, often shared her feelings regarding his slow pace; only because I knew how much she cared for him, and I also sensed her loneliness.

Intellectually, we both knew the right thing to do was for her to let God have His way, but the heart doesn't always want to listen to the wise counsel of the head. Thankfully, my friend aligned her heart with God's Word. Her friendship with this gentleman grew, and they both grew in their relationship with their Lord and Savior. As of this writing, the end has not been determined, so we will have to leave it: To be continued...

When we align our lives with Jesus Christ, we can rest securely in Him, knowing that the outcome will always be for our best, and His timing will always be perfect. Now, that is some confidence to have.

Words of Love: Wait on the Lord; Be of good courage, and He shall strengthen your heart; Wait, I say, on the Lord! Psalm 27:14

DAY 231
IMPLICIT TRUST

Scripture: Also, I say to you, whoever confesses Me before men, him the Son of Man also will confess before the angels of God. But he who denies Me before men will be denied before the angels of God... Luke 12:8-10

Where does one find this kind of trust? I hope you are not looking to find it in a spouse, a parent, a child, or a friend. If you do, there is the strong possibility they will fail you. There is only one person in whom we can put this level of trust, and it is Jesus. He will never fail you. That is a guarantee you can "take to the bank." It has surety, not from the Federal Reserve Bank, but from "Heaven's Bank," with the seal of the character of the Living God. When He says something, He stands behind it. He will not allow it to fail, because His Word never fails. There is a song titled: "He's Never Failed Me Yet," and I want to shout it from the rooftop and everywhere I go, that Jesus Christ has never failed me.

There are many stories, both in the Bible and in modern times, of trust gone awry. You would think that by now everyone would learn the sad truth that human beings will fail you. Our only hope is in Jesus. He is a restorer, not a destroyer. He is a giver, not a taker. He created, and He sustains. His goal is restoration, not condemnation. We can trust Him with our lives. That is implicit trust.

Words of Love: For the word of the Lord is right, and all His work is done in truth. He loves righteousness and justice; The earth is full of the goodness of the Lord... Psalm 33:4-6

DAY 232
STANDING FIRM

Scripture: Let us hold fast the confession of our hope without wavering, for He who promised is faithful. Hebrews 10:23

In my lifetime, I have watched people take a position on issues; standing firm on what they believed, however misguided that belief might have been. I, too, have had occasions to stand firm on issues. As I have matured in age and in my Christian experience, I have replayed some of those "tapes" and wondered what I had been thinking. The only guarantee of being right is when what we say is based on the pure Word of God, and expressed in love.

Carlton was a young Christian who was excited about the Bible truths he was learning. He encountered fierce opposition from family and friends that tested him severely and shook his tender faith. He sought refuge in fasting and prayer, and an intense study of the scripture. His faith was strengthened as he drew closer to God, and he resolved to stand on the Word of the Almighty.

What is testing your faith today? Is it family, your career, educational advancement, financial security? Whatever it is, search God's word for answers. There is a principle to guide every decision we face. As you study and search for truth, ask God's guidance to apply the principles to your circumstances, and stand firm, even if the heavens fall.

Words of Love: Therefore, take up the whole armor of God, that you may be able to withstand in the evil day, and having done all, to stand. Ephesians 6:13

DAY 233
NOT DOUBLE-MINDED

Scripture: If any of you lacks wisdom, let him ask of God, who gives to all liberally and without reproach, and it will be given to him. But let him ask in faith, with no doubting, for he who doubts is like a wave of the sea driven and tossed by the wind... James 1:5-8

A friend of mine uncovered some very unethical practices in her organization, and brought it to the attention of those in authority. She was harassed for not having looked the other way, so that her department would not come under scrutiny and possibly have to pay back a lot of money. In an effort to cover up the wrongdoing of others, my friend, who is honest and straightforward, was terminated. Her trials matured her on many levels; especially in her Christian walk. She went on to complete graduate studies in her profession. She later worked in academia where she helped prepare the next generation to work in that career path.

Her double-minded colleagues are in God's hands. One was later terminated for good reasons, and the fates of the others are sealed, even if not yet revealed. The same passage of scripture says in (V. 11) that "the rich," those people who seem to be prospering now, should take pride in their humiliation, because they will eventually fade away like wild flowers; their seeming beauty being destroyed by the scorching sun.

God is faithful in His promises to vindicate His children of the injustices of the evil one. We are all encouraged to be true to Him in our daily lives, letting our yeas be yeas, and our nays be nays, as guided by the principles and examples of the Master Teacher, Jesus Christ.

Words of Love: Draw near to God and He will draw near to you... James 4:8

DAY 234
TWO FACES

Scripture: I know your works, that you are neither cold nor hot. I could wish you were cold or hot... Revelation 3:15-17

The story is told of a woman who always said negative things about her friend in the presence of her young child, and she kept referring to her friend as being "two-faced." The next time the friend came by for a visit, the child ran to her, all excited, and exclaimed, "Can I please see your other face? My mommy said that you have two faces." Do we have two faces in our Christian walk: one reserved for church once a week, and another for the remainder of the week? Do we have one face for the company president, but another for the customer?

Are your comments behind your colleagues' backs as genuine as the smile you flash them to their faces? Is your behavior reflective of "Dr. Jekyll and Mr. Hyde?" Can you be counted on to act as courteously to the poorly dressed woman who is seeking the services you offer, as you do to the well-dressed one in her business suit and carrying an expensive-looking briefcase? Christ wants us to have one face that we present to everyone: the face of His matchless love for all humanity alike.

Words of Love: I counsel you to buy from Me gold refined in the fire, that you may be rich; and white garments, that you may be clothed, that the shame of your nakedness may not be revealed; and anoint your eyes with eye salve, that you may see. As many as I love, I rebuke and chasten... Revelation 3:18-19

DAY 235
HEALTHY SELF: HEAL THYSELF

Scripture: And do not be conformed to this world, but be transformed by the renewing of your mind, that you may prove what is that good and acceptable and perfect will of God. Romans 12:2

When you look closely at the two sets of words in the title above, you will notice that they have the same letters, organized to form different words. They are not to be mistaken as meaning the same thing. A healthy self is one which recognizes its place in the universe: one which knows the Creator, recognizes and appreciates His creation, and does everything to treat its body well; thus, bringing God the honor and glory which He so richly deserves for His creative genius.

A healthy self does not subscribe to the "heal thyself" notion; recognizing that in the same way it cannot create, it cannot heal. Instead, it yields to the philosophy that true health of body, mind and spirit is attained when one recognizes that the body is fearfully and wonderfully made by an all-wise God, and does everything in its power to maintain that health. The scripture tells us in 3 John 2, that God desires us to have good balanced health of mind and body, even as He desires our souls to be healthy.

Words of Love: Beloved, I pray that you may prosper in all things and be in health, just as your soul prospers. 3 John 2.

DAY 236
HIS PROMISE TO FEED ME

Scripture: Give us day by day our daily bread. Luke 11:3

At the request of Jesus' disciples that He teach them how to pray, He taught them this model prayer, called The Lord's Prayer. He told them, among other things, to ask the Father daily for their food: "Give us this day our daily bread." It is not God's desire that any of His children should go hungry or begging for bread. He has all the resources of the world at His command, and has made those resources available to His children. It may mean that those of us to whom more is given help those who are less fortunate.

I recently met a very kind gentleman who owns a café. He made all his pastries and other baked goods daily, and discarded any leftovers at the end of the day. He was used to donating the leftovers to a soup kitchen. To his surprise, they stopped the daily pickups, stating that if someone choked on his products, he would be liable, and could be sued.

With the knowledge of potential lawsuits, but still wanting to help, this generous business owner began putting the bakery items in a separate bag, by the garbage dumpster, in hopes that the homeless would retrieve it before the garbage truck picked up the garbage. The laws of our land and the litigious nature of our society were contributing to the waste, as well as to the continued problem of hunger in communities, he rightly pointed out.

Lord, I pray for wisdom to prevail in our land, and for love to guide all our actions, so that both the giver and the receiver will be protected and blessed. Amen.

Words of Love: Bear one another's burdens, and so fulfill the law of Christ. Galatians 6:2

DAY 237
LORD, SHOW YOURSELF STRONG TODAY!

Scripture: For the eyes of the Lord run to and fro throughout the whole earth, to show Himself strong on behalf of those whose heart is loyal to Him... 2 Chronicles 16:9

The forces of darkness were bearing down heavily on Malcolm, and he felt powerless to shake them. He knew he needed the light of Christ to enshroud him, heaven's angelic host to guard him, and Christ Himself to walk beside him. So, he cried out in despair: "Lord, show Yourself strong on my behalf today."

Christ is never far from a repentant heart that cries out to Him for mercy and salvation. Jesus said that for this He came. Satan wants you to think that you are beyond God's reach, that your sins have made you undeserving of His love, and undesirable in His kingdom. Jesus says, however, that He did not come to call the righteous, but sinners to repentance.

Malcolm's confidence began to build. At first, they were baby steps. He read the scripture, but lacked the confidence to even pray in private, feeling that he did not have the right words to say. Gradually he began to trust Christ enough with his broken words, then sentences, and then phrases. Eventually a conversation began, as between two friends, which it was.

As their friendship grew, Malcolm became less afraid. He knew that he did not have to face the forces of evil by himself; His new Best Friend, Jesus, went everywhere with him, and Satan had to go through Christ to get to him. Malcolm became strong, though not in his own strength, and in Christ, he became a force to contend with.

You and I have the same privileges today. God wants to show Himself strong in our lives, but we have to yield the reins to Him. We must stand behind Him, and let Him answer the door. Then, the forces of evil that are allowed to attack us will only be those which are intended to mature us in our Christian walk, and prepare us for eternity. Together, we should all cry out: "Lord, please show Yourself strong on our behalf today." Victory will then be guaranteed.

Words of Love: Call upon Me in the day of trouble; I will deliver you, and you shall glorify Me. Psalm 50:15

DAY 238
CHRIST THE RESTORER

Scripture: So, I will restore to you the years that the swarming locust has eaten… You shall eat in plenty and be satisfied, and praise the name of the Lord your God, who has dealt wondrously with you; And My people shall never be put to shame. Joel 2:25-26

Toga was very much in love. He met his beautiful bride in school, and it was not too long afterwards that with all customary cultural norms satisfied, they became man and wife. Things were going very well for the young couple. They both obtained work in their fields of study, and they were talking about a family, as both sets of parents were eager for grandchildren.

The couple tried, but Toga's wife could not conceive. This was not taken very well by Toga's parents, and they began to withdraw from their daughter-in-law. Gradually there was a split in the family that threatened to tear the marriage of this young couple apart.

Christ had not been a strong part of either side of the family, but along the way, Toga and his wife were introduced to Him, and their faith began to grow. They believed that in God's time they would have a child, if it was His will. Several years passed, and the couple immersed themselves in their growing relationship with Christ, strengthening their marriage relationship, and building their careers.

When Toga's family observed the happiness in the young couple's lives, they sought the reason, and in the process, they, too, came to know Jesus as their Lord and Savior. The relationship between both sets of parents improved, and the stress level of all parties was greatly reduced. In time, Toga's wife conceived, and gave birth to twins. This was perceived as a special blessing from God, confirmation of His love and approval. The entire family came together with the goal of loving and raising these two precious gifts from God for His service. One can only exclaim, "What a mighty God we serve."

Words of Love: "For I will restore health to you and heal you of your wounds," says the Lord… Jeremiah 30:17

DAY 239
THE POWER OF THE TONGUE

Scripture: Death and life are in the power of the tongue, and those who love it will eat its fruit. Proverbs 18:21

The words, "You add no value to," are crushing not only to one's ears but also to one's heart. They are words which, seriously meant or carelessly spoken, can never be retrieved. Actions may counter those words to some degree, but they will always linger in the mind of the one to whom they are spoken.

I have determined that the best exchange of words is done in person, where body language and intonation can be paired with the words, for better interpretation. Because this is unrealistic, if not almost impossible, in the mobile world in which we live, we should endeavor to ensure that our words convey positive and uplifting sentiments.

There was a recent exchange between two aunts and a nephew. The exchange began with all three parties in different locations, and continued when the two sisters met together in one place. They communicated with the nephew via text and email, then finally by telephone, but each exchange seemed to complicate the issue further. How they wished for a face-to-face session with all parties present. Apologies have since been made and accepted, but the damage has been done and some of the hurt lingers.

What words will fly off your tongue today? Will they be words of life or words of death? Will they inspire or will they crush? Will they elevate or will they denigrate? Remember, once spoken, they cannot be retrieved, so, think before you speak.

Words of Love: Out of the abundance of the heart his mouth speaks. Luke 6:45

DAY 240
ADDICTED TO THE WORD

Scripture: Your Word I have hidden in my heart that I might not sin against You. Psalm 119:11

When was the last time you came across someone who was addicted to the Word of God? If you know of such a person, what is the impact of this addiction on this person's life? Is the change that is inevitable obvious in the way this person lives? When one is ingesting the Word, there will be evidence of the fruit in the life. There will be love, joy, peace, longsuffering, kindness, meekness, faithfulness, gentleness and self-control.

The person who is "addicted" to the Word will spend time daily, searching the scripture. There will be no feasting on physical food until some spiritual food has been ingested. There will be an eagerness to "come aside" and spend time with Jesus, the Master Teacher. There will be a prayerful search for the answers to life's troubling questions, and there will be an acceptance of those answers, even if they are not making sense now. These same scriptures tell us that now we see darkly, as looking through a glass, but then we will see Him face to face, and get clarity to the puzzling issues of life.

Prayer: Father, of all the addictions to the things of this world: food, exercise and fitness, work, and accumulating wealth; various forms of entertainment, gossip and tearing others down, and self-gratification in its many forms; how awesome it would be to be addicted to seeking after You. Help us today to have a longing for Your Word, and not to be satisfied with any substitute. There is nothing like the real thing, Father, and substitutes do not satisfy our lasting hunger. Fill us now we pray, in Jesus' name. Amen.

Words of Love: But be doers of the word, and not hearers only, deceiving yourselves. James 1:22

DAY 241
CAST YOUR NET ON THE OTHER SIDE

Scripture: And He said to them, "Cast the net on the right side of the boat, and you will find some." So they cast, and now they were not able to draw it in because of the multitude of fish. John 21:6

I reconnected with a friend with whom I had lost contact for many years. When I got her address, I sent her a card with my telephone number, and one morning she called. It was a wonderful reunion. We caught up on each other's lives, and shared God's goodness to both of us. My friend told of some difficulties she was experiencing, and her commitment to "Trust God." Those two words were her mantra for the year.

During the conversation, she mentioned an experience she had the night prior to her calling me. She was reading the Bible on her phone, and was directed to the book of John, where Jesus appeared to His disciples on the beach, after His resurrection. He told them to cast their net on the other side of the boat. They had fished all night, and knew that at that time of the morning, a catch was unlikely. However, they decided to trust Him, and what a catch it was.

Doubts and fears had plagued my friend for several years, and she saw this story as a personal directive from God to cast her net of faith on the other side. For too long she had had her eyes set on a certain path, and God was telling her to look elsewhere. He had blessings "on the other side of the boat" just waiting for her obedience and trust.

Don't miss out on your blessings because of fear of casting your net on the other side. Jesus is waiting to give you the catch of a lifetime.

Words of Love: And all these blessings shall come upon you and overtake you, because you obey the voice of the Lord your God. Deuteronomy 28:2

DAY 242
HIS BEAUTY IN ME

Scripture: One thing I have desired of the Lord, that will I seek: That I may dwell in the house of the Lord all the days of my life, to behold the beauty of the Lord, and to inquire in His temple. Psalm 27:4

Let the beauty of Jesus be seen in me;
All His wonderful passion and purity.
May His Spirit divine, all my nature refine;
Till the beauty of Jesus be seen in me.

Those words are part of the lyrics of the beautiful song, Let the Beauty of Jesus, by Albert W. T. Orsborn, asking God to fill us with His likeness, with the beauty of His character. What would it actually look like, to have the beauty of Jesus shining forth from my life? Certainly, I would be more loving, more kind and gentle, and definitely more forgiving. I would not hold grudges, and would turn the other cheek more often.

The scripture says that there was nothing "comely" about Jesus' outward beauty. It was what emanated from within that drew others to Him. So, what were some of those character traits that made Jesus so beautiful, and His presence so desirable?

Jesus said He came to serve; not to be served. The King of the universe put aside His outer garment, picked up a basin and towel, and washed His disciples' feet. He sought to ease the suffering of others. He was generous and fair, and He believed in good citizenship, such as honoring Caesar with the taxes that were due him. He believed in hard work, and set the example of stellar work ethics as He labored in His father Joseph's carpentry shop.

He was obedient, as He said His purpose was to do the will of God the Father. Ultimately, He has an abiding love for all humanity, and we are all equal in His eyes.

What a legacy to live up to. What exemplary beauty to emulate. That beauty is attainable, though, for by beholding Christ we become changed.

Words of Love: Thine eyes shall see the king in his beauty: they shall behold the land that is very far off. Isaiah 33:17

DAY 243
AN ACCEPTABLE RELIGION

Scripture: Pure religion and undefiled before God and the Father is this, to visit the fatherless and widows in their affliction, and to keep himself unspotted from the world. James 1:27

Have you ever met someone who lived such a sanctimonious life that they were ineffective Christians? I had an aunt who was so righteous that the rest of the family, regardless of their Christian walk, were never "saintly" enough. "You are so heavenly-minded that you are no earthly good" might be a fitting quote for such. A quick-witted friend of mine says some people miss church going to church. These sayings, both true, are bad reflections on people who profess religion.

I am grateful that God is not looking for "religious" people; but for Christians who practice true religion, as defined in the passage above. When we know Christ, and are called by His name, we will live as He lived. In James 1:22, he says that Christians should be doers of the word, and not hearers only.

James concludes the passage by saying, "Pure and undefiled religion before God is to visit orphans and widows in their trouble, and to keep oneself unspotted from the world." How sad, that many have had overlooked the first part of this sentence, in their misguided desire to live the second part. It is hard, if not impossible, to live lives of purity, while ignoring the plight of the needy among us.

Words of Love: Inasmuch as ye have done it unto one of the least of these my brethren, ye have done it unto me. Matthew 25:40

DAY 244

RIGHTEOUS BEFORE THE LORD

Scripture: He has shown you, O man, what is good; And what does the Lord require of you but to do justly, to love mercy, and to walk humbly with your God? Micah 6:8

I read an article about a newly elected president in one of the South Pacific islands who was questioned about living his Christian principles as a public figure. He said he had asked all Christians in his country to be prayerful with him, and to live righteous lives before the Lord. What does righteous living before God entail? I polled my prayer partners, and here are some of their thoughts:

"On a daily basis, as much as humanly possible, be of service to others; remembering that all we say and do must be to bring glory and honor to God."

"Righteous living is being careful to put God first in my life, moment by moment; and to be ever mindful of His presence; by praying continuously. Also, a lot of 'what would Jesus do?' and plenty of, 'Jesus, please take the wheel.'"

"Living according to God's will. It is the work of a lifetime."

Righteous living is giving God total control, and letting Him live out His life in us. Lyrics of the beautiful song, Live Out Thy Life Within Me, by Frances R. Havergal, state: "Live out Thy life within me, O Jesus, King of kings; Be Thou Thyself the answer to all my questionings. Live out Thy life within me, in all things have Thy way; I, the transparent medium, Thy glory to display." Righteous living is truly "living right" for, and before God. This is only possible with the aid of the Holy Spirit.

Words of Love: And do not be conformed to this world, but be transformed by the renewing of your mind, that you may prove what is that good and acceptable and perfect will of God. Romans 12:2

DAY 245
LIVING WITH ETERNITY IN VIEW

Scripture: But, beloved, do not forget this one thing, that with the Lord one day is as a thousand years, and a thousand years as one day. 2 Peter 3:8

Is it true that eternity is possibly just around the corner? If this is so, what impact should it have on how we live our lives?

The scripture tells us that no one knows the day or the hour of Christ's appearing. It is written that His coming will be as a thief in the night; not silent, just unannounced before it happens. His children have been told, however, to look for the warning signs that He is near. They are everywhere.

The devil is on the prowl, seeking diligently to enlarge his host. He knows he has lost out on eternity, and his desire is to deny that privilege to as many of earth's inhabitants as he possibly can. He takes this task very seriously, and will use any method at his disposal to accomplish his goal. However, each one of us still has that power of choice, given to mankind at creation. Exercise it, and let Satan know that eternity with Christ is far more appealing than the alternative.

People can endure almost any hardship when they know there is an end in sight. The trials will be short-lived; relief is just around the corner. The skeptics say that this promise of Christ's return has been for a very long time. One thing I know is that we are closer today than we were yesterday. The signs foretell that it won't be much longer now.

I believe eternity is on the horizon, and I am living with great expectancy. It may be tomorrow, the next decade or century, or, it may be today. I want to be ready, whenever He comes.

Words of Love: But seek first the kingdom of God and His righteousness, and all these things shall be added to you. Matthew 6:33

DAY 246
THE FUTURE... TODAY!

Scripture: Whatever the activity in which you engage, do it with all your ability, because there is no work, no planning, no learning, and no wisdom, in the grave, where you're going. Ecclesiastes 9:10

Only yesterday, today was the future. We had no guarantee it would be here, or that we would exist in it. What a foreboding thought, but a poignant one. And what a privilege to be living in yesterday's future. Let us make the best of this awesome gift; and live to make a difference.

Let's process this scenario: Yesterday I prayed that God would open a way for me in a particular area of my life. I had no idea what the future held, and how my prayer would be answered, but God was already working through you, and today you have helped to open a door.

Today each of us can be the future someone prayed about yesterday. We can help to make today a brighter day for somebody, giving hope to a situation that seemed hopeless. We can turn a potential negative outcome into a positive one. We can lift a dark cloud and let a ray of sunshine in. The future is any time after the present: this moment. So, we don't have to wait for some prescribed time yet to come. Let us make a difference for Christ today. We will be glad we did, and the lives touched by our efforts will be tremendously blessed. We might even find that we receive the greater blessing.

Words of Love: Whatever your hand finds to do, do it with your might; for there is no work or device or knowledge or wisdom in the grave where you are going. Matthew 5:16

DAY 247
GIVING THANKS ALWAYS FOR YOU

Scripture: I thank my God upon every remembrance of you. Philippians 1:3

One morning, after my prayer call, and during my personal prayer time, I was impressed to reach out to my family and friends with a special note of thanks to them for being in my life. No, it was not during Thanksgiving, and I did not feel that I was dying. It was just a moment to pause, and express my love and appreciation to the people close to me.

I selected the graphic of a young woman, out in nature, running into the wind with her arms raised heavenward, and the inscription: "Gratitude is the best attitude."

O, that we would pause more often, and let the people in our lives know how much they mean to us, and how much we thank God always for them. Why not do it now? Take a break right now, and ask God who needs to be affirmed with that kind of acknowledgement. He will reveal it to you, and what a blessing it could be to the receiver. "No special occasion; just thinking of you and letting you know how blessed I am to have you in my life, or, to have your friendship." Wouldn't you be touched to have those sentiments from a family member or friend today? Start a trend, and be a blessing. You will, in turn, be blessed.

Words of Love: It is good to give thanks to the Lord, and to sing praises to Your name, O Most High;. Psalm 92:1

DAY 248
UNMERITED FAVOR

Scripture: So, she fell on her face, bowed down to the ground, and said to him, "Why have I found favor in your eyes, that you should take notice of me, since I am a foreigner?" Ruth 2:10

The story of Ruth is one of my favorite Bible stories. I was intrigued by the passage that says, "Entreat me not to leave thee, or to return from following after thee... your people will be my people, and your God my God." The story has much more depth, however. That was only the beginning of this young woman's journey of faith and trust in the One True God. I assume she was a very attractive young woman, and/or she displayed a demeanor that was attractive. She evidently stood out from the rest of the young women gleaning in Boaz's field; so much so that she caught the attention of the wealthy landowner.

Boaz inquired of the men who she was, and when he learned of her connection to Naomi, he gave special instructions towards her. Ruth did not take the generosity shown her for granted, however. Instead, the passage said Ruth identified herself as a foreigner, and expressed a feeling of being undeserving of such favor.

Are you the recipient of some unmerited favor from the hands of our loving God? How do you thank Him?

Words of Love: For His anger is but for a moment, His favor is for life; Weeping may endure for a night, but joy comes in the morning. Psalm 30:5

DAY 249
PRACTICING FORGIVENESS: LIFE'S BEST MEDICINE

Scripture: For if you forgive men their trespasses, your heavenly Father will also forgive you. But if you do not forgive men their trespasses, neither will your Father forgive your trespasses. Matthew 6:14-15

Unforgiveness is like chaining yourself to the person with whom you are upset, and spending the whole day with them. Forgiveness is a way of letting go, rather than hanging on. Forgiveness is freeing. It is like being given wings, and having the freedom to fly. It has been said that an unforgiving spirit is the equivalent of drinking poison and expecting the other person to die.

I participated in a group exercise at a training workshop I attended. We were to select a topic from a list provided, discuss the topic within the smaller group, and then share with the larger group. My group selected the topic: "Reframing unforgiveness." A member of the group shared how hurt she once was by actions of a brother in her church. She said her anger and unforgiveness had been eating away at the core of her heart like a poison.

God helped her to reframe the whole experience, and she pledged to take action. She and the brother were at a meeting together, and God impressed on her to settle the differences there and then, which she did. She approached the gentleman, expressed how much he had hurt her, but that she was choosing to forgive him.

God's grace abounded, and at a later event attended by both the gentleman and the lady telling the story, he joined her and her husband at their table for dinner. She said, "Not only had I been freed from bitterness, but a brother in Christ had been restored into our fellowship." Her heart muscles no longer tightened whenever she saw him, and neither did her blood pressure rise. She said she had drunk of the medicine of forgiveness, and her heart had been healed. For that we all shouted, "Hallelujah."

Words of Love: To the Lord our God belong mercy and forgiveness, though we have rebelled against Him. Daniel 9:9

DAY 250
ONE FORK, ONE KNIFE AND ONE SPOON

Scripture: Let your conduct be without covetousness; be content with such things as you have. For He Himself has said, "I will never leave you nor forsake you." Hebrews 13:5

A friend told me the following story. She said that in her late twenties she met a very accomplished middle-aged gentleman who took a liking to her. She was college-educated and had a promising professional career; he was nearing retirement. They dated for three years. As the months turned into years, my friend got the impression that the gentleman felt he had more to offer the relationship than she did, so she sat him down for a heart-to-heart conversation. She told him, "I can only eat with one fork and one knife; eat from one plate, and a bowl will suffice, because I can use it for soups as well; I can only sleep in one bed, and a twin bed will be enough, because I don't take up much space when I sleep."

She added, for good measure, "The point I am trying to make is that I am content with little, but I have the necessary tools to achieve much, with God's help, so I am not impressed by what you have." Needless to say, that relationship ended, with my friend achieving great success in the ensuing years; and her suitor living a very miserable life, before he died, alone and lonely.

The blessings that God bestows on us are for the purpose of blessing others, never to be used to elevate ourselves above them. My friend was confident in the God she served, knowing that He would supply all her needs. This gave her the strength to walk away from a life of entrapment by material things.

Put your trust in a God who can give us peace and contentment in whatever state we find ourselves; a God who opens doors to those who walk in His footsteps. Remember, no matter your achievements, you can only eat with one fork, one knife and one spoon at any given time.

Words of Love: Now godliness with contentment is great gain. 1 Timothy 6:6

DAY 251

LIVING ABOVE YOUR CIRCUMSTANCES

Scripture: In My Father's house are many mansions; if it were not so, I would have told you. I go to prepare a place for you... John 14:2-3.

This world is a mixture of joy and sorrow, progress and failure, sunshine and rain. There seems to be a greater abundance of the negatives, but one thing is certain: neither is forever. The circumstances of life are temporary, because life itself is temporary. With this knowledge, the child of God can endure any situation that life imposes, and live above our circumstances:

- She was a normal full-term birth, and was healthy until the age of one year, then disaster struck out of nowhere. She teetered on the brink of death for weeks in the hospital, and when it was over, both sight and hearing had been lost...

- He volunteered to serve his country, and the experiences left him so distraught, he attempted to take his life...

- They had been married for fifty years and were inseparable; then the accident happened, and she was killed by a drunk driver.

How do you live above the circumstances of life that challenge you to the core, and test your faith? With the confidence born out of a personal relationship with Christ, and the knowledge that He is true to His word. What He promises, He will fulfill.

His Word assures us that He is coming back, and in a restored world, all our trials will be over. All that causes us anxiety now will vanish from memory. I don't know about you, but with such blessed assurance, I can endure the temporary hiccups. I can live above life's challenging circumstances.

Words of Love: These things I have spoken to you, that in Me you may have peace. In the world, you will have tribulation; but be of good cheer, I have overcome the world. John 16:33

DAY 252
LORD, MAKE ME THE CEO

Scripture: Therefore comfort each other and edify one another, just as you also are doing. 1 Thessalonians 5:11

Lord, make me a blessing to someone today, should be our constant prayer. We should earnestly pray to be the CEO, Chief Encouragement Officer to those we encounter: those who feel hopeless, downtrodden, misunderstood, unappreciated or helpless. Lord, help us lift them up; pray for them; open doors of opportunity for them, where possible; comfort them in their sorrows; and rejoice with them in their successes.

Sometimes, all people need in life is a cheerleader in their corner. Just as a sports team is energized by their fans or a group of cheerleaders, so too, each of us is encouraged by someone who says, "You can do this; go for it; I know you are well prepared for this task; God's got your back."

So, Lord, as I go about my activities of the day, give me discernment and help me to identify someone who needs a little encouragement. I don't need all the details of their life story, unless they are impressed to share as a means of release. What I need are ears to listen, a heart to connect and understand, and lips to speak encouraging words. May I direct them to You and Your words, and may they come to know that all power in heaven and on earth is Yours. Father, I want to be Your appointed CEO to someone today, so make me a blessing, I pray.

Words of Love: Let the word of Christ dwell in you richly in all wisdom, teaching and admonishing one another in psalms and hymns and spiritual songs, singing with grace in your hearts to the Lord. Colossians 3:16

DAY 253
OVERCOMING THE ODDS

Scripture: Trust in the Lord with all your heart, and lean not on your own understanding. Proverbs 3:5

Are the cards stacked against you? You do not have to succumb to despair. You can overcome and beat the odds. Let me tell you Melisma's story. Melisma never knew her father, and her mother did not know who he was either, but that was not the worst of her story. She was born to a drug-addicted mother, and as if that was not enough, she was born behind bars. You see, Melisma's mother was not only a drug user, but she also worked the streets. She was serving a long prison sentence for a crime she committed while under the influence of drugs.

After she was born, Melisma was placed in the custody of the courts, and spent many years in foster care, until family members petitioned the courts and got custody of her. Melisma did not have a "chip on her shoulder," in spite of her circumstances. She was a bright, mannerly and hard-working child. A very affluent family watched her from a distance, and decided to get close. This God-sent family mentored Melisma, and she flourished under their love and guidance. Melisma graduated at the top of her class and obtained an academic scholarship to a very prestigious university.

So, what is your story? Are you feeling sorry for yourself and blaming the world for your circumstances? The course of your life is not fixed by your beginning. You can take the reins and turn even the most stubborn old mule around. Melisma did, against all the odds. With determination and God's help, you can too.

Words of Love: Casting all your care upon Him, for He cares for you1 Peter 5:7

DAY 254
WITH WINGS LIKE EAGLES

Scripture: But those who wait on the Lord shall renew their strength; They shall mount up with wings like eagles, they shall run and not be weary, they shall walk and not faint. Isaiah 40:31

"I want to soar like an eagle," Connie said one day, as the family worshipped together and read the scripture above. The thought seemed to have come out of nowhere, but it was only the first of many times that Connie would voice that comment. Her family sensed a yearning in Connie's heart for adventure, and they began to pray for God to intervene and give direction to her life. Connie had overlooked the first part of the verse which said: those who wait on the Lord would have this privilege to soar like the eagle.

In obedience, Connie yielded to the wise counsel of her elders. As she prepared herself academically for her chosen career, God was preparing her heart, and setting in motion the direction He wanted for her life. When the time was right, God opened doors of opportunity for Connie, and she reached for the heights. She blazed trails and attained heights that she thought were only possible in dreams, and she grew strong in the strength of the Lord.

Connie confessed that had she not waited on the Lord, her "wings" might not have been strong enough to sustain the heights which she achieved. Are you running ahead of God? His timing is always right, and the higher you climb, like the eagle, the stronger those wings will need to be, so be patient in your preparation. Patience pays rich dividends.

Words of Love: And my God shall supply all your need according to His riches in glory by Christ Jesus. Philippians 4:19

DAY 255
CONFESSION: THE FIRST STEP TO PARDON

Scripture: He who covers his sins will not prosper, but whoever confesses and forsakes them will have mercy. Proverbs 28:13

The story is told of a governor who visited a prison. He asked the first prisoner he met why he was there. He replied that he did not know. The judge sent him there. The question was repeated to one inmate after another, and each respondent became more and more indignant with their answers. They all made excuses, refusing to take responsibility for the actions that caused then to be incarcerated.

Finally, the governor came to a young man and posed the same question. This young man, unlike the others, was very remorseful. In tears, he confessed that he had done wrong. He expressed how sorry he was and how he wished he could undo his poor choices. The governor turned to the guards with orders to get him out of there, as he was likely to contaminate all the other innocent prisoners. Needless to say, he was pardoned and given a chance at rehabilitation.

Christ is ready and eager to offer pardon to repentant sinners, but we have to acknowledge that we have done wrong to obtain His pardon. If we remain in denial, blame others for our failures, and refuse to take responsibility for our actions, it is hard to expect to obtain forgiveness. After all, in our eyes, we have done nothing wrong, and therefore there is nothing for which we need pardon. At least, so we think.

The scripture says that we have all sinned and come short of God's glory. I definitely need pardon, and the quicker I confess my sinfulness, the sooner I will be on my way to living a forgiven life. Do it today. Sin is too heavy a burden to carry around on your shoulder, and Christ wants to give you the freedom of forgiveness.

Words of love: I acknowledged my sin to You, and my iniquity I have not hidden. I said, "I will confess my transgressions to the Lord," and You forgave the iniquity of my sin. Psalm 32:5

DAY 256
THE PUBLICAN'S PRAYER

Scripture: And the tax collector, standing afar off, would not so much as raise his eyes to heaven, but beat his breast, saying, 'God, be merciful to me a sinner!' Luke 18:13.

The story is told of two men who went into the temple to pray: one, a Publican; the other a Pharisee. The Bible tells us that the Pharisee went before the altar, and with his eyes raised heavenward, he expounded on his goodness. He told God he was thankful that he was not like other men, such as the poor wretched Publican standing in the back of the temple. He was arrogant and boastful, self-centered and self-righteous.

The Publican, on the other hand, stood afar off. He felt unworthy to come too close to the holy altar of God. With head bowed low, he confessed his sins to Almighty God. His prayer was one of humility. With a few short and simple words, he prayed, "Lord, have mercy on me, a sinner." The scripture tells us that he, of the two men, went home justified that day.

There are two groups of people standing before God today. You and I are in one group or the other. Some of us stand in need of God's forgiveness, and are conscious that there is no goodness in ourselves to justify us and make us worthy. Others stand in their own righteousness, believing that their own goodness justifies them.

Scripture tells us that our righteousness is as filthy rags. No goodness of ours can earn us God's salvation, so I am choosing to adapt the mode of the Publican, and throwing myself on God's grace. He always hears the cry of one who says, "Chief of sinners though I be, Jesus shed His blood for me." You are invited to approach Him in like manner.

Words of Love: Blessed is the man to whom the Lord does not impute iniquity, and in whose spirit there is no deceit. Psalm 32:2

DAY 257
I WIN EITHER WAY

Scripture: For to me, to live is Christ, and to die is gain. Philippians 1:21

It takes a special person to face death with a smile on their face, and a win-win attitude. You have to be confident in the God who walks at your side day by day. Your relationship with Him has to be secure. You have to be able to claim the words of 2 Timothy 1:12, which says: "for I know Whom I have believed, and am persuaded that He is able; to keep that which I have committed, unto Him against that day."

Facing death with a win-win attitude was how my friend's sister lived her life after her second cancer diagnosis. At her funeral, after only a three-month illness, a family member shared the following story: This special daughter of God was facing yet another surgery in her battle with brain cancer. It was an emergency surgery, and the surgeon counseled against going forward with the procedure, as there was a greater than ninety percent chance she would not leave the operating table alive; and if she did, she would not return home from the hospital.

The family was amazed at her words, "Scrub up doctor. If I live I win, and have more time with my family; and if I die I win, and get to rest in my Savior, wherein the first voice I hear when I awake will be His, welcoming me home." When we die in Christ, we gain, not lose: we gain rest, relief, release and reward. These blessings are gifts that we obtain through the shed blood of Jesus, our precious Lord and Savior.

Words of Love: Come to me, all you who labor and are heavy laden, and I will give you rest. Matthew 11:28

DAY 258
TEACH THEM HOW TO FISH

Scripture: Every good gift and every perfect gift is from above, and comes down from the Father of lights, with whom there is no variation or shadow of turning. James 1:17

Her water had been cut off, because the bill had not been paid, so the church stepped in to help. Then the wise pastor did something very unusual. He visited the family, after the water had been turned back on, and he asked the little boy to demonstrate how he brushed his teeth. He discovered that the child had the water running from start to finish. Further questioning alerted the pastor that this was routine practice of the entire family. Not only was the environment not considered in this family's water usage, but their high monthly water bill was indicative of wasteful use of water. The pastor decided it was time for lessons on budgeting and general money management.

It is great to provide a fish in times of crisis. God wants us to provide for the needs of the poor in our midst, especially those of the household of faith. He also wants us to be good stewards of our resources, however much, or little, they may be. This requires that we teach the poor how to fish for themselves, so they can have a steady source of fish to meet their ongoing needs.

Prayer: Father, please help me to be generous with the blessings You have bestowed on me. Help me to not foster dependency in those needing my assistance, but to teach them how to "fish" for themselves, so that they develop some confidence in their ability to do for themselves. May both those who help and those who are helped recognize Jesus as the source from whom our greatest help comes.

Words of Love: Trust in the Lord with all your heart, and lean not on your own understanding; In all your ways acknowledge Him, and He shall direct your paths. Proverbs 3:5-6

DAY 259

WHAT IS YOUR PURPOSE FOR LIVING?

Scripture: He has saved us and called us to a holy life; not because of anything we have done, but because of his own purpose and grace." 2 Timothy 1:9. (NIV)

Have you ever stopped to ask yourself the questions, "For what purpose was I born? Why am I here on this earth?" If you have, what answer did you arrive at? And, if you haven't, why not prayerfully ask God that question now?

Each of us has a special purpose in life. It is our responsibility to find out what that purpose is. It is so sad to see people everywhere, from every age group, and from every socioeconomic status, living as though life is meaningless. They have lost their sense of purpose, if they ever felt they had one.

Evaluate your strengths. What brings a smile to your face or gets you excited when it pops into your mind? Best of all, ask God to show you, and see where He lights a spark. That is only the first step, however. A critical next step is to get some action going.

Around the age of five years, I discovered my affinity for books, and I told my family that I wanted to be a teacher, and write books. At the age of twenty, I graduated teachers' college, but it has taken me to retirement years to fulfill the other "itch" I felt was a part of my purpose.

Along my journey, I have taken steps to hone those skills. I read with an intent to share what I have read, which helps to sharpen my teaching skills, and I journal my life experiences. God finally said it was time to overcome the fear of not being gifted enough. I am choosing to honor Him and fulfill this purpose I believe I was called to. I believe this project is as much of a blessing to me as I hope it will be for those of you who read it. All glory is given to God for the abilities He gives us, and the calling He places in our lives.

Words of Love: Therefore, my beloved, as you have always obeyed, not as in my presence only, but now much more in my absence, work out your own salvation with fear and trembling; for it is God who works in you both to will and to do for His good pleasure. Philippians 2:12-13.

DAY 260
NOT AGAIN!

Scripture: Therefore, let him who thinks he stands take heed lest he fall. 1 Corinthians 10:12

I had completed the manuscript, so I thought. Then as I began to edit, I realized that I had written a few devotions twice. I was eager to complete the work, so I was frustrated for repeating the error. Wherever that discovery was made, I had to stop and write a completely new devotion. This was the case with this particular day's devotion: I had repeated Day 218. In my frustration, I cried out "Not Again," and then I paused to reflect on the devotion. Although this title was slightly different:"Jesus Watches from Every Angle," the content was exactly the same.

Jesus' vision is telescopic and He sees from a 360-degree angle. I am thankful that He does, and I feel secure under His watchful gaze. I am also thankful for the opportunity to refocus, and instead of questioning, "Again Lord?" to see the big picture of the work that He desires to accomplish in my life. Yes, His eyes are watching us, and He wants us to be purposeful and intentional in how we worship Him through all the events of our lives.

I will not be overconfident in my abilities, but will entrust all my activities to Him, and follow His footsteps on any path He leads me. When He chooses to lead me down the same path twice, I will seek to learn the new lessons He desires to teach me, and enjoy the experience.

Words of Love: Behold, God is my helper; The Lord is with those who uphold my life. Psalm 54:4

DAY 261
IS YOUR BOAT UNSINKABLE?

Scripture: But He was in the stern, asleep on a pillow. And they awoke Him and said to Him, "Teacher, do You not care that we are perishing?" Then He arose and rebuked the wind, and said to the sea, "Peace, be still!" And the wind ceased and there was a great calm. Mark 4:38-39

It was a terrible storm on the Sea of Galilee, and the disciples feared for their lives. There was another boat touted to be unsinkable. Everyone on that boat was having a good time, having placed confidence in the engineering feat of the vessel. The alarms were sent out late, and at first, they appeared to be flares of festivities instead of a signal for help.

What made the boat on the Sea of Galilee, in that life-threatening storm, unsinkable? The waves were crashing over the sides and the disciples could barely stay in the water-filled vessel. Yet, there was One resting in the stern of the boat, unfazed by the howling wind and crashing waves. Yes, Jesus was in the boat.

Is Jesus in your boat for the journey across the stormy sea of life? Have you invited His presence? When Jonah was running from his assignment to Nineveh, a great storm threatened to sink that boat, and it was only after the crew reluctantly cast him overboard that there was calm. Unlike that scenario, we need Jesus in our boat to prevent it from sinking. He is the only one who can calm the storms of life, and bring us to safe harbor.

Take advantage of His willingness to walk the journey with you. He is the only guarantee of a safe passage.

Words of Love: He replied, "You of little faith, why are you so afraid?" Then he got up and rebuked the winds and the waves, and it was completely calm. Matthew 8:26 (NIV)

DAY 262
PRAY MORE AND WORRY LESS

Scripture: But you, when you pray, go into your room, and when you have shut your door, pray to your Father who is in the secret place; and your Father who sees in secret will reward you openly. Matthew 6:6

Pray without ceasing. This is an admonition to stay in a constant attitude of prayer. Pray about everything. It is difficult to pray and worry at the same time. Pray big and bold prayers; pray with confidence that God will hear and answer according to His will for your life. Regardless of the status of the issue you have placed before the Lord, never doubt His desire for your good.

Marlin was young but wise beyond his years. He had witnessed a lot in his war-torn community, and had lost most of his family members in the ongoing turmoil. He lived in a refugee camp, and from all appearances, he did not have a very promising future. Marlin was not deterred by his bleak prospects. He had learned to trust God.

Instead of spending his days worrying, Marlin went about the refugee camp relieving the suffering of the children and the elderly. He was a ray of sunshine and a breath of fresh air around the camp. Marlin's bright and helpful disposition caught the attention of visiting officials, who are now helping him accomplish his educational goals. He is eager to gain the knowledge and skills to help the people of his impoverished community. He is dedicated to the mission of relieving human suffering, and sharing the love and hope that he found in Jesus.

Words of Love: You ask and do not receive, because you ask amiss, that you may spend it on your pleasures. James 4:3

DAY 263
HIS PEACE FOR YOUR WORRIES

Scripture: Be anxious for nothing, but in everything by prayer and supplication, with thanksgiving, let your requests be made known to God; and the peace of God, which surpasses all understanding, will guard your hearts and minds through Christ Jesus. Philippians 4:6-7

Worry kills. We need peace. This was Monique's sentiment, as she walked out the hospital's waiting room door. She and the family paced the hospital floor, anxiously awaiting the outcome of their loved one's surgery. It was a long and tedious procedure, and the prognosis for a successful outcome was only fifty percent.

Most of the family members did not profess Christ as their Lord, and without His abiding peace they worried incessantly. Some were so tense that they themselves were becoming ill. Monique knew Jesus personally, and she tried to share her faith and confidence in Him, and to encourage the others to trust Him.

Midway through the procedure, one of the medical team came with an update, and left with this parting word: pray. Monique invited the family to the chapel next door, where they prayed to the Great Physician. Some prayed silently, others who had never prayed publicly pleaded with God for mercy. Monique thanked God for His divine power over illnesses, and asked Him for peace for the family.

The waiting became easier, and the surgery was successful, leading to a full recovery. Many of those family members are now enjoying a closer walk with Jesus, and they credit the turning point to be the peace they felt in that hospital chapel when they surrendered their worries to Jesus.

What is on your heart today? What is causing you to lose sleep tonight? Exchange your worries for the peace that Jesus gives. Sing the words of the beautiful song, Wonderful Peace, by Warren D. Cornell: "Peace, peace, wonderful peace; Coming down from the Father above. Sweep over my spirit, forever, I pray; In fathomless billows of love," and feel the peace and calm that floods your being.

Words of Love: Peace I leave with you, My peace I give to you; not as the world gives do I give to you. Let not your heart be troubled, neither let it be afraid. John 14:27

DAY 264
THE LAMB WHO DIED IS THE LORD WHO LIVES

Scripture: Behold! The Lamb of God who takes away the sin of the world! John 1:29

They nailed Him to a cross, thinking it was the end of His ministry, but Christ's death was the beginning of His heavenly role as our Lord and Redeemer. "He is risen; the grave could not hold Him down."

For thirty pieces of silver, Judas betrayed Him. He never defended Himself, though He could have summoned the forces of heaven to His rescue. He was interrogated like a common criminal, but like a lamb to the slaughter, He answered them not a word. He knew that He would have His time to speak, when before His throne, they would one day stand.

The roles will be reversed. He will have plenty to say as the books are opened, and both their deeds and the opportunities for salvation that they spurned are revealed. Christ's justice will silence them. There will be no need for pleas of mercy, as probation will be closed. Their fates will have been sealed, and now they will be standing before the Lord of the universe to receive their just reward.

While there is still mercy, let us fall on Him and plea for pardon. He will not turn a deaf ear to the cries of repentance.

Words of Love: Behold, I stand at the door and knock. If anyone hears My voice and opens the door, I will come in to him and dine with him, and he with Me. Revelation 3:20

DAY 265

OVERCOMING OR BECOMING?

Scripture: For whatever is born of God overcomes the world. And this is the victory that has overcome the world—our faith. 1 John 5:4

I read an article which included the two concepts, overcoming and becoming, as being at opposite ends of the spectrum. The author stated that it was negative fear-based thinkers who focused on overcoming, while positive freedom-based thinkers focused on becoming. It is true that when our feelings are based on fear, there is a constant struggle to overcome something. It is also true that freedom-based thinkers see every day as a new beginning, an opportunity for a fresh start.

Our Creator is a God of abundance, and He desires to bestow good things on us, but we have to partner with Him in this endeavor. Fear has the ability to prevent us from becoming the person that God created us to be.

When I was contemplating the purchase of my first house, I knew I needed an additional source of income, so I worked for a company that paid me less than one-fifth of what they charged clients for my services. I was grateful for the opportunity, and understood quite well that it was a for-profit organization. Twenty-one years later I was offered a position by the same company, for little more than the wages of those yesteryears. I finally knew my worth, however, and I negotiated elsewhere, getting compensated for my education and experience. Declining was not because I had overcome and moved beyond those hard times, but because I had grown and become the person God had created and prepared me to be. I finally knew my value in my Father's eyes. Our journey may have begun by "overcoming," but we have the opportunity to grow into "becoming."

Words of Love: For I know the thoughts that I think toward you, says the Lord, thoughts of peace and not of evil, to give you a future and a hope. Jeremiah 29:11

DAY 266

IF RICHES WOULD CHANGE ME

Scripture: Search me, O God, and know my heart; Try me, and know my anxieties; And see if there is any wicked way in me, and lead me in the way everlasting. Psalm 139:23-24

A friend said he begged God that if riches would change him, not to give him any. God heard and answered his prayer by keeping him poor of this world's wealth. How many of us, knowing the scripture which asks the question, "What does it profit a man to gain the whole world, but lose his soul?" would earnestly beg God to keep us poor if riches would change us, and cause us to lose out on eternity?

In the story of the widow's mite, in Mark 12:41-44, we are told that other worshippers gave of their abundance, but the widow, out of her poverty, gave all that she had to live on. Another scripture states that it is easier for a camel to go through the eye of a needle, than for a rich man to enter heaven.

Greed makes it difficult for us to part with wealth. It is easier to give up one tenth of a dollar or even a hundred dollars, than it is to part with the same tenth of a larger sum, such as a million or ten million. That large amount of money seems too much to give away, but it is the God of the universe, in His generosity, who opened the opportunity for us to achieve all that we have, great or small. If the wealth hasn't changed us, we will open our hands to give back freely what has been so graciously given to us. It is into the open hands from which we give that God pours even more riches.

Words of Love: For the love of money is a root of all kinds of evil, for which some have strayed from the faith in their greediness, and pierced themselves through with many sorrows. But you, O man of God, flee these things and pursue righteousness, godliness, faith, love, patience, gentleness. 1 Timothy 6:10-11

DAY 267
WALKING IN HIS AMAZING GRACE

Scripture: For by grace you have been saved through faith, and that not of yourselves; it is the gift of God, not of works, lest anyone should boast. Ephesians 2:8-9

The following are among some of the beautiful songs about God's grace. I encourage you to obtain the lyrics and sing them throughout the day:
- Amazing Grace, by John Newton
- My Chains Are Gone, I've Been Set Free, By Chris Tomlin
- Grace Greater Than Our Sin, by Julia H. Johnston

Camille spent her late teens and early adulthood dedicated to serving God. No one knows what happened, because she refused to talk about it, but in her early thirties, she walked away from her Christian faith, and embraced the ways of the world. She behaved as though she was making up for lost time in the world.

I met Camille when we both taught at a local high school. She was smart, polished, and very well liked, but she had a wild and unstable character. There was a battle waging within her. Something in the world was pulling her in one direction, and Jesus Christ was gently pulling her back towards Him.

God's tender love finally won Camille's heart for the second time, and she surrendered to His mercy and kindness. For the remainder of her tenure at the school, she faithfully walked in God's grace, and demonstrated what that walk can and should look like. We lost contact when we both moved to pursue our career goals, but I am looking forward to reuniting with Camille around God's throne, where the evidence of His amazing grace will be fully manifested.

Words of Love: And of His fullness we have all received, and grace for grace. John 1:16

DAY 268
PRAY FIRST

Scripture: And whatever you ask in My name, that I will do, that the Father may be glorified in the Son. If you ask anything in My name, I will do it. John 14:13-14

I attended a screening of the powerful movie, **War Room**, and left with a coin on which was inscribed the words, "Pray First." This was but a reminder of what all Christians should already practice routinely.

If we prayed first, we would worry less. Prayer relinquishes our hold on the situation, and places it squarely on the shoulders of the Mighty Deliverer, Jesus Christ. He has proven Himself by healing broken hearts, and setting captives free, so I know He can handle any problems I have. I only have to pray and trust.

This practice of praying first is not the normal human tendency. We are hard wired to jump into action, often before processing the whole scenario first. In fact, with our limited perspective, we cannot process the whole scenario. Without all the information, is it any wonder that we so often fail? Failure then frustrates us, and we either give up or we flounder, with much worry, until we wear ourselves out.

Jesus sees the big picture. He knows the end. Let us commit all our needs to Him in prayer. Nothing is too hard for Him. Remember, He is only a prayer away.

Words of Love: Ask, and it will be given to you; seek, and you will find; knock, and it will be opened to you. Matthew 7:7

DAY 269
WHATEVER YOU ARE, BE A GOOD ONE

Scripture: And whatever you do, do it heartily, as to the Lord and not to men, knowing that from the Lord you will receive the reward of the inheritance; for you serve the Lord Christ. Colossians 3:23-24

Denny griped a lot about his work: they didn't appreciate him; he was worth more; he was tired of his position, which in his eyes was the lowest on the totem pole. One day, Denny complained to an older gentleman, who was a father-figure and mentor. Denny valued this highly respected Christian gentleman's opinion, and when he spoke Denny listened, even when the advice was not something he was eager to hear.

On this particular day, the older gentleman, who was tired of hearing Denny's complaints, invited him over to his home so they could talk. Denny gratefully accepted the gracious invitation. After a lovely dinner, prepared by the gentleman's wife; the gentleman invited Denny to his study for conversation over coffee.

It did not take very long for the conversation to get around to Denny's unhappiness with his job. The gentleman listened to Denny's frustrations, then he asked him a series of questions. One poignant question was, "Denny, do you believe you are good at the job you currently do?" The question took Denny by surprise and threw him off guard. "Be very honest now," the gentleman added.

After Denny got his composure back, he responded that he could be better, but he blamed it on his dissatisfaction with his situation. The wise mentor looked Denny in the eyes and said to him, "I have one piece of advice for you: 'whatever you are, be a good one.'"

Denny left his friend's home that evening with those words ringing in his ears. He pondered them, and changed his attitude toward his work. As he excelled in his duties, management began to take notice. In time, Denny was promoted; and he continued to excel in each new assignment. Denny climbed to the top of the company, all because his perspective was redirected, and he began to bloom wherever he was planted.

Words of Love: Whatever your hand finds to do, do it with your might; for there is no work or device or knowledge or wisdom in the grave where you are going. Ecclesiastes 9:10

DAY 270
TO DIE FOR

Scripture: Fight the good fight of faith, lay hold on eternal life, to which you were also called and have confessed the good confession in the presence of many witnesses. 1 Timothy 6:12

The young man was only thirty years old, and he had spent half of his life in prison. The Holy Spirit drew him to some evangelistic meetings being held in the neighborhood, upon his release from prison. When he heard the personal testimonies that people shared, something stirred within him and he gave his life to Jesus Christ. The preacher studied with him and he requested baptism.

Jonas confided to the preacher, after the date was set for his baptism, that it was not easy to leave a gang. "Pastor," Jonas said, "they may kill me, but my decision to walk with Christ is firm." Those words were a self-professing prophecy, as two days before his baptism, Jonas was gunned down by members of his gang who felt he was a traitor for planning to leave the gang.

Jonas joins the thief on the cross, who was promised a place in God's kingdom, and Christians through the ages who have been faithful to the end. They will rise in the first resurrection, to spend eternity with the Savior. It is not how you begin the race of life, but how you end it, that counts. Jonas' start in the race left much to be desired, but he made it to the finish line with Jesus by His side.

How willing are you to die for your faith? Eternity with Christ is worth dying for, and there are many who, like most of the apostles of old, and Jonas, paid the ultimate price. There is something intriguing about a willingness to die for your faith. However horrendous the prospect, these committed followers faced it with grace, knowing that to die for Christ is great gain.

I am praying to be more than talk, to be willing to take my stand for righteousness, and die rather than deny my Lord and Savior. This level of self-surrender is required of all His followers. There is no straddling the fence.

Words of Love: Stand firm, and you will win life. Luke 21:19 (NIV)

DAY 271
WORRIER OR PRAYER WARRIOR?

Scripture: Don't worry about anything; instead, pray about everything. Tell God what you need, and thank him for all he has done. Philippians 4:6 (NLT)

You have probably heard or read stories of God's miraculous intervention, when people prayed. At first, Myrna did not pray; she was a worrier. She worried about everything, to the point where her worrying was becoming very debilitating. It was hard for her to grasp that it was not her worrying that brought about the breakthrough with Christ, instead it was prayer. She even worried whether or not she should be worried.

There was a traumatic event in Myrna's life that brought things to a head. Family and friends knew that this would either completely break her, or it would be the catalyst to restore her to wholeness, and it was. It drove Myrna to her knees, where she wrestled with God about her own issues and those of others.

Myrna began to see results from her prayers: people were healed; relationships were restored; hurts were forgiven; broken hearts were mended; and hardened hearts were broken. Myrna the worrier had become Myrna the prayer warrior.

Words of Love: Therefore, do not worry, saying, 'What shall we eat?' or 'What shall we drink?' or 'What shall we wear?' Matthew 6:31

DAY 272
DO MORE THAN JUST SURVIVE: THRIVE

Scripture: I have come that they may have life, and that they may have it more abundantly. John 10:10

We were meant to thrive, not just survive. Caleb understood this very well, so he maintained a positive and upbeat attitude. His faith was constantly being tested, but he purposed in his heart to live his life to the fullest, in Christ. He was in his late teens when tragedy struck his family, causing what was once a stable and happy family to crumble. It looked like his dreams of college and the pursuit of an engineering degree were going to be an unlikely reality. Friends told him, "Man, you will survive;" but at the back of his mind was the constant thought: "Caleb, you were meant to thrive, not merely survive."

The months that followed the family tragedy were very bleak for Caleb, but the thought was never out of his mind, "You were meant to thrive, not merely survive." A year passed, and then two, and when depression threatened, Caleb drew strength from that thought which would not leave his head. Then two-and-a-half years after the tragedy, God opened a window through which Caleb crawled. Then He opened a door, and then another. Those years of waiting had made Caleb "hungry" for opportunities, and when they came, he seized them.

Caleb focused on his goals; something he might not have done as well had he began his program of studies earlier. He was bright and disciplined, and with the guidance of faculty whose favor he had gained, Caleb completed an accelerated program in record time. He went on to do an MD/PhD, became a professor and researcher, and influenced many young minds.

Caleb credits his success to the foundation of faith, discipline, and trust in God that his parents had laid, and a loving Jesus who walked beside him all the way. He is a living testimony to the fact that a partnership with Christ will produce results beyond mere survival. You will thrive, blossom, and bear fruit to God's glory.

Words of Love: These things I have spoken to you, that in Me you may have peace. In the world, you will have tribulation; but be of good cheer, I have overcome the world. John 16:33

DAY 273
WALKING ALONE OR FOLLOWING THE CROWD?

Scripture: I have been crucified with Christ; it is no longer I who live, but Christ lives in me; and the life which I now live in the flesh I live by faith in the Son of God, who loved me and gave Himself for me. Galatians 2:20

It is better to walk alone than to follow a crowd going the wrong way. Walking alone can be very lonely, however, if you are not well grounded and confident in the knowledge that an unseen army walks beside you.

June was in an uncomfortable position. The wrath of the group settled on her like an ominous cloud, and she felt their anger and disdain at every turn. She was singled out with falsehoods, and denied the opportunity to properly defend herself. "Guilty as charged," seemed to be the verdict with every accusation. There was no justice for her, yet she was committed to standing for what she knew to be right and just.

There were many days when she cried quietly; and sometimes not so quietly. Her health suffered, and her family and friends became quite concerned. What recourse did she have? She must be wrong, some thought. She was the only one who was willing to take a stand. When it seemed like she was alone, her unseen Friend made His presence felt by whispering words of comfort and encouragement. He gave her the strength to carry on.

The crowd was wrong, and she maintains her confidence in the One who went to Calvary to right all wrongs and deliver justice. He went to the cross alone; all others fled and denied Him. He knows the agony of standing alone, but knew He would stand for truth even if the heavens fell. It is His example which enables you to stand alone instead of following the crowd heading in the wrong direction.

Words of Love: You shall not follow a crowd to do evil; nor shall you testify in a dispute so as to turn aside after many to pervert justice. Exodus 23:2

DAY 274
LOVE, NOT JUDGE!

Scripture: Judge not, and you shall not be judged. Condemn not, and you shall not be condemned. Forgive, and you will be forgiven. Luke 6:37

In God's eyes, there are no little sins or big sins. The scripture is quite emphatic that if we break one of God's commandments, we are guilty of all. The scripture also says that we have all sinned and come short of the glory of God. That leaves me begging for mercy, because my righteousness is truly like filthy rags. Without the blood of Jesus Christ to wash our sin-stained lives, you and I would not stand a chance of being saved.

Thank God, that although my Savior hates my sins, His love is so far-reaching that His mercy reached me in the depths of my degradation. If you are saved, that is what He did for you as well, and that is what it will take for everyone to be saved. Yes, Christ hates the sin, but O, how He loves each sinner.

When I am tempted to be Pharisaical, I am reminded of the two men who stood in the synagogue praying. The scripture talks about one being very self-righteous, saying he was glad that he was not like the other man. That "other man," recognizing that he had fallen short, asked for mercy and forgiveness; and went home more justified than the self-righteous Pharisee.

Mother Theresa said, "If you judge people, you have no time to love them." I will add that if you spend time loving them, you won't have time to judge them. Christ reaches down and takes hold of us where we are, but thankfully He does not leave us in the sin-sick state He finds us. He cleans us up and says, "Go and sin no more." He who created us is the one who saves us, and He is the only One who can judge us. So, in spite of my sin, love me, and let Him judge me.

Words of Love: Love suffers long and is kind; love does not envy; love does not parade itself, is not puffed up. 1 Corinthians 13:4

DAY 275
NO MISTAKES

Scripture: When I consider Your heavens, the work of Your fingers, the moon and the stars, which You have ordained, what is man that You are mindful of him, and the son of man that You visit him? For You have made him a little lower than the angels, and You have crowned him with glory and honor. Psalm 8:3-5

We all have different features, unique in every way. He said He made no mistakes, so how dare us to try to redesign the work He calls perfect? It must have been a dream, because I was being moved from room to room. "It's a hospital," I thought. No. Then it is a school. No. Is it a business complex? No. Then, it must be a church.

Everywhere I looked, I saw "different." Different? Yes, unique differences. Different shapes, different skin tones, different hair colors and textures, different eye colors and shapes. Listen, there is talking: but the languages and accents are all different. Look at the activities and interactions: they like different things, and they have different tastes. There were even those who required different levels of assistance to function.

I was tempted to ask the point of this tour, but then I looked in His eyes, and I saw the tenderness with which He viewed everyone. He loved and valued them just the way they were. Then He turned back to me and said, with such longing in His voice, "If you are called by My name, you will love them like I do, just the way they are."

The scene vanished from my view, confirming it was only a dream, but it was more than just a dream: It was a lesson in acceptance. If I am His disciple, called by His name, "Christian," then I must view all of His creation through His eyes of love. He made no mistakes when He selected the special characteristics unique to you or to me. He said, "You are as I intended you to be. You are one of a kind; and you are Mine."

Words of Love: Therefore, you shall be perfect, just as your Father in heaven is perfect. Matthew 5:48

DAY 276
IN PURSUIT OF HAPPINESS

Scripture: Do not fret because of evildoers, nor be envious of the workers of iniquity. For they shall soon be cut down like the grass, and wither as the green herb. Trust in the Lord, and do good; Dwell in the land, and feed on His faithfulness. Delight yourself also in the Lord, and He shall give you the desires of your heart. Psalm 37:1-4

What would it take to make you happy? What price are you willing to pay to achieve this "happiness"? Do you seek God's guidance before your relentless pursuit of the happiness you so greatly desire?

What do the answers to the questions above tell you about yourself and your relationship with the Father? Are you on the right path to achieving your desired goal, and if not, what will it take to build the intimacy you need with Him to achieve true and lasting happiness? These questions are not intended to be an inquisition, but to create an awareness of the process, and provide a means for honest self-assessment.

Christ desires your happiness, and He knows that you will never achieve true happiness outside of a relationship with Him. Happiness is not achieved from the many good things that the Father places in your path: not wealth or health; not beauty or brains; not pleasure or treasure; not friendships or fame. Absolutely nothing external will fill the void within.

My visit to the Waldensian Valley, in Torre Pellice, Italy, and the opportunity to trace the history of the Waldensians, have given me a new appreciation for the pure joy found in a true relationship with Jesus. These Christians endured significant hardships. Their happiness was found in serving Christ, and theirs was the testimony of a relationship in which no sacrifice was too great, and no hardship too much to endure for Him. Yes, true happiness is possible in a life totally committed to Christ.

Words of Love: For I know the thoughts that I think toward you, says the Lord, thoughts of peace and not of evil, to give you a future and a hope. Jeremiah 29:11

DAY 277

BY BEHOLDING WE ARE CHANGED

Scripture: But we all, with unveiled face, beholding as in a mirror the glory of the Lord, are being transformed into the same image from glory to glory, just as by the Spirit of the Lord. 2 Corinthians 3:18

The story is told of a reclusive bachelor, whose life had fallen into a slump. On his occasional trip into town, he always stopped and admired a beautiful vase in a window display. The business owner observed his admiration of the vase and asked him why he didn't just buy it. At first, he resisted, but with the encouragement that he could have it to admire whenever he liked, he eventually purchased the beautiful vase.

The reclusive bachelor found a place of honor on the mantle for this choice possession. Then a strange thing happened: suddenly he noticed the dust on the mantle, and the chipped paint on the wall behind the mantle. He dusted the mantle and painted the wall, then he noticed other repairs that had been neglected for years. One by one the repairs were made, and the home looked like new. The recluse began to take better care of himself, and even became more neighborly.

If a beautiful vase could inspire such change in one man's life, just imagine the change that can and will take place when we look upon Jesus and behold the beauty of His character. There is a song which references the transformation that takes place when we survey the cross on which our Lord and Savior died, and contemplate what it means to our salvation.

There are wonderful blessings that come to those who have the presence of God with them. If we want transformation in our lives, let us keep our eyes fixed on the Savior. By beholding His character, we will be transformed into His likeness.

Words of Love: And the glory which You gave Me I have given them, that they may be one just as We are one. John 17:22

DAY 278
THE WRONG DOOR

Scripture: Look to Me, and be saved, all you ends of the earth! For I am God, and there is no other. Isaiah 45:22

The tour group that my husband and I were a part of was visiting the Sistine Chapel in Rome. I was getting sicker by the moment, having caught some bug which caused many uncomfortable symptoms. The smart thing to do would have been to stay behind in the hotel, but I had come too far and paid too much to miss out on the total experience, so I went along with the group.

The shoulder-to-shoulder crowd in the Sistine Chapel had become overwhelming. I became clammy with cold sweat and was near fainting. My husband led me out as I became somewhat disoriented. Our tour guide had clearly said we would exit at a door on the right, but I chose to ask directions of a security officer, who did not ask where I was trying to go, but simply directed us to the main exit. That caused us a thirty-minute delay in reconnecting with the group, and missing the inside tour of St Peter's Basilica.

There are many paths in life that lead to some destination, but Christ is the only way that leads to eternal life. He is the door to the Father, and His instructions are very clear on how to gain access. It behooves us to follow His loving instructions. Stop asking others for directions along the way, because they do not have the same interest in our ultimate goal. Life's trials may make us sick and faint, but we should never get weary. We should not follow the crowd or let them overwhelm us to the point of disorientation. It is Satan's tactic to distract us. He tells us that any door will get us to our destination. Don't believe his lies. You lose precious time, miss out on many blessings, and if not for the grace and mercy of God, you could completely lose your way and miss out on eternity.

Words of love: In all your ways acknowledge Him, and He shall direct your paths. Proverbs 3:6

DAY 279
AN ALL-FORGIVING GOD

Scripture: If we confess our sins, He is faithful and just to forgive us our sins and to cleanse us from all unrighteousness. 1 John 1:9

"No ifs, ands, or buts; our God is an all-forgiving God." This was an emphatic statement made by one member of a touring music group to the rest of the team.

"You speak as one with experience," another team member ribbed.

"I bet, if we think about it honestly, every born-again Christian can make that statement emphatically," the first student responded.

One of the chaperones decided to join the conversation for some mature perspective, and what followed was a deep, heart-searching discussion on why Jesus was so forgiving.

When God created man, He desired to have an intimate relationship with him. He spent time communing with Adam and Eve in the garden, daily. Sin entered, however, and short-circuited this relationship. The disobedient pair hid from God when He came for His usual visit with them.

God knew the likelihood of sin and disobedience entering mankind, because of the power of choice He had given them. He had a plan in place to save His creation, should they go down this wrong path. Because of His great love and forgiveness, He chose not to totally annihilate humanity and start over, though He certainly had the power to do so.

Words of Love: For by grace you have been saved through faith, and that not of yourselves; it is the gift of God, not of works, lest anyone should boast. Ephesians 2:8-9

DAY 280
CAPTAIN OF MY SHIP

Scripture: For it was fitting for Him, for whom are all things and by whom are all things, in bringing many sons to glory, to make the captain of their salvation perfect through sufferings. Hebrews 2:10

My brother learned to sail at a very early age, and eventually became a sailboat captain. I was never privileged to sail with him, but I believe, from all reports, that he was good at what he did.

There is one Captain, however, whom I would sail with any day, and I have asked Him to be the Captain of my life. The waterways of planet earth are too treacherous for me to trust my life to anyone else. Captain Jesus knows how best to navigate every channel, and even when the waves are high and threatening to capsize us, I am confident in His ability to bring us safely to harbor.

With Jesus as the Captain of my ship, I can lie down in peace and sleep, for He will keep me safe. I am going to the stern to take a nap. When I awake, I know He has some work for me to do, but it certainly won't be bailing water or lowering the sails. He's got that.

Words of Love: He makes me to lie down in green pastures; He leads me beside the still waters... Psalm 23:2-3.

HEARD, ACKNOWLEDGED, UNDERSTOOD

Scripture: But now God has set the members, each one of them, in the body just as He pleased. And if they were all one member, where would the body be... And if one member suffers, all the members suffer with it; or if one member is honored, all the members rejoice with it. Now you are the body of Christ, and members individually. 1 Corinthians 12:18-27

Early in my career, I worked with a colleague who could not stand for anyone to disagree with her. She would hold a grudge and be mad at you for days. I was very new to my position and she was my senior. I respected her position, because although our qualifications were the same, I valued her knowledge in the particular duties we performed. Even though my experience was varied and extensive, I was still a rookie on this job and had much to learn.

I sat down with my colleague one day and I said, "We are both educated adults, and qualified to perform the work we do. We are independent thinkers, not robots, so we will likely disagree on some issues. However, disagreement does not have to result in discord. Let us listen and try to understand each other, respectfully acknowledging each other's point of view, even when we don't agree." Thing got better after that.

We all want to be heard, understood and acknowledged. I believe it is a God-given need, if not a right, which should not be denied any human being. I recall, growing up as a very young child, telling my mother as she whipped me for challenging a wrong point of view: "I am a person, please hear me out before you decide that what I am saying is wrong." In essence, I was begging to be heard, understood and acknowledged. People are so deprived of these needs that it leads some to depression and suicide.

God has placed us in families and communities, because He knew that human beings have these needs. Let us learn to embrace each other, and help each other thrive as individuals with unique, innate abilities. We will be a stronger family, workplace, community, nation and world when we do.

Words of Love: As each one has received a gift, minister it to one another, as good stewards of the manifold grace of God. 1 Peter 4:10

DAY 282

REJOICE!

Scripture: Now after the Sabbath, as the first day of the week began to dawn, Mary Magdalene and the other Mary came to see the tomb... But the angel answered and said to the women, "Do not be afraid, for I know that you seek Jesus who was crucified. He is not here; for He is risen, as He said. Come, see the place where the Lord lay." Matthew 28:1-6

Christ's resurrection is something to rejoice about. Even after His death, Satan was trying to distort the truth about His body being absent from the grave. So that no one would believe He had fulfilled what He said, that in three days He would rise, they tried to concoct stories about His body being removed by His disciples.

Christians know the truth, however. Jesus Christ, our Lord and Savior, has indeed risen. The grave could not hold Him. His resurrection confirmed that the victory to secure our salvation had been won. Can you imagine the futility His death would have been, if He remained in the grave? His resurrection provided the assurance that if we confess our sins, and ask His forgiveness, those who die in Christ will rise in the first resurrection. This is reason for rejoicing.

I am moved to tears whenever I reflect on what Jesus Christ bore to ensure my salvation. He took what was ours, so we could have what was His. This is reason to rejoice.

Words of Love: He is not here, but is risen! Remember how He spoke to you when He was still in Galilee. Luke 24:6

DAY 283
LIVING HOLY LIVES

Scripture: But you are a chosen generation, a royal priesthood, a holy nation, His own special people, that you may proclaim the praises of Him who called you out of darkness into His marvelous light. 1 Peter 2:9

How can I live in His presence, beholding His beautiful character day after day, and remain the same as before I met Him? It is not possible. I will either begin to take on His characteristics, or they will irritate me so that I will walk away from following Him.

The beautiful lyrics of the song Turn Your Eyes Upon Jesus by Helen H. Lemmel in 1922 say, "Turn your eyes upon Jesus, look full in His wonderful face; and the things of earth will grow strangely dim, in the light of His glory and grace." Wow, I will lose interest in the things of this world. They will no longer hold an overpowering attraction for me. I will hunger and thirst after righteousness, and will not be satisfied, until Jesus fills me up.

I find myself very drawn to people who exemplify the character of Jesus Christ. They are the face of Christ to everyone they encounter, and it brings delight to see the light of Jesus shining forth from within them. I pray constantly for that same beauty of Jesus to be seen in me. I don't want to have a "holier than thou" attitude. I want to reflect His goodness, kindness, mercy, and love. I want to look at others with His eyes of compassion, and His spirit of forgiveness.

I pray that we will commit our ways to Him, and with the help of the Holy Spirit, endeavor to live holy lives; lives that reflect His beautiful character.

Words of Love: Therefore, as the elect of God, holy and beloved, put on tender mercies, kindness, humility, meekness, longsuffering. Colossians 3:12

DAY 284
SEPARATION ANXIETY

Scripture: Coming out, He went to the Mount of Olives, as He was accustomed, and His disciples also followed Him. When He came to the place, He said to them, "Pray that you may not enter into temptation..." Luke 22:39-46

It has been stated or implied in much Christian literature that our Lord and Savior did not die from the nails that crucified Him, but from a broken heart over the sins of humanity. Christ experienced separation from the Father, with whom He had shared an extremely close bond, because of the sins that He bore for us.

When Christ took on humanity, He depended on the Father for guidance every step of the way. He said His meat was to do the will of the Father. He was on a mission to restore lost humanity to God, who missed the communion He had with mankind in Eden.

Christ often spent entire nights alone with His Father, connecting with Him and obtaining strength for the journey. There had not been a time in His thirty-three-and-a-half years that He did not have access to the Father. Imagine then how He must have felt, facing the toughest decision of His life: to face Calvary, without the presence of His Loving Father.

Children face separation anxiety on the first day of school, be it kindergarten or college. The anxiety is often caused by the unknown. Christ, however, knew what He was facing, but He desired to do the Father's will.

There was no other way to save us from the death penalty of sin, so our Savior faced "The last mile of the way" alone; with the Father's face veiled from the sins of the world that He carried to Calvary. Christ's sacrifice is demonstrative of love beyond measure, and gratitude is to accept the priceless gift He has given us. We can say, in the words of the song When I Survey the Wondrous Cross by Isaac Watts: "Were the whole realm of nature mine, that were a present far too small; Love so amazing, so divine, demands my soul, my life my all."

Words of Love: Through the Lord's mercies we are not consumed, because His compassions fail not. Lamentations 3:22

DAY 285
WISDOM'S POWER

Scripture: If any of you lacks wisdom, let him ask of God, who gives to all liberally and without reproach, and it will be given to him. James 1:5

It is amusing to hear comments like, "He or she is so bright, but as foolish as they come." What I take from such comments is that the person, though having good book knowledge, does not exercise much common sense. That shows a lack of wisdom, but then, wisdom comes from God, with the guidance of the Holy Spirit to help you make right decisions.

In 2 Chronicles 1:11, God said to Solomon, "Since this is your heart's desire and you have not asked for wealth, possessions or honor, nor for the death of your enemies, and since you have not asked for long life, but for wisdom and knowledge to govern my people, over whom I have made you king; therefore, wisdom and knowledge will be given you. I will also give you wealth, possessions and honor, such as no king who was before you ever had, and none after you will have."

Two women had an issue between them concerning two infant boys; one dead and the other alive. Each woman claimed that the living infant was hers. Solomon offered a solution. He said to cut the child in two and give a half to each woman. The true mother was horrified at the decision, and agreed that the other woman could have her child, rather than any harm coming to him. The woman whose child was dead agreed with the horrible decision, saying that neither of them should have the child. Solomon in his wisdom knew immediately to which woman the infant belonged, and gave the infant to its true mother. This decision was shared throughout Israel as an example of the power of true wisdom.

Yes, there is power in God-given wisdom. This requires thoughtful and prayerful deliberation, and it is available to all who will allow the Holy Spirit to direct their thoughts and actions.

Words of Love: The fear of the Lord is the beginning of wisdom… Psalm 111:10

DAY 286
VICTORY IN JESUS

Scripture: For whatever is born of God overcomes the world. And this is the victory that has overcome the world—our faith. 1 John 5:4

Sometimes life throws us curve balls, and we think, "There is no way I can catch that and run with it." Sometimes it appears to be certain defeat, and you cry out, "Lord, am I ever going to make it?" Then the answer comes back, "Hold on tight to Jesus."

As a new follower of Christ, Amos felt all alone when his family and friends gave him a hard time about his newly found faith. He no longer enjoyed the places he used to go, the sights and sounds he used to view and listen to, and the activities he used to participate in. Now, he wanted to go to church, read the Bible and participate in ministries to help others.

Jesus Christ did not promise His followers a life without trials. In fact, He said we should take up our cross and follow Him. This request for unfailing commitment does come with one guarantee, however: He would accompany us to the battle front and secure our victory. We may not win every skirmish, but ultimate victory of the battle will be won by and for our Commander, Jesus Christ.

We must encourage all believers to stay strong and not give in to the pressures of the fight. There is nothing sweeter than a victory song: "O victory in Jesus, my Savior forever." Knowing that Satan has lost his grip on our lives, and we have been secured by the blood of Jesus, will be victory indeed.

Words of Love: Today, if you will hear His voice, do not harden your hearts. Hebrews 3:15

DAY 287
CHANGED INTO HIS IMAGE

Scripture: But we all, with unveiled face, beholding as in a mirror the glory of the Lord, are being transformed into the same image from glory to glory, just as by the Spirit of the Lord. 2 Corinthians 3:18

There is an American folk hymn, Lord I Want to be a Christian, sung by artists such as Fernando Ortega, with lyrics stating: "Lord, I want to be like Jesus, in my heart." Other stanzas exclaim that we should want to be more loving, and more holy, and if true followers of Christ and bearing His name, we should want to be Christians in our hearts. We have to be changed into His image for all these behaviors to take place, but what an exhilarating feeling it is when He is living out His life in us, and we are functioning in His likeness.

Another beautiful song, Live Out Thy Life Within Me, by Frances Havergal says, "Live out Thy life within me, O Jesus, King of kings, Be Thou Thyself the answer to all my questionings; Live out Thy life within me, in all things have Thy way. I, the transparent medium, Thy glory to display."

There is one more song that speaks to my heart regarding the condition of my life, and the need to be changed into Christ's image. It is the song, "Cover with His Life," with words and music written by Franklin E. Belden in 1899. The song says, "Look upon Jesus, sinless is He; Father impute His life into me. My life of scarlet, my sin and woe; covered with His life, whiter than snow."

O, how I want to be like Jesus, how I want to be covered with His pure life, and how I want Him to live out His life within me. Change is guaranteed when all these elements are in place, and I am trusting Him to answer the desire of my heart to have this transformation take place in my life.

Words of Love: Therefore, if anyone is in Christ, he is a new creation; old things have passed away; behold, all things have become new. 2 Corinthians 5:17

DAY 288
FATHER GOD

Scripture: "I will be a Father to you, and you shall be My sons and daughters," says the Lord Almighty. 2 Corinthians 6:18

Whenever I hear or read those two names of our Heavenly Father, "Father God" used together, it always brings a smile to my face and fond memories of a former pastor's wife. Several years ago, she spoke at a weekend retreat sponsored by our church's Women's Ministry Department. There was a special tenderness and awe with which she used that endearing name for the Creator, so that I have associated the endearment to her. It is as though she has put claim to it, and now owns it.

We can all stake the same claim to our loving Father, however, and every time we use the endearment, it should conjure up respect, love and adoration for the gift of His love to us. He loves us so much that He sent His Only Son, Jesus Christ, to bring us back home to Him. This journey requires some preparation, and the third person of the Godhead, the Holy Spirit, has been sent to help prepare us for the long-awaited trip home.

Father God is eager for our arrival, and like any loving dad who is waiting for his beloved children to come home from their travels, He cannot wait for us to turn the corner toward home. In our absence, He has been preparing our residence. No one on this earth can compare with the skills of the Master Builder: our beloved Father, God.

I wonder how much time I will spend in that beautiful mansion, however, because I will want to enjoy the delight of God's company forever. There will be so many questions to ask, and so much to learn, that it will take all eternity. My Abba, my Savior, my Jehovah, is mine and April Langley's Father God. I pray He is yours too.

Words of Love: The Lord has appeared of old to me, saying: "Yes, I have loved you with an everlasting love; Therefore, with lovingkindness I have drawn you." Jeremiah 31:3

DAY 289
HE'S TRUE TO HIS WORD

Scripture: The words of the Lord are pure words, Like silver tried in a furnace of earth, purified seven times. Psalm 12:6

If God can create the innate ability in a flock of birds to fly thousands of miles, across continents, to the same breeding site every year, He is a God I can trust to lead me on my life's path. My implicit trust is based on scripture, which says that heaven and earth would pass before one of His words would come back to Him void.

He is the kind of God who does not speak empty words. When He speaks, it is because He has something to say, and best of all, He is true to His word. The saying that "you can take it to the bank" can be tested on His words only. His Word is His honor; it is His character. When others will flip at the drop of a hat, you can bank on the Word of God. They are the same yesterday, today and forever.

I met a young woman many years ago who considered herself an agnostic. It was hard to have a conversation with her about anything, as she disputed almost everything. We crossed paths again several years later, and I reminded her of the fact that Jesus Christ does not change. His words stand true forever. She blew me off, but I noticed a softening in her stance. Then our paths crossed for the third time. There was excitement in her voice as she sought me out to tell me of her personal encounter with Jesus.

Had I not known God's desire to change lives, I would not believe this transformation possible. Jesus is true to His Word. He did not come for the righteous, if there is such, but to bring sinners to repentance. I believe Christ loves a challenge. The scripture says that those for whom He does more, loves Him more. I must therefore love Him with my whole heart, because He has done so much for me. If God says it, you can believe it. He is true to His Word... He cannot lie.

Words of Love: But the Helper, the Holy Spirit, whom the Father will send in My name, He will teach you all things, and bring to your remembrance all things that I said to you. John 14:26

DAY 290
REPENTANCE OR DESPAIR?

Scripture: And Peter remembered the word of Jesus... so he went out and wept bitterly. Matthew 26:75

When Judas, who had betrayed him, saw that Jesus was condemned, he was seized with remorse and returned the thirty pieces of silver to the chief priests and the elders. Matthew 27:3

On His way to Calvary, Jesus was betrayed by Judas for thirty pieces of silver. In despair, he returned the money when his plans fell apart, throwing the coins at the feet of the high priests, then going out and hanging himself. He acknowledged betraying innocent blood, but his heart never sought forgiveness of the One he had wronged; the One who called him friend, hoping he would turn to Him in repentance.

Peter was also heading down a slippery slope. He accompanied Jesus in the Garden of Gethsemane. Peter who, at supper, had vehemently stated that he would die with Christ before he would forsake Him. He was overconfident, with statements like: I will do this, and I will never do that. Peter drew his sword and cut off the ear of the servant of the authorities who came to arrest Jesus in Gethsemane.

Peter followed Jesus at a distance. He entered the judgment hall where Christ was being tried. There he fulfilled the words of Jesus, that he would deny Him three times before the rooster crowed. Before his final denial, Peter had been told that his speech gave him away; he spoke like one who walked with Jesus, so he tried to use language that would show a distinct separation.

Christ turned and looked deep into Peter's eyes. It was a look of love that reached into Peter's soul. Peter was confused at the events he was witnessing. How could that be happening to his Lord and Master? He cracked under the pressure and confusion, but he was remorseful and repentant. He accepted the love and forgiveness he saw in Jesus' eyes, and he who was weak in his denial of Christ became bold in proclaiming Him to the world. In the end, at his request, he was crucified like his Lord, but upside down.

Despair may be the result of regret at the outcome of events, but only repentance brings forgiveness and restoration. We all have free wills to choose our path, as did Peter and Judas. Choose repentance, and experience God's mercy and forgiveness.

Words of Love: Why do you sleep? Rise and pray, lest you enter into temptation. Luke 22:46

DAY 291
MINDFUL AWARENESS

Scripture: We then who are strong ought to bear with the scruples of the weak, and not to please ourselves. Let each of us please his neighbor for his good, leading to edification. For even Christ did not please Himself... Romans 15:1-13

Central to the new buzz phrase, Mindful Awareness, is the word "me," but life is certainly not all about me. I am not the center of the universe, with everything and everyone revolving around me. With Christ as my model, I must be about serving others.

As I sat on the sideline of a conversation between two business associates about the topic of mindful awareness, a verse of the beautiful song In Christ There Is No East or West, written by John Oxenham in 1908 came to mind. It says, "In Christ there is no east or west, in Him no north or south; but one great fellowship of love, throughout the whole wide earth."

Christ desires that in our interaction with each other, we demonstrate His selfless character. He was purposeful and intentional in His interaction with everyone He encountered, ever mindful of their needs and desiring their good. His followers must do nothing less.

Words of Love: Where there is neither Greek nor Jew, circumcised nor uncircumcised, barbarian, Scythian, slave nor free, but Christ is all and in all. Colossians 3:11

DAY 292
TELL ME, TEACH ME, INVOLVE ME

Scripture: Then Jesus said to those Jews who believed Him, "If you abide in My word, you are My disciples indeed." John 8:31

A quote which has been attributed to Benjamin Franklin states, "Tell me and I forget, teach me and I may remember, involve me and I learn." This quote reminds me of one by Edgar Guest which I often use: "I'd rather see a sermon than hear one any day; I'd rather one should walk with me than merely tell the way."

There is a common thread in both of the above quotes. They both require an investment of personal time. To involve one in an activity, you have to be personally engaged in some way yourself. To walk a path with someone requires that you take some steps as well.

During Christ's three-and-a-half-year ministry among His disciples, He employed all these teaching strategies. However, there was still something lacking in His followers. They jostled for position; doubted if Christ was really who He claimed to be; wondered at the miracles He performed; and questioned why He didn't do some things they thought He should do. They were unable to perform some of the miracles Christ sent them out to perform, some hated to see the valuable resources that were expended on the Master, and they feared for their own safety, among other things.

This was all to change after the Savior's death, resurrection and ascension, and following the outpouring of the Holy Spirit at Pentecost. The change was nothing short of miraculous. Those who were proud and self-centered became humble and self-sacrificing. The lessons Jesus shared through parables, miracles and personal interactions had finally taken root in the hearts of His disciples. They were now "sold" on the truth about the Savior, and were ready to give their lives to proclaim this truth.

Words of Love: And you shall know the truth, and the truth shall make you free. John 8:32

DAY 293
A POSITION OF TRUST

Scripture: And I said: "I pray, Lord God of heaven, O great and awesome God, You who keep Your covenant and mercy with those who love You and observe Your commandments, please let Your ear be attentive and Your eyes open, that You may hear the prayer of Your servant which I pray before You now, day and night..." Nehemiah 1:5-2:9

Nehemiah's position as cupbearer to King Artaxerxes was one of great trust. The cupbearer, in addition to serving wine to the king, was also an advisor. Nehemiah was a faithful servant, and had earned the king's favor, so when he became troubled about the fate of his fellow Jews and the city of Jerusalem, which lay in ruins, the king granted his request to go and rebuild the walls and restore the city.

God wants to entrust us with His resources. There is much soul winning to be accomplished. He wants to determine our faithfulness, because He knows if we are faithful in the little things, we will be faithful in much. Have we earned the Savior's trust? Have we used the blessings He has given us for His glory, or have we squandered them on things that are not of eternal value?

The king gave Nehemiah letters to the governors of the surrounding states, so he could obtain all the resources he needed for the work at hand. Nehemiah and his team lacked nothing to accomplish the job they had to do. Likewise, when by our diligence and faithfulness we have earned God's trust, He will make available to us what we need to accomplish the work entrusted to us.

We honor God when we are faithful to those we serve. Being good stewards earn us positions of trust, which bring glory to Christ's name. Like Nehemiah, let us fulfill the duties of our calling, so that God can use us to help build up His kingdom, and hasten His return.

Words of Love: Righteous lips are the delight of kings, and they love him who speaks what is right. Proverbs 16:13

DAY 294
FOR THIS I COULD HAVE SAVED ONE MORE

Scripture: For we are God's fellow workers; you are God's field, you are God's building. 1 Corinthians 3:9

The movie, **Schlinder's List**, tells the story of the factory owner who hired many Jews in order to save them. At the end of the war, he looked at possessions he had, and lamented, "For this I could have saved one more." I was very moved by the story, and in awe at the sincerity of a man who had done so much, putting himself at great risk, yet sensing that he could have done more.

I looked around me, as I watched the clip, and took mental note of my possessions. I felt compelled to ask myself the question, "How many more souls might I win for Christ, if I relinquish some of what I have?" Many of us desire to "build more barns" so that we can store up more stuff. It seems to give us a false sense of security and accomplishment to acquire more, and still more; be it one more pair of shoes, in a slightly different shade of the same color, or maybe just a different style or height heel. Or, maybe it is another car, for church and weekend activities. There is much work to be done, and Mr. Schlinder had the right mindset.

The only possession that will last through eternity is that which is used to advance the kingdom of God, by helping to spread the good news of His love, and drawing a dying world into the light of His truth. All the resources of the world belong to God, but in His mercy, He has allowed Believers to share in the ministry of servanthood, being His hands and feet, and His heart of love and compassion. Let us use what God has placed at our disposal to help save the world for Him.

Words of Love: We then, as workers together with Him also plead with you not to receive the grace of God in vain. 2 Corinthians 6:1

DAY 295
MY CONSTANT COMPANION

Scripture: I will never leave you nor forsake you. Hebrews 13:5

Jesus said that He would be with us always, even to the end of the age. He does this through the person of the Holy Spirit. Jesus said it was expedient that He go back to the Father, so that the Holy Spirit could come to us. He promised that when He, the Spirit, comes, He would be everything to us: teacher, guide, friend, counselor, encourager, healer of broken hearts and spirits, restorer of broken dreams.

Christ could only be in one place at a time, when He walked this earth in human form. As in the case of the death of His friend, Lazarus, Mary and Martha had to send for Him, and wait until He got there, traveling on foot. The Holy Spirit, on the other hand, is as close as a thought. What an amazingly kind and generous Lord, to have given us the gift of the third person of the Godhead to be our constant companion.

I am taking advantage of this companionship. In the midnight hour, I don't have to worry that I am interrupting His sleep, and I don't have to get upset that someone else has selfishly taken up all His time. Take all the time you need. He is available to me just as much as He is to you. Amazing! What an honor to have such a friend. My secrets are secure with Him. I will never hear them repeated. When I mess up, all I have to do is confess my wrongs, and He lovingly wipes the slate clean.

He is happy and rejoices at my successes, and He is available to share in my grief and sorrows, offering me a hand up, and guidance to improve the opportunities going forward. I cannot be any happier to have the Holy Spirit as my friend, always at my side. Thank You, loving Savior, for being true to Your Word. I love having the Holy Spirit on this journey with me. I would be lost without Him as my Constant Companion, Counselor, Guide and most wonderful friend.

Words of Love: "They will fight against you, but they shall not prevail against you. for I am with you," says the Lord, "to deliver you." Jeremiah 1:19

DAY 296
TOUCHING LIVES FOR ETERNITY

Scripture: Assuredly, I say to you, unless you are converted and become as little children, you will by no means enter the kingdom of heaven. Matthew 18:3

A friend shared a text message she received from a former student teacher. At the time of the communication this young lady was teaching kindergarten, and loving it. She had the following to say, "Some days I get emotional because our students are so innocent and, yes, poor; yet so street wise. I am blessed to be able to provide them with a foundation that will set them on the road to a better life."

Jesus loved children, and when He was on earth He rebuked His disciples who tried to block them from coming to Him. He said, "Suffer the little children to come unto me, and do not stop them, for of such is the kingdom of heaven." He touched the lives of young and old, but He had a special love for the innocent children. This young teacher is in good company.

You don't have to be a school teacher to touch a young life, though. You can help a child or youth in your community of faith or home community who needs some mentoring. You can volunteer to read to children in the schools. The children's division of most churches is usually short of teachers, so offer to help. Remember that the lives you touch, regardless of the age or the setting, may be of eternal significance.

Words of Love: But Jesus said, "Let the little children come to Me, and do not forbid them; for of such is the kingdom of heaven." Matthew 19:14

DAY 297
RECONCILED

Scripture: Now all things are of God, who has reconciled us to Himself through Jesus Christ, and has given us the ministry of reconciliation. 2 Corinthians 5:18

The dictionary defines reconcile as bringing to agreement or harmony; making compatible or consistent; to win over to friendliness or cause to become amicable. Sin has made us hostile toward God. Jesus Christ came to reconcile us to Him, to make us more responsive to His great love.

I don't know your experiences, but I have witnessed people spurning the love of others. If we are to be honest, we ourselves may have spurned the affections that others extended to us. I was only nineteen years old when a suitor sent me something I could not accept. I politely returned it to him, and received an apology.

Christ's love and mercy are never inappropriate. They are always for our good and should be accepted with gratitude. When we are drawn into the warm fellowship of God's family, He sends us out into a broken world, to help reconcile fallen humanity to Himself, and to each other.

The scripture says that if we bring our gifts to the altar, and the Holy Spirit brings to our minds that we are at odds with others, we should leave our gifts at the altar, go, and be reconciled to them; then return to the altar and present our gifts to the Father. Christ asks the question, "How can you say you love Me, whom you do not see, yet hate your brother, who you see?"

The summation of the commandments is that we should love God and our fellow man. Through the power of the Holy Spirit, Christ draws us to Himself. I pray that we will put aside all hostility and be at peace with God and man.

Words of Love: Therefore, if you bring your gift to the altar, and there remember that your brother has something against you, leave your gift there before the altar, and go your way. First be reconciled to your brother, and then come and offer your gift. Matthew 5:23-24

DAY 298
TRANSFORMED

Scripture: Create in me a clean heart, O God, and renew a steadfast spirit within me. Psalm 51:10

I don't like caterpillars. I suppose it is because of the way they move, lacking a backbone. I know these feelings are not shared by everyone, as we all have our preferences. On the other hand, there are not many people who do not enjoy butterflies. What makes the difference? I believe it is the transformation.

Have you ever known someone who was despicable when you first met them, and then something happened? Your jaws dropped and you questioned if this was the same person. Sometimes they themselves are amazed at their own transformation. That is the life-changing power of the Holy Spirit. He meets us where we are, but He does not leave us there. He breaks us, molds and reshapes us, and makes us into something brand new, something functional, that can then be used for God's glory.

If you are living a self-centered life, you need the Creator. The One who formed you is the only One who can transform you. He wants to wash you white by His shed blood, and make you brand new. Like the ugly caterpillar, now a beautiful butterfly; Christ will make us into His likeness, so that others will drop their jaws when they see His life being lived out in us. What a transformation that will be.

Words of Love: Therefore, if anyone is in Christ, he is a new creation; old things have passed away; behold, all things have become new. 2 Corinthians 5:17

SIN BY ANY NAME

Scripture: for all have sinned and fall short of the glory of God. Romans 3:23

I came across a sign that stated that we should not judge someone because they sin differently than we do. What is the message here? The scripture says that all have sinned and come short of God's glory. The scripture also says that there are no little sins and big sins in God's eyes. Finally, God says that judgment should be left to Him. He is the only One qualified to do so, because He is the only sinless one.

On a hot summer afternoon, I waited for my friend in the outer waiting room of the doctor's office. I passed the time watching the talk show being shown on one of the two television screens. I was amazed at the family drama being played out in the public arena.

There were accusations of abuse and infidelity, alcoholism and drug use. Fingers were pointed at each other, and each person minimized their sins as they elaborated on the sinfulness of the others. They all professed to know God, but the God of love and forgiveness was not being exhibited in their lives.

While there is truth to the words that "by their fruits you will know them," it is also true that man looks at the outward appearance, but God judges the heart. Sin by any name, description or degree in still spelled: Sin.

Words of Love: For the wages of sin is death, but the gift of God is eternal life in Christ Jesus our Lord. Romans 6:23

DAY 300
THE MIDNIGHT CRY

Scripture: And at midnight a cry was heard: 'Behold, the bridegroom is coming; go out to meet him!' Matthew 25:6

The pastor was preaching on the topic of the midnight cry, and I was very engrossed in his development of the subject. His central theme was about readiness, and he used the story of the ten virgins as the main characters. He said it was not unusual for wedding parties, during that historical period, to take a nap as they waited for the bridegroom and his entourage to arrive for the wedding ceremony. This might have seemed foreign to many in the congregation, because in most western cultures we are used to waiting for the bride.

What spoke to my heart, however, was the reminder that the five foolish virgins were not totally unprepared. The fact that they were not fully prepared made all the difference to them missing out on the marriage ceremony. Partial readiness will not gain us entrance into eternity. Christ does not want ninety-nine percent of our commitment. It is an all or nothing relationship that He desires. What does partial readiness look like, you might ask? Maybe going to church every time the doors are open; returning a faithful tithe, and supporting various causes; serving on multiple committees; and even going on mission trips, or supporting the missionary field work.

Those may all sound good to you, and you may be asking yourself, "What is missing? What else does God want?" What He wants is all of you and me. He wants hearts that are totally dedicated to Him, that put Him before everything else. He is not interested in sacrifice of things. What interests Him is the sacrifice of a broken spirit and a contrite heart. He wants us to be so in love with Him that we wait for Him with eagerness, with our eyes fixed on the eastern sky. When we are waiting with this kind of anticipation, the midnight cry will not take us by surprise.

Words of Love: Watch therefore, and pray always that you may be counted worthy to escape all these things that will come to pass, and to stand before the Son of Man. Luke 21:36

DAY 301
HOPE KEEPS THE "TICKER" GOING

Scripture: Eye has not seen, nor ear heard, nor have entered into the heart of man the things which God has prepared for those who love Him. 1 Corinthians 2:9

It was supposed to be a happy occasion. Rain had fallen most of the early morning, but the sun had come out, and with just the right wind, it was the perfect afternoon for a gathering of family and friends on the beach. Everyone was having a good time, when Lamont walked toward the water.

There was an unusual look about Lamont in those final moments. He appeared to be in a daze. It was a look that caused his friend Marvin to call after him. Lamont turned and looked at Marvin, just before he stepped into the deep water of the pier, never to resurface again, alive. "I cannot understand it," Marvin moaned, "he was an excellent swimmer, who once worked as a lifeguard."

Everyone looked on in disbelief, and immense sorrow. By all appearances, Lamont had so much to live for. He had beautiful family, a good job, and a host of friends. Word spread quickly around the island. A crowd gathered, and there were more questions on everyone's mind than there were answers.

As the days passed, and funeral arrangements were made, some semblance of Lamont's mind, in the days leading up to his death, began to surface. The pieces began to come together, and the culprit was determined to be a sense of hopelessness. He had simply lost the will to live. Hope is what keeps us going through the lonely valleys; having the assurance that there is sunshine on the other side of every dark cloud, and knowing that there is a special Friend who walks beside us. In the poem, "Footprints," we are reminded that the single set of footprints we see, when we can barely make the next step, does not mean we are walking alone. It means that we are being carried in the tender arms of the Savior. If only Lamont had that conviction, he might not have given up when he did. Never give up... with hope, it gets better.

Words of Love: Beloved, now we are children of God; and it has not yet been revealed what we shall be, but we know that when He is revealed, we shall be like Him, for we shall see Him as He is. 1 John 3:2

DAY 302
THE MANY FACES OF A MOTHER

Scripture: Children, obey your parents in the Lord, for this is right. Honor your father and mother, which is the first commandment with promise: that it may be well with you and you may live long on the earth. Ephesians 6:1-3.

It is said that when God wanted us to experience His great love for us, in a tangible and human way, He placed us in the arms of a mother. I remember my mother with great fondness, and those memories always bring a smile, sometimes a chuckle; and sometimes when the family gets together, much laughter. She was quite a disciplinarian, and I often felt her "wrath," which was not fun when it was being administered. My mother was the kindliest of women, always available to lend a hand, even to those who were not friendly towards her. She taught us to not hold grudges, and to leave vengeance to God. That has helped me very well throughout life.

Aunt Tine, as she was fondly called by family and close friends, had only an elementary school education. However, she read and wrote very well, mingled with those who were well educated, and exposed my siblings and me to books, always encouraging us to read. At a very early age, I developed such a love for books that I would often choose a book over a meal, reading late into the nights by the light of a kerosene lamp.

I recall tender moments during times of illness, when my mother would place a blanket on the floor, sit down beside me as I lay on the blanket, and cradle my head in her lap, as I groaned in pain. I often saw the tears in her eyes, as she softly cried with and for me. Those moments and many like them remind me of the tenderness of our loving Savior. He rejoices in our happiness, and grieves with us in our sorrows.

My mother, for all her love, could only do so much, but there is no limit to what God can do. When Jesus comes again and restores us to Himself, I want to linger awhile to gaze upon His face, and then I want to look into the face of my mother again. Her face of love will be the image of Christ reflecting from her. What a day of rejoicing that will be, when the faces of my Jesus and my mother, I see.

Words of Love: As one whom his mother comforts, so I will comfort you... Isaiah 66:13

DAY 303
MY ANXIETIES STYMIE ME

Scripture: Search me, O God, and know my heart; Try me, and know my anxieties. Psalm 139:23

Anxiety has a paralyzing effect. It feels like a hundred-pound brick has been tied to your feet, and you cannot go anywhere. There also appears to be a cloud or fog over your brain, preventing productive thought processes. How do you break free from this apparent paralysis? How do you turn the tide of this sinking feeling that threatens to drown you in despair?

Joni's story is a comfort to hurting hearts. It shows that there is healing, salvation and restoration in Jesus. Joni was successful, at least she had been, before her anxieties began to paralyze her. She lacked energy, wasn't eating well and rarely left her house, except for work. Then she began to withdraw from friends and associates. Her work began to be affected, as it required her to interact with others.

Eventually, Joni was told she had to get help or she would lose her job. Her friends encouraged her to check into a Christian retreat center, where a holistic and Christ-centered team approach was used to treat Joni's anxieties and the issues that developed, subsequent to her illness. Joni learned that she could not fight the demons of her past in her own strength, and when she relinquished the struggle to Jesus, she found relief.

Joni learned to stop making associations between everyone and everything in her present life, with someone or something from the past. She learned coping mechanisms and life skills that advanced her healing process. Most importantly, Joni found Jesus Christ, who became her Rock. All of us, in our own strength, can be stymied by the heavy burdens that sometimes back us into a corner. We often feel like running and hiding, but Jesus is waiting at the foot of the cross to wipe our beaded brows and calm our pounding hearts, so don't run away, run to Him. At the foot of the cross is where burdens are lifted, and true life begins. That is where Joni's began, and yours can, too.

Words of Love: Say to those who are fearful-hearted, "Be strong, do not fear! Behold, your God will come with vengeance, with the recompense of God; He will come and save you." Isaiah 35:4

DAY 304
PRAYER: IT'S THE BEST WE CAN DO

Scripture: Be anxious for nothing, but in everything by prayer and supplication, with thanksgiving, let your requests be made known to God... Philippians 4:6-7

The father was found slumped over in his chair, and unconscious, but by the grace of God and the good work of a medical team that responded quickly to the call, he survived. He was placed on a ventilator, and was unresponsive for several days. Family members later shared that the hospital chaplain, who knew the family well, came in to pray for the gentleman. A very distraught son exclaimed, "He needs to get out the way and let the professionals do their job. If that doesn't work, then he can pray."

We live in a world where people consider prayer as a last resort, but prayer is not the least we can do. For God's children, it should be the first thing we do. Before Christ performed any miracle, He prayed to the Father. We should do no less, and we should not be afraid of being ridiculed and scoffed at.

The network news had a field day when a prominent sports figure, who provided assistance to someone in a crisis, invited the presence and guidance of the Great Physician, Jesus Christ, at the onset of the emergency. Like the Good Samaritan, help was provided until the crisis was over, but prayer was the first step. We must remember that miracles happen when God's children pray.

Words of Love: Rejoicing in hope, patient in tribulation, continuing steadfastly in prayer. Romans 12:12

DAY 305
LIVING WORRY-FREE

Scripture: Look at the birds of the air, for they neither sow nor reap nor gather into barns; yet your heavenly Father feeds them. Are you not of more value than they? Matthew 6:26

What if you were to be given a million dollars today, without any strings attached? Would that allay all your worries and fears? What if you received a clean bill of health? Would that restore all your joy? And what if you had a great family: parents, spouse, children, siblings; and a great network of extended family and friends? Would that guarantee happiness? "Not necessarily," you might say. So, what guarantees a worry-free life? It is trust in the Almighty who is all-powerful, all-loving, merciful, kind, and gracious; the One who is patient and long-suffering; the One who has the power to still the winds and calm the waves. Yes, He is our only guarantee.

The story is told of a flight that became very bumpy along the way. Everyone was instructed to stay in their seats with their seatbelts securely fastened. Panic struck the passengers as the plane dipped and swayed, soared and dipped again. A child was observed calmly reading a book amid all this turmoil. During a period of temporary calm, she was questioned regarding her lack of concern for the danger they faced during the upheaval. She answered with confidence and pride, "My daddy is the pilot, and he is taking me home."

What confidence to have in our Heavenly Father. He never promised that the road would not be rocky, nor did He say the winds of strife would not blow. He never said that the sea would always be calm, or that the bushes would not have thorns on them. He never said sickness would not befall us, nor did He say death's sting would not come nigh us. What He did promise, however, is that He is coming back for us; coming to take us home.

Words of Love: Therefore, I say to you, do not worry about your life, what you will eat or what you will drink; nor about your body, what you will put on... Matthew 6:25

DAY 306
AN EXTRAORDINARY GOD

Scripture: The heavens declare the glory of God, and the firmament shows His handiwork. Psalm 19:1

The earth and the heavens above give evidence of an extraordinary God. What's the evidence, you may ask? Well, there are so many that time and space cannot record them. Let me identify a few, however, that bring a smile to my face:

- A baby's laughter. I saw a video of babies laughing, and I cannot recall it without an unexplainable joy filling my heart. There is so much innocence and pure delight in the smile or laughter of a baby.
- The beauty of fall, as well as springtime. Who but the Almighty, the Extraordinary God, can delight us with such beauty?
- The pure delight of a rainbow. On her way to work one morning, a friend and prayer partner sent the prayer team a picture of a rainbow she had just taken. There was this perfectly arched rainbow, as if it were caressing this high-rise building that houses a behavioral hospital. It was as if our Lord and Savior was saying, "All those within are mine, and I have them under My care." Amazing.
- The flower that closes up at night and opens brightly with the morning sun; or the flower that only blooms at nights. These are not coincidences; they are designed by the hands of an Extraordinary God who delights in bringing joy to the hearts, and smiles to the faces of His children. He never ceases to amaze me, and I believe we have seen nothing yet. I can hardly wait to explore the new heavens and new earth. What delights we have been promised.

Words of Love: "For My thoughts are not your thoughts, nor are your ways My ways," says the Lord. "For as the heavens are higher than the earth, so are My ways higher than your ways, and My thoughts than your thoughts." Isaiah 55:8–9

DAY 307

A PROMISE KEPT

Scripture: Let your conduct be without covetousness; be content with such things as you have. For He Himself has said, "I will never leave you nor forsake you." Hebrews 13:5

I visited my friend's sister in the hospital, and observed the dedication and care that my friend provided her. She had been in the hospital for six weeks when I visited again, and my friend had moved into the room with her, leaving for church and other necessary engagements when she had a family member or friend to relieve her. Why was she so faithful, some may ask? She was keeping a promise to her sister, to be there for her, if and when she needed her assistance or care. My friend was being true to that promise.

That family had even greater challenges ahead, as the sick sister was facing some life-altering surgeries. She was confident, however, that she could count on her sister and the promise she had made. That confidence gave her peace to face the difficult future.

My observation was another moment of reflection on the mercies and goodness of God, and His great love for us. We have His assurance that regardless of our circumstances, He will never leave us or forsake us. What a promise, and how wonderful to know that He keeps His promises.

If a promise between two sisters held so much weight, how much more confident we can be that Christ will never fail us. And He won't. This is the kind of God whom Christians serve; One who is true to His word, and keeps His promises.

Words of Love: Through the Lord's mercies we are not consumed, because His compassions fail not. They are new every morning; Great is Your faithfulness. Lamentations 3:22-23

DAY 308
OVER YONDER, DOWN BY THE CRYSTAL SEA

Scripture: We grow weary in our present bodies, and we long to put on our heavenly bodies like new clothing. 2 Corinthians 5:2 (NLT)

Besides sitting at the feet of Jesus, and learning from Him throughout eternity, have you contemplated what you might want to do in heaven? Well, one of my friends sent me a text with a picture of two beautiful fish they had just purchased for their new aquarium. Having grown up by the seaside, with the privilege of watching sea life, up close and personal, aquariums make me nostalgic.

As I sat and admired the tranquil scenery in the aquarium, with several colorful fish swimming by, the chorus of the song Over Yonder, written by Henry de Fluiter in 1918, flooded my mind: "Over yonder, down by the crystal sea; Over yonder, there's where I long to be. No more sorrow, toil, grief, nor care; In that homeland, bright and fair: Over, over there."

One of the great things about heaven, I believe, is that we will be able to pursue our individual interests: whether it is hanging out by the sea, scaling mountain peaks, wind gliding or exploring fascinating caves and caverns. We will have eternity to develop and enjoy multiple interests, but I don't think I will ever get tired of the beautiful underwater life. The scripture reminds us that eyes have not seen, nor ears heard what Christ has in store for us. I don't want to miss out on the adventure.

Words of Love: Behold, I tell you a mystery: We shall not all sleep, but we shall all be changed. 1 Corinthians 15:51

DAY 309
HE SPECIALIZES IN CLEANING UP MESSY LIVES

Scripture: I have not come to call the righteous, but sinners, to repentance. Luke 5:32

I have often heard people say, "When I get my life right, I am going to start going to church and living for Christ." I believe many of these people yearn for something better; they have a sincere desire for a different experience. The problem is that none of us can make ourselves right. We cannot clean up our own messes, but there is One who can. He specializes in cleaning up messes; He is in the business of restoration.

Jesus Christ is the best in the cleanup business. As a matter of fact, He is the only One who can do the job. He has the patent on the cleaning solution: His blood. It is the only thing that can wash away the stains of sin.

While you and I can do absolutely nothing to clean ourselves up, there is one thing that we alone can do. We have to give Jesus permission to do the dirty work for us. He delights in this kind of work. That was His sole purpose for coming to earth and taking on our humanity: to do this job for us that we cannot do for ourselves. All we have to do is cry out, "Lord Jesus, I long to be perfectly whole, I want you forever to live in my soul; break down every idol, cast out every foe, now wash me and I shall be whiter than snow."

Words of Love: Jesus answered and said to them, "Those who are well have no need of a physician, but those who are sick." Luke 5:31

DAY 310

COUNTDOWN TO FRIDAY

Scripture: And whatever you do, do it heartily, as to the Lord and not to men. Colossians 3:23

Some people only endure Mondays because they have Friday to look forward to, and they "stomach" 8:00 a.m. Monday through Friday, living in anticipation of 5:00 p.m. Sam Levenson said, "Don't watch the clock: do what it does. Keep going." We would be happier and more fulfilled, and so much more productive, if we heeded that advice.

Samantha and Arlene worked side-by-side on the assembly line, doing the same job day after day, and week after week. Sam was fed up with the work, and constantly grumbled as she worked. Others around her took sides, depending on their mood; sometimes they shared her feelings, and at other times they were tired of hearing her discontent.

Arlene, on the other hand, was a ray of sunshine on the line. She was friendly, positive, a fast and talented worker, and never too busy to lend a hand to someone in need. Every Monday, she greeted the team by telling them how much she missed them over the weekend; and every Friday she told them how she would miss seeing them for the two days.

Word got around that business was not as good as expected, and there was the possibility of downsizing. Then a strange thing happened that surprised management: unsolicited letters began to come in to the office, telling them that whatever happened, they had to keep Arlene, as she was the motivator in their production area.

Life is ten percent what happens to us, and ninety percent how we handle it. Clock watchers are often not very successful, and they definitely are not very happy. Let us take Christ to work with us on Mondays, and our perspective regarding Fridays will change. Let us create a new culture where, instead of "Thank God it's Friday," we can exclaim with exuberance, "Thank God for another Monday; another opportunity to give of my best service." Can you imagine what such a change might do? I think we would see amazing results.

Words of Love: Commit your works to the Lord, and your thoughts will be established. Proverbs 16:3

DAY 311
I WANT TO GET TO KNOW YOU

Scripture: And when Jesus came to the place, He looked up and saw him, and said to him, "Zacchaeus, make haste and come down, for today I must stay at your house." Luke 19:5

Sometimes people say that they know another person after only a short meeting or a brief conversation. You only get to know someone by spending time with them, however.

Jesus wanted to get to know the real Zacchaeus, not the one who sat in the seat of custom and stole from rich and poor alike. Christ saw the person that Zacchaeus could become, if he allowed Him into his heart. This was the person He wanted to get to know, so He said to Zacchaeus, who had positioned himself in a sycamore tree for a better view, "Come down, Zacchaeus, because today I must spend time with you at your house."

As in the case of Zacchaeus, Christ is inviting Himself to spend time with us; and like Zacchaeus, we should let Him know how delighted we are to welcome Him. When we welcome Christ into our lives, He will change us, just as He did Zacchaeus.

Most of us would like to say to a world that is quick to judge us, "Don't judge me too harshly. When I accept Jesus' invitation to spend time with me, He will not leave me as He finds me, but will change me into who He sees I can become."

Prayer: Thank You, Gracious Lord, for loving me enough to want to get to know me. Please change me into Your likeness.

Words of Love: That the God of our Lord Jesus Christ, the Father of glory, may give to you the spirit of wisdom and revelation in the knowledge of Him. Ephesians 1:17

DAY 312
HEAD OVER HEELS IN MY TRUST OF YOU LORD

Scripture: Whenever I am afraid, I will trust in You. Psalm 56:3

I was seated in the waiting room of a local hospital, waiting for my friend who was there for a medical procedure. Promptly at 8:00 a.m., the voice of the hospital chaplain came over the intercom, drawing everyone's attention to prayer. It was not intrusive, and no one was forced to stop what they were doing. She was simply inviting the presence of the Great Physician, Jesus Christ, to be actively involved in all the procedures taking place at the hospital on that day. I was very intrigued with her words, "Lord, I am so head over heels in my trust of You."

I began to think on her words, carefully chosen, I am sure, for the hospital setting. Trust was critical for the patients who were placing themselves and their well-being in the hands of the medical professionals who worked there. How important it is for us to put our trust in the Almighty, and ask Him to guide the medical and allied health teams that provide us with care. How awesome it would be, to be head over heels in love with God, and equally head over heels in our trust of Him. With this level of trust, we will not fear the outcome of any lab tests, diagnostic or surgical procedures, knowing that, however difficult, our loving Savior will walk the rough path with us.

Trust is key in any relationship, and when it comes to my spiritual health, there is only one person I trust: Jesus Christ. He is the only One with the antidote to the poisonous venom of sin. I am grateful that His emergency room is open round-the-clock, and I do not have to wait for the arrival of an ambulance. While physical restoration is not guaranteed, my spiritual health and wellbeing are guaranteed, in the skilled, and loving hands of the Creator. I trust Him implicitly.

Words of Love: He who trusts in his riches will fall, but the righteous will flourish like foliage. Proverbs 11:28

DAY 313

TENDER MOMENTS

Scripture: Jesus, knowing that the Father had given all things into His hands, and that He had come from God and was going to God, rose from supper and laid aside His garments, took a towel and girded Himself... John 13:3-10

Are you a softie, for moments that either bring a smile to your face, an Ah... to your lips, or a tear to your eyes? Some of those moments for me include seeing babies or toddlers hugging each other, and elderly couples publicly displaying their devotion to each other. The following tender moment was somewhat different; but evoked all three of those emotions mentioned above, and still brings a smile to my face when I remember it.

My friend's two boys, ages sixteen and twelve at the time, sang a beautiful duet in church. Although they did a fantastic job singing the song, that is not what I will remember fondly. These are two boys who, although they love each other dearly, experience the typical sibling rivalry. It was, therefore, very touching to see the older brother, at the conclusion of the song, reach over and embrace his younger brother. It was a moment for the record books, and one that had a very positive and lasting impact on several people in the congregation. Their tender moment prompted one member to tweet, "Yep, kids are like that. They act like they are rotten to the core, but they are just bruised on the surface with good hearts inside."

Scripture records some of Jesus' tender moments. Here are a few that are memorable for me: Him taking the children on His lap; Him making breakfast on the shore for some of His disciples, after they had experienced a hard night of fishing; and His kind and forgiving treatment of the woman caught in the act of adultery.

Moments of tenderness are relational moments that display actions from hearts of love. Christ created us for relationships, and He desires to experience these tender moments with us.

Words of Love: And let us consider one another in order to stir up love and good works. Hebrews 10:24

DAY 314
HE IS STILL MY SAVIOR

Scripture: Therefore, He is also able to save to the uttermost those who come to God through Him, since He always lives to make intercession for them. Hebrews 7:25

My relationship with Christ is not based on feelings. My feelings may waver, based on what is going on around me, or as my friend describes it, "Depending on the flavor of the month." My mood may swing with the flavor of the month, but God does not change. His love for me is not based on my feelings, or even my actions. As a matter of fact, He sought me when I was in the grasp of the enemy, and He fought for me. I resisted, but He lovingly pursued me and won my heart.

I would love to say that this pursuit was a one-time event, but unfortunately it has been repeated many times. I have been hot, I have been cold, and there are times I have teetered on being lukewarm. The latter is the state most difficult for the Savior to help me, because in that state I think everything is well with my soul. This is a state that Satan likes us to be in; this self-righteous state that locks Jesus out. Regardless of my feelings, however, Jesus is still my Savior.

I am ecstatic that Christ loves me, no matter what. Although His love knows no limit, I don't have unlimited time, so at some point during the pursuit, I must accept His love, or stand to lose out on eternity with Him. How awesome it is to accept His love and love Him in return.

Words of Love: In this is love, not that we loved God, but that He loved us and sent His Son to be the propitiation for our sins. 1 John 4:10

DAY 315
HE WOULD NOT GO IN

Scripture: And he said to him, 'Your brother has come, and because he has received him safe and sound, your father has killed the fatted calf.' But he was angry and would not go in. Therefore, his father came out and pleaded with him. Luke 15:27-28

The story of the Prodigal Son is very well known to Christians. The part of the story that is often overlooked, however, is that of the angry older brother. Why was this older brother so indignant that he refused to enter the welcoming party for his brother who had been lost out in the world, but had finally come home? I believe he had a sense of entitlement. In verse 29 of the same chapter, he complained that he had served his father all these years, and had never been given a party.

Fear denies us the relationship with Jesus Christ that is necessary for our salvation. The older brother, by refusing to go in to the welcoming party and give thanks for his brother's safe return, denied himself God's forgiveness for his own sins. He feared that his brother's return would cut into his share of his father's inheritance. Fear also causes us to elevate our self-righteousness over everyone else. This older brother did not see that the hatred in his heart, which prevented him from entering the party, was no less sinful than the prodigal son who spent his inheritance in riotous living.

The older brother had the mentality of a slave rather than an heir. He was jealous of his brother who had ventured out into the world, and had experienced life on the other side. What he did not know, because he refused to join in the celebration, was that his younger brother had not come back feeling entitled to an inheritance. The prodigal son begged to be taken back as a hired servant. He had a repentant heart, and came looking for mercy. A beautiful song says that there is room at the cross for you; and there is room in God's kingdom for every prodigal child, son or daughter.

Words of Love: For the commandments, "You shall not commit adultery," "You shall not murder," "You shall not steal," "You shall not bear false witness," "You shall not covet," and if there is any other commandment, are all summed up in this saying, namely, "You shall love your neighbor as yourself. Romans 13:9

DAY 316
GIVING YOUR LIFE TO AND FOR CHRIST

Scripture: I have been crucified with Christ; it is no longer I who live, but Christ lives in me; and the life which I now live in the flesh I live by faith in the Son of God, who loved me and gave Himself for me. Galatians 2:20

What does it mean to you to give your life to Jesus Christ? Is there a difference between giving your life to Him and giving your life for Him? To have a personal walk with Christ, we have to give Him our lives, and though we might not all be asked to give our lives for Him, we have to be willing to do so as well.

An amazing young woman spoke on the topic of "The Impossible Life," at a youth gathering. "It is impossible to live a life for Jesus Christ without the indwelling of the Holy Spirit," she said. One of the examples she used was David Livingston, who had dedicated his life to the service of Christ in Africa. He buried his wife there, after she succumbed to illness and died, and he himself eventually died there, in service for his Master. Yes, he had both given his life to Christ, and for Him.

I am also reminded of a story of missionaries who were killed by cannibals to whom they had gone to witness. What they had not gained in life, they gained by their death, however, as many in the tribe were later converted to Christianity. Many Christians are still giving their lives for Christ, as they dedicate themselves to His service.

"I will follow thee my Savior, whatsoever my lot may be." These are the words of one who desires a life of total surrender to Jesus Christ. Are you willing to go all the way with Jesus? Are you ready to make that kind of surrender today? If not, what is holding you back?

Words of Love: Jesus said to him, "I am the way, the truth, and the life. No one comes to the Father except through Me. John 14:6

DAY 317

THE WIND AND THE WAVES OBEY HIM

Scripture: And they feared exceedingly, and said to one another, "Who can this be, that even the wind and the sea obey Him!" Mark 4:41

What a sight that must have been, to see the silhouette of a man walking toward you on a stormy sea. Second only to the fear of their small boat sinking and the whole team drowning, was the sight of this "ghost." At least, that was what they thought.

Then came the reassuring voice of their Master, telling them to not be afraid. What does He mean, "don't be afraid"? Can He not see the disaster which is about to happen momentarily? Then Peter had the guts to challenge Him, "Master, if it is truly You, bid me come to You." Jesus bid him come, and stepping out of the boat, Peter headed toward Jesus. Good progress was being made, until the consciousness of walking over turbulent waves caused him to take his eyes off the Savior. Immediately he began to sink. In desperation, he cried out to Jesus, who in an instant was by his side, to lift him from the angry waves.

After Jesus and Peter stepped into the boat, Jesus spoke to the wind and the waves to be still. Immediately there was a great calm. A God who can calm the storms on the Sea of Galilee can calm the storms in your life. Cry out to Him, and ask Him to save you. He will not disappoint. He will come to your rescue. Yes, He will rescue the perishing, He will care for the dying. He is ever wonderful, and He will save.

Words of Love: Come and see the works of God; He is awesome in His doing toward the sons of men. He turned the sea into dry land; They went through the river on foot. There we will rejoice in Him. Psalm 66:5-6

DAY 318
NEVER ALONE

Scripture: No man shall be able to stand before you all the days of your life; as I was with Moses, so I will be with you. I will not leave you nor forsake you. Joshua 1:5

Charlene enjoyed her externship in the "Land of Opportunity." She loved her host family, and learned a lot about international trade at the headquarters of the corporation to which she had won this fellowship, as a part of her graduate studies. Charlene was from a Christian home, and grew up with strong Christian values. Her host family practiced their faith openly, and Charlene was delighted to participate in their worship and church fellowship.

The Christmas holidays drew near, and there were celebrations in many offices of the large headquarters where Charlene worked. She was caught up in the holiday spirit and did not want to seem odd, so she went to some of the office parties. At one of those parties, she observed practices that took her by surprise. She prayed and asked God to keep her strong and safe, and she was comforted by the words of the song, "No Never Alone," Anonymous, published 1892. Charlene silently repeated the words: "No, never alone, alone; no never alone. I promise never to leave you, never to leave you alone."

What a comfort it is to know that when the tempter tries to break our will, we can draw strength and comfort from the promise of Christ to be by our side, and never to leave us alone. Hold fast to that promise and find strength for the journey.

Words of Love: And I will pray the Father, and He will give you another Helper, that He may abide with you forever. John 14:16

DAY 319
CHECK YOUR PULSE

Scripture: Giving thanks always for all things to God the Father in the name of our Lord Jesus Christ. Ephesians 5:20

I drove past the marque at my church, and reversed to take a second look. The new sign read, "If you think you have nothing for which to be thankful, check your pulse." It reminded me of a plaque I came across on a door on one of my evening walks, which read, "Thankful. Grateful, Blessed."

I know that you experience challenges. We all do. But if you have a pulse, you have an opportunity for a new life. That is something amazing for which to be thankful. When given the right perspective, life and the opportunity of a relationship with and service for God are all that truly matters. News came from home that a neighbor's mother, who was well known to my family, had died. She had multiple complications from the primary diagnosis of diabetes, and had languished in her suffering for many years.

The news sent me into one of those moments of reflection that I frequently have. I wondered how she spent her last years, months, weeks, days and even hours. Did she use them to thank God for all the blessings He had showered on her, and she enjoyed many; or did she spend them bitter about her fate of double amputations and blindness, among other things?

What are the things that agitate you today? Get out your hypothetical scale, and weigh them in the balance. A pulse is a very significant blessing and carries a lot of weight, so I bet that your advantages far outweigh your disadvantages. Stop the pity party, and get on your knees. Thank God for all His wonderful gifts, and don't forget to include a special "Thank You" for that pulse.

Words of Love: Every good gift and every perfect gift is from above, and comes down from the Father of lights, with whom there is no variation or shadow of turning. James 1:17

DAY 320
GOD ALREADY KNOWS

Scripture: Two men went up to the temple to pray, one a Pharisee and the other a tax collector. The Pharisee stood and prayed thus with himself, 'God, I thank You that I am not like other men—extortioners, unjust, adulterers, or even as this tax collector...' And the tax collector, standing afar off, would not so much as raise his eyes to heaven, but beat his breast, saying, 'God, be merciful to me a sinner!' I tell you, this man went down to his house justified rather than the other; for everyone who exalts himself will be humbled, and he who humbles himself will be exalted. Luke 18:10-14

In the story of the Pharisee and the Publican, there are many elements that stand out, but the ones that speak to my heart are pride and arrogance of the one, versus the humility of the other. The scripture says the Pharisee stood and prayed thus with himself. He was, in essence saying, "Hi there, God. I want You to take a good look at me. I am thankful, and I want You to know it. I am a cut above the rest. I perform all these great rites, and I don't do bad things like these others named. Neither am I like this other man standing before You." Wow, what an overrated value he placed on himself and his deeds. The problem with his boasting, however, was that God already knew all that he had done, and He was not impressed by his works, because He knew the motive behind each deed.

The other man in this story, the Publican, was keenly aware of his shortcomings; so much so, that he was reluctant to look into the "face" of the Almighty. Smiting his breast, a sign of penitence, he pleaded with God for mercy and forgiveness. God heard his cry and saw his repentant heart, and he left with the weight of sin lifted from his shoulders. The proud and boastful Pharisee left the way he came: empty. Simply a sounding brass and a tinkling cymbal.

God's mercies are free and new every morning, but if we are full of ourselves, we have no place to hold them. Just like oil and water do not mix, self and God's grace cannot operate in the same space. We must be emptied of self, so that we can receive the abundant grace and mercies available from the hands of a kind and loving Savior.

Words of Love: A broken and a contrite heart—These, O God, You will not despise. Psalm 51:17

DAY 321
MAKING THE CROOKED PATHS STRAIGHT

Scripture: I will go before you and make the crooked places straight; I will break in pieces the gates of bronze and cut the bars of iron. Isaiah 45:2

The island nation of my birth is very mountainous, with some narrow winding roads. There is no way to get around the entire island without going across some precipitous mountain ranges. It is quite the norm, or even an expectation, for drivers to blow their horns as they navigate many of the dangerous corners along the way.

Life is full of narrow, winding paths, and the devil has many traps for us around every bend. When we commit our ways to the Lord, however, He promises to go before us and make the crooked paths straight. I believe that as Christians, we sometimes misunderstand the promises of God, and I don't dare to pretend to have answers for the many questions that verses such as the one above generate. What I do know for certain is that life without Christ, even if smooth at the onset, will have a very bumpy finish. The Christian's path, on the other hand, may have a rough and winding start, and Satan may even threaten to throw us off paths with steep declines, but Christ's promise to smooth out the rough paths is worth holding out for.

I don't believe I am alone in my preference for straight and smooth roads, where you can see for miles ahead. We have a tendency, however, to travel along at high speeds on such roads, without thought for what is happening to our left or right. When the roads are rough and winding, on the other hand; we need bulldozing capability to make them passable. Christ Jesus has the power to move all the obstacles placed by Satan, if we let Him go before us. He knows the way through the wilderness, as the song says, and all we have to do is to follow.

Words of Love: Every valley shall be filled and every mountain and hill brought low; The crooked places shall be made straight and the rough ways smooth. Luke 3:5

DAY 322

WHAT IS IT ABOUT HOPE?

Scriptures: We are hard-pressed on every side, yet not crushed; we are perplexed, but not in despair; persecuted, but not forsaken; struck down, but not destroyed. 2 Corinthians 4:8-9.

Hope transcends our circumstances. It gives us something better than the present to look forward to. Hope says to us, when things are not going so good, "There are better days ahead." And when things are good, hope says, "It only gets better."

My friend told me the story of a man who went onto a bridge, with plans to end his life by jumping off the highest point. As he ascended the bridge, he encountered a man who evidently had the same plans in mind. Suddenly a voice spoke to him and said, "I know you thought you came to this bridge to end your life, but I have other plans for you. You have been sent on a mission to save this other man's life."

Suddenly a life that had been without purpose had a purpose. There was a reason for his existence, if nothing more than to save this other man from taking the easy way out. He walked over to the man and engaged him in conversation. He shared his story of hopelessness, which had suddenly seen a light of hope. His genuineness caused this other man to step back from the turbulent waters below, to a future of promise.

There was no judgment, no "What were you thinking?" questions, just the ears of understanding that listened, a voice of kind and encouraging words, and a heart that seemed to genuinely care. Hope is what brings you back from the brink of death, and gives you a purpose for living. Both men found hope that day. Jesus wants to give you that hope today, if you will open your heart to His gentle voice.

Words of Love: These things I have spoken to you, that in Me you may have peace. In the world you will have tribulation; but be of good cheer, I have overcome the world. John 16:33

DAY 323
RESIGNED TO HER FATE

Scripture: For there is hope for a tree, if it is cut down, that it will sprout again, and that its tender shoots will not cease. Though its root may grow old in the earth, and its stump may die in the ground, yet at the scent of water it will bud and bring forth branches like a plant... Job 14:7-12

On my walk one late afternoon, I met a young lady who I engaged in conversation. She told me she worked in the cardiology department of a local hospital. I remarked that it was a pleasure to meet her, but hoped that I would never need their services, to which she responded, "We will all need it sooner or later, with the way we eat." She seemed resigned to a diagnosis of heart disease in her lifetime. How sad, I thought, to be resigned to something over which you have some control.

In the same way, a poor physical diet leads to cardiac problems from cholesterol-clogged arteries, a poor spiritual diet will lead to hearts clogged by the residue of sin: hate, greed, unforgiveness and envy, among others. There are many who seem resigned to a life that they believe has nothing to offer beyond the grave. They have lost sight of the blessed truth about eternity with Jesus Christ.

That brings up the question: Are people not seeing the joy in our Christian lives; something different that makes them want what we have: that blessed assurance? When we are filled with this joyful anticipation, it will radiate from within us to those we encounter; and maybe, just maybe, we can help someone find a ray of hope beyond resignation to life's true "heart disease,": sin.

My prayer is that we are not failing to exemplify the blessed hope, which lifts us beyond resignation to a fate of doom, to a heavenly anticipation. Christ is the answer.

Words of Love: Jesus said to him, "I am the way, the truth, and the life. No one comes to the Father except through Me." John 14:6

DAY 324
THE CLOCK IS TICKING

Scripture: Lord, make me to know my end, and what is the measure of my days, that I may know how frail I am. Psalm 39:4

Everyone has a finite lifetime on this earth, and in that sense, our time clock is ticking. There is a beautiful poem that speaks to the life we live between birth and death. Our clock begins ticking from the moment of that first breath, and every one of us is given the same number of minutes and hours for each day we live. For some people, the clock did not tick for very long; and for others, they enjoyed a very long life.

I have witnessed the joy that accompanies many births; and I have seen and experienced the grief of losing many friends and loved ones. What I find touching and memorable, however, is not the length of one's life, but the impact of that life on those it encountered. I have seen young children who, in their short lives, have left an indelible mark on those who knew them, or knew of them. On the other hand, there have been many who lived selfish lives, who took much, but gave little in return; and who are remembered, not for the joy they brought, but for the sorrow they caused.

Your clock is ticking, as is mine. We have no guarantee of the date the "battery" will stop running, and when it does, we don't have the option to replace it. What each of us has, however, is a choice as to how we use the time given to us. If we knew the time we have allotted, I believe we would plan to use it advantageously. But we don't know, and our clock could stop ticking today. So, starting right now, why don't we choose to make any changes necessary to ensure a closer walk with Jesus? Let's leave a legacy of love that will last throughout eternity.

Words of Love: I am He who lives, and was dead, and behold, I am alive forevermore. Amen. And I have the keys of Hades and of Death. Revelation 1:18

DAY 325

RUN!

Scripture: For the wages of sin is death, but the gift of God is eternal life in Christ Jesus our Lord. Romans 6:23

Life is exciting, and sin is very tempting. We are reminded that Satan does not present himself as the little man in a red suit, with a pitchfork. That would be too obvious, and unappealing. No, sin entices us with things that look and feel good. There are often promises that it will not hurt; it will take away our pain, low self-esteem, and lack of confidence. We are told that it will energize us and recharge our batteries. We are told that we will be accepted and loved, and often these lies are coated with just enough truth to entrap us. Things look good at the beginning, but what is promoted is not what we usually get.

There is an old adage which says, "If it seems too good to be true, it probably is." Our eternal salvation is worth far more than the pleasures of sin for a season; so, with every offer of sin's momentary pleasure, ask yourself the question, "What is this worth in the realm of eternity?" When the answer does not line up with the Word of God, make haste to put some distance between you and the temptation. Run…Run as fast as you can. Run to Jesus and live.

Words of Love: My sheep hear My voice, and I know them, and they follow Me. And I give them eternal life, and they shall never perish; neither shall anyone snatch them out of My hand. John 10:27-28

DAY 326
LOVE AT ANY AGE

Scripture: Yet in all these things we are more than conquerors through Him who loved us... Romans 8:37-39

During the weeks when I work at my consulting job in the state capital, I live in a fifty-five and older apartment community. It is fun to watch the interactions between these senior citizens, some of them in their nineties. The complex forms a square, with an inside wraparound corridor that overlooks the courtyard with swimming pool and clubhouse. The corridor offers residents a place to walk, protected from the elements.

I was taking a break from writing one afternoon, and getting in my daily walk, when I met another resident from the third floor. She was accompanied by a gentleman who was pulling her small foldable grocery cart. As I got closer, I smiled and was getting ready to greet her when the gentleman, who was probably ninety years old, greeted me first with the comment; "We just started dating," referring to the elderly lady whose cart he was pulling. She, just as quickly, responded, "Isn't he a kind gentleman to offer to bring my groceries up for me?" As they passed me, she asked him a question about where he grew up, clearly indicating that they were recent acquaintances, not a dating couple, as he had indicated.

The encounter made me smile for the remainder of my walk, and even as I wrote this devotion. God created us as relational beings, who need to love and be loved, regardless of our age. This gentleman was evidently a new resident, and even in his senior years he was looking for companionship. I hope he found my third-floor neighbor receptive.

Prayer: Lord, there are many ways that we can show love for each other. Help us to seek out opportunities to touch some lonely soul with the agape love that comes only from You.

Words of Love: Beloved, let us love one another, for love is of God; and everyone who loves is born of God and knows God. 8 He who does not love does not know God, for God is love. 1 John 4:7-8

DAY 327
HE COULDN'T DO IT ALONE AND NEITHER CAN WE

Scripture: But Moses' hands became heavy; so they took a stone and put it under him, and he sat on it. And Aaron and Hur supported his hands, one on one side, and the other on the other side; and his hands were steady until the going down of the sun. So Joshua defeated Amalek and his people with the edge of the sword. Exodus 17:8-13

It was unprovoked, and yes, all the surrounding nations, at one time or another, sought to pick a fight with the Israelites. Their off-again, on-again relationship with God often left them weak and unable to endure the attacks against them; because God sometimes had to withdraw His divine protection in order to get their attention, and lead them to repentance. This particular battle was against the Amalekites, and Moses told Joshua that they would not just sit around and take their assault. Israel would prepare for battle and launch an attack.

With the plan in place, Moses stood on top of the hill, with the staff of God in his hands. As long as Moses held up his hands, the Israelites were winning the battle, but whenever he lowered his hands, the Amalekites were winning. It became obvious to Aaron and Hur that Moses needed help to keep the staff of God lifted high. They sat Moses on a stone, and standing on either side, whenever Moses' hand became tired, they helped to hold them high. Moses' hand remained steady until sunset, and Joshua overcame the Amalekite army with the sword.

You and I are not unlike Moses: we need support to fight the enemy. We need a Joshua who will lead the fight, and we need an Aaron and a Hur, to stand by our side and hold up our hands with their encouragement. Sometimes, we will find ourselves in Moses' position. At other times, we may be called upon to be Joshua, and yet at other times we may have to be Aaron or Hur. Whatever our position in the battle against Satan and his army, however, none of us can go it alone. Every man needs to do his part, under the guidance and leadership of our Captain, King Jesus, if we want a successful outcome.

Words of Love: For the Lord your God walks in the midst of your camp, to deliver you and give your enemies over to you; therefore, your camp shall be holy, that He may see no unclean thing among you, and turn away from you. Deuteronomy 23:14

DAY 328

MAYBE TOMORROW

Scripture: Give no sleep to your eyes, nor slumber to your eyelids. Deliver yourself like a gazelle from the hand of the hunter, and like a bird from the hand of the fowler. Go to the ant, you sluggard! Consider her ways and be wise... A little sleep, a little slumber, a little folding of the hands to sleep—So shall your poverty come on you like a prowler, and your need like an armed man. Proverbs 6:4-11

I often think it is just human tendency to do only what has to be done, and put off the rest for later. Contrary to the scripture text above, some people's philosophy is, "Why do today what you can put off till tomorrow?" People with this mindset will not prosper, however. They are the people who sit on the side and watch others work hard, then strategize how to benefit from their success, or destroy it. This mindset carries over into all aspects of people's lives, though it may be different for each person.

Some people work very hard on the job, but make every excuse possible to not exercise or eat well. For others, it is getting routine wellness checks; and for others, it is furthering their education or pursuing a more fulfilling career. Procrastinating with one's relationship with God is the most dangerous thing anyone can do. King Agrippa said to Paul, in Acts 26:28 "Almost you persuade me to be a Christian." That may have been his last opportunity, as there is no record that he ever accepted Christ.

Paul went on to say in a later verse that he wished that everyone who heard him speak would accept the truth of God's Word and become as him, except for his chains. When you hear the good news of salvation, do not put it off for tomorrow, for tomorrow is not promised to anyone. Don't let your last opportunity pass you by. Today, if you hear His voice, harden not your heart.

Words of Love: I will give you a new heart and put a new spirit within you; I will take the heart of stone out of your flesh and give you a heart of flesh. Ezekiel 36:26

DAY 329
EXCEEDING ALL EXPECTATIONS

Scripture: And not only as we had hoped, but they first gave themselves to the Lord, and then to us by the will of God. 2 Corinthians 8:5

The setting for the scripture in 2 Corinthians is Paul's encouragement to the believers in Corinth, to give generously of their means to help finish the work of God. They were among the first to give to the work, and now more resources were needed to bring it to completion. Paul commended them for the resources they had given previously, and encouraged them to stretch themselves as they were able, in the second round of giving, to go beyond all expectations. He told them it was very important that they give in the right spirit, and with the right motive.

There are many books and articles written about sacrificial giving. The Bible tells us that many give from their abundance, not missing what they give. Others give until they feel it, as in the story of the widow's mite. They give out of their want, being in need themselves of the resources they have so very generously given. This level of generosity exceeds all expectations, and brings abundant rewards from the storehouse of a generous God.

So, what worthy cause is God impressing on your heart to support; be it with your time, talent or treasure? Or, what adjustment do you need to make in your current level of giving, to be a more generous giver? Remember, only that which we store in the bank of heaven will accompany us beyond this life. It is a blessing to have someone say, "You did more than we could have asked or hoped for." Giving blesses both the giver and the receiver; and given with the right spirit, I often wonder who is more blessed.

Words of Love: Now to Him who is able to do exceedingly abundantly above all that we ask or think, according to the power that works in us, to Him be glory in the church by Christ Jesus to all generations, forever and ever. Amen. Ephesians 3:20-21

DAY 330
CELEBRATING THE SUCCESSES OF OTHERS

Scripture: Let nothing be done through selfish ambition or conceit, but in lowliness of mind let each esteem others better than himself. Philippians 2:3

I have two friends who met in a community service organization, and became great friends. They were both accomplished and successful, in their careers as well as in the organization where they met. Intellectually, they were very compatible, and they enjoyed many stimulating conversations. They were good communicators and wherever they met, they enjoyed introducing the other in their circle of friends.

A few years went by and then, as both their careers advanced, one became very competitive. Instead of celebrating each other's success, jealousy entered the relationship, and an amazing friendship waned.

I have observed this unfortunate human tendency in many relationships: among lovers, colleagues, and families; in the home, the church, and the classroom; on the sports team, and in any setting where humans interact. We are admonished to cry with those who grieve, and seek ways to relieve their sorrow; and laugh with those who are happy, finding ways to help them celebrate their accomplishments and further their successes.

Words of Love: Rejoice with those who rejoice, and weep with those who weep. Romans 12:15

DAY 331
STOP STRETCHING THE TRUTH

Scripture: Lying lips are an abomination to the Lord, but those who deal truthfully are His delight. Proverbs 12:22

I went to one of my doctors for an annual check-up, and observed a book of popular church signs sitting on a table nearby. Church signs, like any quote, are among the things that fascinate me, so I picked up the book, and for once, hoped that my doctor would delay coming into the room. One of the early entries in the book was a sign that read, "Nothing ruins the truth like stretching it."

A dear friend confessed that she has a problem with telling the truth. Those of us who know and love her are keenly aware of this tendency. She said that many acquaintances who value her profession of faith share stories of their lifestyles, and ask her opinion, maybe trying to trap her into passing judgment.

This young lady is smart and diplomatic, and I believe her thoughtful answers to these frequent probing questions were guided by the Holy Spirit. She said she sometimes shares with them her tendency toward stretching the truth, and simply lying on too many occasions. She tells them that in God's eyes, both they and she are equally guilty of sin and need to change their ways and walk in the precepts of God, if they are to see His face.

I was impressed with her honesty, which got many of these acquaintances to open up with more questions, providing an opportunity for her to share Jesus. While her personal testimony has often been an icebreaker that opens doors for sharing, she realizes that she needs to be believable about the love of God for all humanity, and His desire to change us from our sinful ways. That is not just another truth stretched to ruin, but the One Truth that can withstand the test of time, and hold firm to the very end.

Word of Love: Therefore, putting away lying, "Let each one of you speak truth with his neighbor," for we are members of one another. Ephesians 4:25

DAY 332
GIVE TO GOD WHAT IS RIGHT, NOT WHAT IS LEFT

Scripture: And he blessed him and said: "Blessed be Abram of God Most High, Possessor of heaven and earth; And blessed be God Most High, who has delivered your enemies into your hand." And he gave him a tithe of all. Genesis 14:19-20

When God blesses us with resources, we should return to Him a tithe, not out of a sense of obligation or a means of invoking His blessing; but rather, in response to His blessing. We should give from hearts of love and gratitude, realizing that He didn't have to give us what He did. Someone I once knew, very foolishly said, "God didn't give me what I have, I worked hard for it." Should we be inclined to think that foolishly, let us pause for a moment and ask ourselves a few questions: Who gave us the breath we breathe, so that we could wake up to work for what we have? Who made the job available, and then gave it to us instead of someone else? Who gave us the health and strength to perform the work?

The one and only correct answer is: Jesus. It seems, then, that He deserves all of what we have earned, or at least ninety percent. Instead, all He asks of us is a tenth, and we dare to give it to Him grudgingly from what is left over. Let's do the right thing and give God what is rightfully His, not what is left after we have satisfied our needs, and often, our wants.

Do you have a problem making ends meet, and wonder why you are simply shuffling the bills around, and not getting ahead? Have you tried returning to God what is His first, and trust Him to help you take care of the rest? You may have to accept His budget guidance, but He promises to never fail you when you honor Him first. He says to prove Him, and He doesn't lie.

Words of Love: Honor the Lord with your possessions, and with the firstfruits of all your increase; So your barns will be filled with plenty, and your vats will overflow with new wine. Proverbs 3:9-10

DAY 333

A SIGN OF GOD'S PROVIDENCE

Scripture: The Lord shall preserve you from all evil; He shall preserve your soul. Psalm 121:7

We arrived in Wittenberg, Germany on a rainy Friday afternoon. Knowing that our time was limited in the city and there were several things of interest to see, my husband and I, along with another couple, ventured into the town square; with raincoats on and umbrellas in hand. We planned to have dinner while we were there. There was one main street through the town center, and thankfully some parts appeared to be blocked to through traffic. We sauntered to the end of the historic street, and turned around to go back to a highly-recommended restaurant, The Potato House, for dinner.

As we turned to face the direction of our hotel, the most breathtaking double rainbow arched across the sky. It reminded us of the promise God made to Noah after the flood. He pledged to never again destroy the earth by a flood, and the rainbow was the symbol of His great promise. It was a promise of His divine protection.

Words of Love: I set My rainbow in the cloud, and it shall be for the sign of the covenant between Me and the earth… the waters shall never again become a flood to destroy all flesh. Genesis 9:13-15

DAY 334
SURVIVING OR THRIVING?

Scripture: God is our refuge and strength, a very present help in trouble...The Lord of hosts is with us; The God of Jacob is our refuge. Psalm 46:1-11

When was the last time you asked someone how he or she was doing, and got the response, "I am surviving"? How sad that life is merely an existence for some people. The Giver of life and all good gifts wants His children to thrive, not merely survive. So, how do we thrive in this sinful and selfish world, focused on a lot of "I" and "me" messages? "I want 'this' because I am entitled to it." "I did not get 'that,' but someone else did." "Don't blame me, it is your fault."

A part of thriving is accepting responsibility for my own life and my own actions. I am only surviving when I blame everyone else for my failures and shortcomings. On the other hand, when I learn from my mistakes and allow them to be my teacher, I grow and thrive. My Heavenly Father says that whom He loves, He chastens. I am grateful for His willingness to meet me where I am, but not leaving me there. He knows my potential, and wants to help me to achieve it. His storehouse is full of blessings, ready to be poured out into the lives of His waiting children.

Words of Love: Have I not commanded you? Be strong and of good courage; do not be afraid, nor be dismayed, for the Lord your God is with you wherever you go. Joshua 1:9

DAY 335
FINDING WHAT IS REAL

Scripture: Let love be without hypocrisy. Abhor what is evil. Cling to what is good. Be kindly affectionate to one another with brotherly love, in honor giving preference to one another... Romans 12:9-13

On a flight from Atlanta to Amsterdam, en route to Berlin, I passed the long hours reading and watching a couple of movies, which I rarely take the time to do when I am at home. For the first time, I watched the movie, "Breakfast at Tiffany's," in which Holly Golightly, played by Audrey Hepburn, was in search of a rich husband to satisfy the lifestyle she thought she wanted. What she found instead was someone who could not offer her any of this world's riches, but loved her in spite of who she was.

Jesus Christ offers us what is real: eternal life. He knows that what this world offers is phony. All the glitter and glory of the limelight is fleeting, and offers no real joy. Lasting joy is found only in Him. He is the real deal, and life is pretty empty without Him, regardless of how much of this world we try to fill it with. It is like buying a piece of cheap jewelry, only to find that it tarnishes after a short time. Jesus tells us to buy of Him gold tried in the fire. That gold is real and has eternal value. It is the gold of His character, His likeness; the only thing that we can take from this world into the next.

Words of Love: Jesus said to him, "You shall love the Lord your God with all your heart, with all your soul, and with all your mind." Matthew 22:37

DAY 336
SNATCHED

Scripture: Be sober, be vigilant; because your adversary the devil walks about like a roaring lion, seeking whom he may devour. 1 Peter 5:8

The newscast reported, "Child snatched from under mother's eyes." Nearby cameras showed this young mother, with one child in her arm, being momentarily distracted from the toddler who had wandered a few feet away. This short distance was enough for this predator and pedophile to snatch the child and make a run for it. Within seconds of the child's screams, the desperate mother and others standing close by gave chase. The child was rescued and the criminal apprehended, thanks be to God, and people who cared enough to get involved.

Satan is on the prowl, looking for easy targets to snatch and destroy. Christians must be vigilant, so we do not become his next victim. We must also be alert to the needs of our brothers and sisters, so we can run to their rescue when there is a cry of distress. The scripture says that we are our brothers' keeper, so, we cannot be complacent, with a hands-off approach, while the devil and his evil angels snatch and destroy innocent victims. We are called to bear one another's burden, and so fulfil the law of God.

Words of Love: Therefore, submit to God. Resist the devil and he will flee from you. James 4:7

DAY 337
FINDING COMMON GROUND

Scripture: And a servant of the Lord must not quarrel but be gentle to all, able to teach, patient, in humility correcting those who are in opposition, if God perhaps will grant them repentance, so that they may know the truth. 2 Timothy 2:24-25

Our similarities are greater than our differences, and we need to focus on what unites us rather than what divides us. Discord abounds, because we live in a world where people groups look for and focus on what is different about others. We don't like them because "they" don't look like us, talk like us, or worship like us. The foods they eat are different, the entertainment they enjoy is different, their belief systems, ideologies and philosophies are different. Simply put, they are just different, and they change the status quo. We don't like change: we want everyone to eat grits and eggs, greens and cornbread, and drink sweet tea; or eat Cream of Wheat cereal, bagels, cream cheese and lox. We don't want variety... no, we cannot stand it.

How dare you clap your hands during the service, or say, "Hallelujah, praise the Lord," when the preacher makes a point that touches your heart? And what is this about "praise and worship songs"? What was wrong with the old hymns of Zion? It seems sacrilegious to make any sound, except for the scripted program, which of course does not include exclamations of praise. I hear what is being said, although I am having a hard time understanding it. God the Father, in His great wisdom, created a world of variety for us to explore and enjoy. He desires us to commingle and enjoy the common threads that bind us: the desire for love and acceptance; for safety for our families; for a clean and healthy environment; for fulfilling careers; for freedom to simply exist and occupy a tiny piece of this planet.

With Christ in our hearts, we can look for and find the good in each other. If we look earnestly, we will find that we all have more in common than we have differences. And with a little effort and open hearts, we can bridge those differences with acceptance and love.

Words of Love: Do not be deceived: "Evil company corrupts good habits." 1 Corinthians 15:33

DAY 338
ROAD RAGE

Scripture: So then, my beloved brethren, let every man be swift to hear, slow to speak, slow to wrath; for the wrath of man does not produce the righteousness of God. James 1:19-20

There have been numerous accounts of road rage that has ruined the lives of individuals and families: man killed while his wife and children watched in fear; victim shot in the head by a man who said he was cut off in traffic; argument ensued after a fender bender, and one man shot and killed in the process. These are just a sampling of the newscasts detailing the craziness that is encountered on the roadways.

One of the sad aspects of this epidemic is that sometimes one of the parties is unaware that they have angered the other, and they are often not given the chance to say they are sorry for the unintentional act. If only the angry party had given the other person a chance to explain, and if necessary, apologize, a peaceful resolution might have been achieved.

What is true of road rage is, unfortunately, true of anger in in any situation. Human lives have become cheap to many, and the way to resolve any dispute is often to permanently remove the other person, who is believed to cause an offense, from the face of the earth. What are we going to tell the Father when He asks us to give an account of our brother or sister? Are we, like Cain, in Genesis 4:9, going to respond that we are not their keepers? We are our brothers' and sisters' keepers, and their blood will be on us, if we are guilty of causing them harm.

Words of Love: Therefore, let us not judge one another anymore, but rather resolve this, not to put a stumbling block or a cause to fall in our brother's way. Romans 14:13

DAY 339
RESPECT

Scripture: Be kindly affectionate to one another with brotherly love, in honor giving preference to one another. Romans 12:10

My daily walk provides many opportunities for meeting people and making acquaintances. On one of those walks, I met an elderly neighbor, who I will call Carmen. We introduced ourselves, and when she told me her name, I said, "It is nice to meet you, Miss Carmen." She responded by saying, "You don't have to call me Miss Carmen," to which I responded, "But I want to. It is my way of showing my respect for you." We met many times after that, and always exchanged the warmest of greetings. She was ninety years old and deserved my respect.

We respect people for many different reasons. Sometimes it is because they have done something to earn that respect. Sometimes it is because of a position they hold, and we respect the office or position, even if they themselves are not deserving of our respect. Sometimes we respect them because of their age. God calls us to respect all human beings, as lives that He has created. We don't always have to attach titles to show respect, but when necessary, it is a sign of our respect.

Jesus Christ is due our ultimate respect, and His is not based on age, as was Miss Carmen's, but rather on His titles: Creator of the universe, King of kings, Lord of lords, and Savior of all mankind. Let's not only respect Him, but let us love, adore, and worship Him. He deserves it all.

Words of Love: Show proper respect to everyone, love the family of believers, fear God, honor the emperor. 1 Peter 2:17 (NIV)

DAY 340
WORSHIP HIM WITH THE PSALMS

Scripture: Oh, worship the Lord in the beauty of holiness! Tremble before Him, all the earth. Psalm 96:9

There are multiple ways to worship God, and sing praises to His name. The Psalms are not short of words of adoration, and I would like to share a few of those with you in this devotion. I invite you to draw near to God, with the assurance that He will also draw near to you.

Unto You, O my Strength, I will sing praises; For God is my defense, my God of mercy. Psalm 59:17

I will abide in Your tabernacle forever; I will trust in the shelter of Your wings. Psalm 61:4

Oh, sing to the Lord a new song! For He has done marvelous things; His right hand and His holy arm have gained Him the victory. Psalm 98:1

The heaven, even the heavens, are the Lord's; But the earth He has given to the children of men. Psalm 115:16

Teach me to do Your will, for You are my God; Your Spirit is good. Lead me in the land of uprightness. Psalm 143:10

I will sing a new song to You, O God; On a harp of ten strings I will sing praises to You, Psalm 144:9

Find your favorite Psalms of praise, and praise God today for His matchless love and kindness towards us. He is worthy and very deserving of our worship.

Words of Love: Oh, give thanks to the Lord! Call upon His name; Make known His deeds among the peoples! Psalm 105:1

DAY 341
ENDURING LOSS

Scripture: And God will wipe away every tear from their eyes; there shall be no more death, nor sorrow, nor crying. There shall be no more pain, for the former things have passed away. Revelation 21:4

My friend lost her husband suddenly and unexpectedly. He was our beloved brother in Christ, who was loved by everyone in our church. I will never forget the day I got the call from her son with the horrific news. He was crying and I was crying over the phone. Disbelief was an understatement. I knew they were not playing a cruel joke, but I didn't want to accept it. My friend was so overtaken with grief that my heart broke for both mother and son, aware that there was little I could do from almost two hundred miles away.

I have lost my father, mother, and a brother, and know that the pain of such loss never completely goes away. In our grief at this latest loss, we consoled each other with the reminder that those who die in Christ will rise in the first resurrection. So, take heart, my beloved sister, and all those who have lost loved ones. In just a short while, the great trumpet will sound, and those of us who live for Christ, along with those who died in Him, will rise together to meet Him in the sky. And the beauty of it all is that we will never part again.

Words of Love: The Lord is near to those who have a broken heart, and saves such as have a contrite spirit. Psalm 34:18

DAY 342
THE COMMAND TO LOVE

Scripture: You have heard that it was said, 'You shall love your neighbor and hate your enemy.' But I say to you, love your enemies... Matthew 5:43-44

To love is not an option, it is a command. In the scripture above, Jesus tells us to love our enemies, and pray for those who do us wrong. He said it is not difficult to love those who love us. That does not require much, and does not come with any special reward. On the other hand, it is not easy to love, pray for, and do good to those who continually lay heavy burdens on our backs: the burdens of hatred, thievery, lies, and deceit, among others. Loving them and doing good for them, in spite of their oppressions, heap coals of fire on their heads.

What would it take for you to honor this command? For most of us, it requires the constant companionship and intervention of the Holy Spirit. It requires letting go of the struggle, and letting God have His way in the situation.

For Jan, it was her hard-earned money, which she had so willingly loaned her niece to resolve one of her many crises. In her retirement, Jan desperately needed the money, which amounted to many thousands of dollars. Her niece refused to answer any of her calls, or respond to her correspondence. Jan had to accept that her money was lost forever, and for a while she wrestled with feelings that were close to hatred. Jan had a deep love for the Lord, and she made the decision to give her anger and resentment to Him. He, in turn, gave her sweet release.

Jan's story is not unlike that of many others, but regardless of the scenario, the command is the same, "Love them with the same everlasting love that I have shown you." It may not be easy, but if you love God, it is not an option.

Words of Love: A new commandment I give to you, that you love one another; as I have loved you, that you also love one another. John 13:34

DAY 343
STAND UP!

Scripture: But Peter, standing up with the eleven, raised his voice and said to them, "Men of Judea and all who dwell in Jerusalem, let this be known to you, and heed my words... Therefore, let all the house of Israel know assuredly that God has made this Jesus, whom you crucified, both Lord and Christ." Acts 2:14-36

The command to stand up is one that many resent, simply because it is a command, and most of us don't like being told what to do. In a court of law; when the judge enters the courtroom, the bailiff bellows, "Will the court please rise." What sounds like a question is in fact a command, because everyone who is able to is expected to stand up. The same is true for high-ranking military officials. Their troops show respect for them by standing at attention in their presence.

We are soldiers in Christ's army, and the song Stand Up, Stand Up for Jesus, written by George Duffield, Jr in 1858 says, "Stand up, stand up for Jesus, ye soldiers of the cross; lift high His royal banner, it must not suffer loss." My pastor preached a dynamic sermon on the topic, and he said that in these last days of earth's history, we need to "stand up and stay up." If we are to see and receive all that Christ has in store for us, we must first stand up, and then stay up to follow Him.

When Jesus called the first disciples, they asked Him where He was staying. Jesus told them to come and see. They got to their feet, left their task behind, and followed Him. In their own strength, however, they could not stand for Jesus as they should. They constantly failed at standing up to the call, and this was most evident during Christ's final hours. They, who had vowed to stand up for Him to their death, fled or denied Him.

We must first fall down at the feet of Jesus before we can stand up for Him. Jesus "stood tall" at Calvary for you and me. The question is, will we now stand up for Him?

Words of Love: Watch, stand fast in the faith, be brave, be strong.
1 Corinthians 16:13

DAY 344
I GAVE MY LIFE FOR YOU

Scripture: I beseech you therefore, brethren, by the mercies of God, that you present your bodies a living sacrifice, holy, acceptable to God, which is your reasonable service. Romans 12:1

Christ desires the Christian's complete devotion, and this is not too much to ask, considering that He gave His all for us. The martyrs of old could respond to the statement and question of the song, "I gave My life for thee; what hast thou given for me?" with the response, "Lord, I willingly give back to You the life that You have given me."

Walking in the footsteps of Martin Luther, through Germany and Italy, is an experience I will not soon forget. Luther and many of his contemporaries suffered great persecution. Thousands of Christians lost their lives for Jesus Christ during the Reformation, and thousands more in the centuries that have followed are answering the question, "What hast thou given for Me?" with their lives.

Luther walked from Wittenberg to Rome in the winter, to answer for his faith, willing to pay with his life, if that was required. The Waldensians were hunted in mountain caves and valleys. They and many others were burned at the stakes, for no other crime than that of loving Jesus Christ more than life itself.

What Christ did for the Christian Reformers, He has done for all mankind. He gave His life on Calvary as a ransom for our sins. Today, His call is the same to all of us, "I have given My life, My all, for you; are you willing to give the same for Me?" The sacrifice comes with great rewards.

Words of Love: Only fear the Lord, and serve Him in truth with all your heart; for consider what great things He has done for you. 1 Samuel 12:24

DAY 345

OUTNUMBERED TWO TO ONE

Scripture: For You have armed me with strength for the battle; You have subdued under me those who rose up against me. Psalm 18:39

Christians have twice the army on our side, and a commander who has never lost a battle; so, tell me, why are we often bewildered and panicking? When Lucifer was cast out from heaven, he took a third of the angelic host with him. That still left two thirds, however, to launch any counter assault on him. The children of God, though besieged by the angry foe, can call on heaven's army when in distress. We have the assurance that God will dispatch forces from heaven to assist us, and we know that Satan and his army are outnumbered two to one.

I must confess, it "tickles me pink" to know that when we are within the will of God, we do not have to fear the enemy. That does not mean, by any stretch of the imagination, that we will glide through life, trouble-free. What it means, however, is that though we may lose some battles, Christ has already won the war for us. His army of angels, seen and unseen, protect us from attacks, many of which we are unaware.

Prayer: Father, we are grateful for the protection You offer us daily. When we are tempted to despair by the trials that threaten to undermine and unsettle us, help us to remember that we have twice the army of the enemy on our side, and that You, our General and Commander, are already victorious.

Words of Love: When you go out to battle against your enemies, and see horses and chariots and people more numerous than you, do not be afraid of them; for the Lord your God is with you, who brought you up from the land of Egypt. Deuteronomy 20:1

DAY 346
LORD, PLEASE CHANGE ME

Scripture: Not that I speak in regard to need, for I have learned in whatever state I am, to be content. Philippians 4:11

My sister lived in the Boston suburbs for most of her adult life, and although she disliked the harsh winters, she loved the freedom of mobility that the area offered. She drove herself around her immediate neighborhood, but whenever she was challenged by driving somewhere, there were excellent bus and transit systems. Nothing was too far away. Everything she needed was in reasonable proximity.

As a part of their retirement plan, my sister and her husband bought land in Florida, and eventually built a house there. For many years, they rented the house, as she inwardly fought the move. After her husband's retirement and one of the hardest winters in Boston, the day came when they finally moved.

Within the first year of their move to Florida, my sister and her husband were enjoying the fruits of his labor, including mangoes, and a variety of vegetables. Although she still misses the easy access to most things in Boston, and sometimes reminisces about the place where she lived for almost forty years, my sister confesses that she would not want to go back to the snow and cold.

What made the difference for my sister was that she asked God to change her, and give her a heart of acceptance and contentment. She acquired a caring church family, and began to get involved. There were also other family members who had made the move to the area before them, and they included them in their activities. She had this to say, "There is never a dull moment."

Prayer: Father God, when Your plans do not involve changing our circumstances; please change us, and give us hearts of praise and thanksgiving. Then, like the apostle Paul, we will be content in all our circumstances.

Words of Love: A little that a righteous man has is better than the riches of many wicked. Psalm 37:16

DAY 347
CAUGHT IN THE RAIN

Scripture: All that the Father gives Me will come to Me, and the one who comes to Me I will by no means cast out. John 6:37

It was a beautiful afternoon. The sun was shining and there was a gentle breeze. Then the rain began. It was a light rain, without lightning or thunder. I opened the front door of my apartment to a surprising sight. Sitting at the poolside was someone in a wheelchair, with a companion standing close by. There was a small tree that blocked a clear view, so I stood for a while and watched, without being intrusive.

There was no appearance of distress on the part of wheelchair occupant, and they seemed in no hurry to move. As I watched from my vantage point, I mused: "Was this a planned adventure, someone reliving their childhood of 'playing in the rain,' or were they caught off guard, and decided to make the best of it?"

After some time, another person joined them and eventually took the wheelchair-bound person up the walkway and out of sight. My afternoon reverie came to a close, but not before another moment of reflection. In the scenario just described, there were several take away lessons for me:

* I saw God's love in both persons who attended the mobility-challenged occupant of the wheelchair. "The love of God, how marvelous, how measureless and strong."
* I saw an acceptance of the situation by all parties involved, and a resolution to not allow it to steal their joy.
* I saw a loving, kind, and merciful Savior, who sent the combination of sunshine and rain, without dangerous lightning or unnerving thunder, so that even if the experience was unplanned, it could be accepted as an adventure without harm.

Words of Love: First of all, then, I urge that entreaties and prayers, petitions and thanksgivings, be made on behalf of all men. 1 Timothy 2:1

DAY 348

YOUR PATH WAS SPECIALLY CHOSEN FOR YOU

Scripture: And it came to pass, when Pharaoh had let the people go, that God did not lead them by way of the land of the Philistines, although that was near; for God said, "Lest perhaps the people change their minds when they see war, and return to Egypt." Exodus 13:17

Two sisters, only a year apart in age, left home at the same time to pursue their dreams. They were both equally prepared for successful lives, and both had the same Christian foundation on which to build. The younger of the two sisters joined the staff of an international nonprofit organization and fulfilled many missions to multiple foreign countries. After many years with this group, she settled at home to marry and raise a family. She did not amass much of this world's wealth, but she enjoyed a life of service, where she was able to make a difference and touch many lives for Christ.

The older sister pursued a very profitable career in their home country. She, too, touched many lives in her work, but she did not have the same sense of fulfillment that her younger sister had. The two sisters had a very close relationship, and they encouraged each other in moments of doubt and stress. The younger sister frequently reminded the older one that their paths were directed by the Lord. They had prayerfully pursued the directions they believed He had laid before them, and they had both served Him faithfully as they felt led, therefore, they should not live with any regrets.

Do you believe your path is chosen for you by the Lord? If there is any doubt, it is not too late to ask for His help in pursuing a path of service for Him; the path He has chosen for you. It is not guaranteed to be an easy path, but it is the path where you will find the most fulfillment. Life is too short to waste it on the wrong path. Give Christ your hands today, and let Him lead you on the path of joyful living.

Words of Love: But the path of the just is like the shining sun, that shines ever brighter unto the perfect day. Proverbs 4:18

DAY 349
PRAYING FOR GRACE AND MERCY

Scripture: Two things I request of You (Deprive me not before I die): Remove falsehood and lies far from me; Give me neither poverty nor riches—Feed me with the food allotted to me; Lest I be full and deny You, and say, "Who is the Lord?" Or lest I be poor and steal, and profane the name of my God. Proverbs 30:7-9

Have you ever felt that your burden was too much to bear? I would guess that for many of you, the answer would be a profound yes. Well, here is another question: Have you ever had too much joy, too many blessings? Sorry... Did I stump you with that question?

How many of us honestly ask God for just enough to keep us at His throne, daily... thanking Him for His goodness, and pleading for His grace and mercy? Yes, no matter how tough the trials, His mercy and His grace are sufficient to meet our needs. And no matter how good our lives are, we should pray for enough grace and mercy to keep us thankful and humble.

Prayer: Lord, I pray for just enough. Enough to meet my needs and share with another. Enough to keep me from hunger, but not too much to make me gluttonous. Enough to meet an emergency, but not too much to keep me from needing Your constant provision. Father, I want enough joy to keep my spirit glad in You, but enough sorrow to remind me of Your sacrifice on Calvary for my sins. Lord, today I pray for Your grace and mercy, and may it be enough.

Words of Love: And He said to me, "My grace is sufficient for you, for My strength is made perfect in weakness." Therefore, most gladly I will rather boast in my infirmities, that the power of Christ may rest upon me. 2 Corinthians 12:9

DAY 350
LOCKED OUT

Scripture: Jesus said to him, "I am the way, the truth, and the life. No one comes to the Father except through Me. John 14:6

A friend told me she was sitting by her front door one afternoon, when one of her neighbors approached, with his hands full. They exchanged pleasantries as he dropped everything by his door and looked for his keys to open the door. No keys were to be found. They were on the same key ring with his car keys that he had just used to drive home, so he knew they could not be far. He retraced his steps, and realized he had locked the keys in the car.

The neighbor insisted on forcing entry into his apartment, refusing to call management to open the door for him. My friend even offered to pay the fee, if he was charged for the service. Recognizing his growing distress, she called anyway, against his wishes, and within ten minutes, management opened the door for him and waved the service charge.

Christ makes it clear that He is the only door through which we must enter to gain eternal life. Any attempts to force our way in another way will fail. His service to us is free, though it cost Him His life. Pride and stubbornness can cause us to refuse His offer of salvation, which will keep us locked out for eternity. Today, if you hear His voice, harden not your heart.

Words of Love: Oh, that my people would listen to me; that Israel would walk in my ways. Psalm 81:13

DAY 351
IN THE PATH OF THE STORM

Scripture: He who dwells in the secret place of the Most High shall abide under the shadow of the Almighty. I will say of the Lord, "He is my refuge and my fortress; My God, in Him I will trust." Psalm 91:1-2

The alert on my phone sounded with the message, "Lightning has been detected close to your area." This verbal alert is usually accompanied by a written announcement that includes the radius in which the lightning has been detected. I was already seeing periodic flashes of lightning, and hearing peals of thunder, as black storm clouds thickened and drew closer.

We were definitely in the path of this storm, and it was predicted to be an electrifying one. I was at about a third of my intended walking goal, but as the alert persisted, I decided it was time to go indoors. I remember my mother covering all the mirrors during a lightning storm, when I was growing up. I also remember a friend who was struck by lightning while on her landline telephone, so, during bad weather, I take the necessary precaution as I am able to.

Then my mind reflected on the many tropical storms and hurricanes that we have endured, living in a coastal city. We cannot escape all the storms that will come our way, and prepare as we may, we often suffer devastating losses. When I have done all that is in my power, however, I will rest in the protecting arms of a loving Savior.

Having lived through Hurricane Katrina, I am reminded that Christ remains in control even in the eye of the storm. He is our anchor amidst the tossing of the waves. Let us thank Him for His love and protection in all the storms of life.

Words of Love: Then they cry out to the Lord in their trouble, and He brings them out of their distresses. He calms the storm, so that its waves are still. Then they are glad because they are quiet; So He guides them to their desired haven. Oh, that men would give thanks to the Lord for His goodness, and for His wonderful works to the children of men! Psalm 107:28-31

DAY 352
WHAT WOULD YOU DO WITH IT?

Scripture: For everyone to whom much is given, from him much will be required; and to whom much has been committed, of him they will ask the more. Luke 12:48

My sister shared the following story with me one morning as we expressed our gratitude to God for His many blessings. She was a certified nursing assistant (CNA) in a hospital in Somerville, MA, where she encountered a doctor who allegedly had the ability to perform hypnosis. He was joking with the nurses on the cluster about hypnotizing people, and at the end of the conversation my sister said she would only want to be hypnotized if she would wake up with a million dollars. Without even as much as a smile, and with a tone and mannerism of disdain, he responded, "You wouldn't know what to do with it."

My sister is one of the most generous people I know. She would not hesitate to give you the last of what she had, if she felt that your need for it was greater than her own. I have no doubt that she would know what to do with a million dollars, if God so chose to give it to her; because she is a good steward of the "little" that He has given her. She would certainly use it to advance His work and help hurting humanity.

The discussion prompted one of those moments of reflection for me, and leads me to ask you the question, "What would you do with a million dollars, or more, if God was to so choose to bless you?" In the story of the talents, the servant who was given ten was a good steward and gained ten more, and the one who was given five returned five more as well. The one who was given one, however, did nothing to produce a return on the Lord's investment, so his one talent was taken away and given to another. If you are faithful and trustworthy with that which God has given you, He will increase your blessings, because He knows that you will do even better with more.

Prayer: Father, we thank You for Your gifts to us, large or small. May we use them for Your glory, by blessing others. And if You so choose to increase those gifts, may our principles of stewardship not change. Help us to remember that it all belongs to You in the first place.

Words of Love: The generous soul will be made rich, and he who waters will also be watered himself. Proverbs 11:25

DAY 353
SITTING ON THE EDGE OF DISASTER

Scripture: But the Lord is faithful, who will establish you and guard you from the evil one. 2 Thessalonians 3:3

The Philippines has over 7,000 islands, many of which are reportedly absolutely beautiful. It is one of the areas that I hope to visit in my lifetime. It is among the areas with the strongest seismic activities, with strengths of 8.3 or higher on the Richter Scale. It is also, reportedly, the third most vulnerable area of the world to typhoons. One of the most recent storms left several of the islands almost totally wiped out, with tremendous loss of lives and livelihood.

Not unlike other areas of the world that are prone to dangers of volcanos, earthquakes, and hurricanes, some of these volcanic islands are experiencing a building boom, as people are attracted to the very thing that poses such great danger. Many people live for the thrill that danger poses.

The world, as a whole, is sitting on the edge of disaster, and while it is true that life was meant for living, and if we live in fear we miss out on some of the most beautiful experiences, we must live and enjoy God's world with the awareness that He is the Creator. We must also be aware that He is coming back to restore it to its former glory. What a sight it will be to behold all the awesome works of His hands, without the fear of the next disaster being just around the corner.

I can't wait to surf at Siargao; laze on the beach at Bacuit Bay and Boracay Island; enjoy the beautiful Chocolate Hills of Bohol Island; or enjoy Cambugahay Falls. There will be so many beautiful sites to enjoy, eternity will be just long enough.

Words of Love: Oh, give thanks to the God of heaven! For His mercy endures forever. Psalm 136:26

DAY 354

THERE'LL BE SUNSHINE IN THE MORNING

Scripture: Be anxious for nothing, but in everything by prayer and supplication, with thanksgiving, let your requests be made known to God. Philippians 4:6

Have you gone through a season of pain and sorrow? Did it seem like the "night" would never end? Things always seem to get worse during the night. Take heart, however, the sun is rising on the horizon, with the promise of a better day.

Each of us may have had a different "nighttime" experience, but our heart's cry has been the same: "Lord, send me some relief in the morning." Now the morning has broken and it promises to be a brighter day. Trust God for answers to your prayers. Others have been praying for you also, and help is on the way.

So, go ahead and say another prayer. This time make it a prayer of thankfulness. Thank God ahead of time for the answers you know He will provide. Let your eyes of faith see the results you desire, according to His will. Submit your will to Him and feel the peace that floods your soul. May you be able to say, like the words of the song, "It is Well with My Soul," by Horatio Spafford, "When peace like a river, attendeth my way, when sorrows like sea billows roll; whatever my lot, Thou hast taught me to say, it is well, it is well with my soul."

May the morning bring you sunshine, for your night of sorrow, and may you find rest in the One who gives us sunshine in our souls. Claim the peace that He offers, and feel the rays of sunshine creeping in.

Words of Love: And the peace of God, which surpasses all understanding, will guard your hearts and minds through Christ Jesus. Philippians 4:7

DAY 355

WHEN THE NEWS IS NOT GOOD

Scripture: He will not be afraid of evil tidings; His heart is steadfast, trusting in the Lord. Psalm 112:7

"It has been another one of those days; and lately there have been too many like it," Billie exclaimed after her most recent diagnosis. She had gone for a follow-up appointment with her urologist and got the bad news that the spot on her kidney had grown over the past year. A biopsy confirmed what the doctors feared; it was cancer, albeit a slow growing kind.

You may be inclined to pity Billie, if you knew all that she had gone through in the previous two years, and now to receive this latest news. However, she was quick to say, "My life is in God's hands." To the surprise of many who heard her, Billie continued with these words, "The Lord gave us life, and He has the right to take it when He chooses. I am not worried, however, because Christ has healing powers in hand. He will see me through this as He has the other crises, according to His will."

I was humbled by the confident trust that Billie had in her Lord and Savior. Trials are sure to come to most of us. The scripture says we are to take up our cross and follow Him. A cross is never an easy thing to bear. It was not easy for Christ, who was already bleeding from the beating that He had received. Billie bore her cross with grace, knowing that she would have to endure only what God allowed, and with the suffering, He would give her the strength to endure.

Oh, for a trust like Billie's. Oh, for a quiet confidence that my life is in His hands. Don't you want this kind of assurance as well? You can have it. He offers it to all of us, but we must first develop a relationship with Him to experience it. Start today. All relationships take time to build.

Words of Love: As cold water to a weary soul, so is good news from a far country. Proverbs 25:25

DAY 356

YOU ARE HERE!

Scripture: Then Jesus spoke to them again, saying, "I am the light of the world. He who follows Me shall not walk in darkness, but have the light of life." John 8:12

One of my friends and prayer partners visited Thailand, and shared an experience she had in the mall in Bangkok. She reported that the mall was large and intimidating, and one could easily become disoriented and lose their way. For that reason, shoppers relied heavily on the signs which say "You are here" to keep reorienting them.

Life's journey is like that mall. It is easy to become disoriented with the layout, and all that is going on around us. To refocus us, there are signs along the way to show us where we are in relationship to where we need to go. There may be more than one way to get to your earthly destination, with some more direct than others. There is only one way to heaven, however, through Jesus Christ. If you follow the path laid out for you, the experience is guaranteed to be much more pleasant.

Christ looks down on us every day, and He sees how disoriented we are from our efforts to find our own way. He bids us, "Slow down, and read the signs I have provided for you. This is where you are in your relationship with Me, and this is how you need to get to Me." Then He goes on to say, "You are working too hard, and your efforts will not get you to Me, so take advantage of the Guide standing beside you. He has been there all along, but you have ignored Him, trying to get to Me by your own works. There are many treasures waiting to be discovered, and the sooner you get to Me, the more time you will have to explore and enjoy them. So, follow your Guide."

Words of Love: My sheep hear My voice, and I know them, and they follow Me. John 10:27

DAY 357

REST ONLY WHEN THE WORK IS DONE

Scripture: And give Him no rest till He establishes and till He makes Jerusalem a praise in the earth. Isaiah 62:7

So, you did a good job on that assignment; you won that well-fought game; you did one good deed: do you now rest on your laurels? The answer is an absolute "no." You do not rest until the work is done. You do not become complacent after one victory. You do not stop practicing after one recital, or sit back after one person of many is pulled from the wreckage.

The work of saving souls is not finished. Your generosity and hard work have not gone unnoticed, but there is still more work to be accomplished. Before the championship game is played or the Olympic finals are staged, there are many elimination games and meets to be won. Only those who prepare for and make it to the end have a chance to take the trophy home to their country. Losers give up along the way, but winners stay until the job is done.

The celebration will begin only after the task is accomplished. Then, and only then, can you afford to rest and celebrate the victory achieved: victory in Jesus. Just hold on a little longer. There is more work yet to be done, and more souls to be won. The rest, however, will be sweet, and the reward even sweeter, when you can stand before the Savior and say, "I have fought a good fight and I have finished the race." There is a crown of life awaiting you. Don't miss out on the final ceremony by giving up too soon.

Words of Love: And let us not grow weary while doing good, for in due season we shall reap if we do not lose heart. Galatians 6:9

DAY 358
STAY ON THE PATH WITH ME

Scripture: In all your ways acknowledge Him, and He shall direct your paths. Proverbs 3:6

"Stay on the path with Me," I hear the Savior say. "Even though it may be arduous; even though it is steep and winding, and sweat furrows your brows, do not give up, for this is the path I have chosen for you, and the reward at the end is worth the journey." Are you ready to be challenged? This is not an optional journey, but one that is required for completing the course. Don't look at the other person's path, wishing that it was yours. You don't know what is around their corner.

"Your path is laid out just for you, and you must walk it. My Spirit is available to you, however, so you do not have to go it alone."

On a visit to the Waldensian Valley in Torre Pellice, Italy, I missed out on two experiences that most of our group enjoyed, because I was unwilling to stay on the narrow precipitous path that led down into the cave; and the steep hill that led up to the dorms, at the School of the Barbs. Reward comes with sacrifice, whether it is the grueling schedule of study or work, or living holy lives.

Christ admonishes us to stay on the path with Him. He is an amazing guide, and it will be an unforgettable experience; with an eternal reward.

Words of Love: Ponder the path of your feet, and let all your ways be established. Proverbs 4:26

SETTING THE STAGE FOR SUCCESS

Scripture: My son, do not forget my law, but let your heart keep my commands; For length of days and long life and peace they will add to you. Let not mercy and truth forsake you; Bind them around your neck, write them on the tablet of your heart, and so find favor and high esteem in the sight of God and man. Proverbs 3:1-4

When you speak positive words about your future, it helps propel actions that are necessary to achieve success. Doing the opposite brings sure failure. The power of both good and evil, failure and success are in the words you speak, so choose your words carefully.

You may have heard people who speak negatively about themselves and their future, or you may have done so yourself: "I am a failure; I will never achieve success; I will never pass this test; they will never hire me; I will never be able to purchase a home... a car," etc. How about turning those words around and say, "I can and I will achieve all that God has in store for me. I will apply myself to the goal with all my energy, and trust the Lord for success."

People often worry about the opinions of others. They may think you will never amount to much or achieve any measure of success, and while that is discouraging, it is what you say and believe about yourself that have the most power to push you forward or hold you back.

There are both life and death in our words, so speak life and success in your future. You have the choice and the power. Exercise them. Let those words motivate you to make the impossible possible, with the help of the Holy Spirit.

Words of Love: For by your words you will be justified, and by your words you will be condemned. Matthew 12:37

DAY 360

SPEAK TO ME, LORD

Scripture: Give ear, O heavens, and I will speak; And hear, O earth, the words of my mouth...Deuteronomy 32:1-2

My heart was crying for answers, and I asked God for an explanation of the evil taking place around me. If only He would speak to me, and answer one question: Why? And then, in the stillness of my soul, God answered. He said, "Child of mine, there is an answer for every question; but some things are better left unsaid at the moment. Trust Me, you will understand it someday." There was no rebuke in His words; they were cushioned with tenderness, and I had to learn to trust Him.

When your heart is breaking and you are searching for answers to questions that seem to have no answer, find a quiet place, and talk to God. Approach Him with an open heart that is receptive to the answer He will give. Remember that His answer may be a yes, a no, or "not now, My child." Whatever His response, it will be what is best for you.

So, Lord, please speak to me and give me willing ears to listen, and a receptive heart to accept Your words. Strengthen me so that I will stand strong on You, the Rock of Ages, and I will help to strengthen someone else who is struggling in the rough waters of life's raging sea.

Words of Love: When You said, "Seek My face," my heart said to You, "Your face, Lord, I will seek." Psalm 27:8

DAY 361
TIME CANNOT BE BOUGHT OR SOLD

Scripture: See then that you walk circumspectly, not as fools but as wise, redeeming the time, because the days are evil. Therefore, do not be unwise, but understand what the will of the Lord is. Ephesians 5:15-17

Time cannot be bought, and the supply is finite. Every day we are given twenty-four hours, and what we do with it is a choice for which we must give an account. There are many things that are bought and sold, but time is not one of them. We must be careful how we use it then, because once gone, it cannot be restored.

A friend of mine dated an older man for a period of time, but the day came when she decided it was time to end the relationship, as she felt they were not making any progress. She said the strangest thing happened when she told him that she was moving on with her life. This man reportedly cried uncontrollably, acknowledging what she had done for him, but stating that he had not gotten the opportunity to do the same for her. The wise young woman responded that God had given both of them the same amount of time with each other. He had simply chosen to withhold his love and care, while she had given hers freely.

Live so that you have no regret. Use the time you have been given wisely. We pass this road only once, and when the moments have passed, they are gone for good. We cannot backtrack or rewind the tape. Those precious moments cannot be restored. The billionaire and the pauper have the same amount, as do the genius and the dunce, royalty and commoner.

Words of Love: In the morning sow your seed, and in the evening, do not withhold your hand; For you do not know which will prosper, either this or that, or whether both alike will be good. Ecclesiastes 11:6

DAY 362
OH, FOR THE PEACE THAT CHRIST OFFERS

Scripture: I will both lie down in peace, and sleep; For You alone, O Lord, make me dwell in safety. Psalm 4:8

The Psalmist says in Psalm 119:165 that those who love the law of God have great peace, and nothing offends them. Lord, I am struggling with the state of our world. There is turmoil on every front; wars and rumors of wars; hatred and intolerance. How I long for the peace that is in You.

Bloodshed has become a daily occurrence worldwide, and one cannot help but wonder if people have become desensitized to the value of human lives. My heart aches within me, and my cry is, "How long, Lord Jesus, how long?" How much longer can we continue to devalue the lives of our brothers and sisters?

We are all created in Your image, Lord, so we are one. Neither politics, religion, nor race; language, culture, nor ethnicity; wealth, education, position, nor profession: nothing should divide us, Lord, because we are all one in You. The sooner we accept this reality, precious Jesus, the quicker we can bridge the divide with Your love.

Lord, I want to live in safety; with the peace and comfort of knowing that those I encounter will take care of me, instead of taking advantage of my naivety, and trust. I long for the peace and safety, and the wellbeing of all of humanity. I know You desire the same for us, good Lord and Master, so, is it too much to ask of each other? I hear You speaking to my soul, "No, it is not too much to ask, but it is only achievable as each of you see Me in the face of the other." Father, each of us have to first know You, to be able to recognize You in the face of a brother or a sister.

There is much work for those of us who profess Your name to do, Lord. Help us to be about Your business of drawing others to You, before we are all annihilated. While the Christian should not fear death by those who can only kill the body, we must fear for the death of those who die without knowing You who have power over both body and soul.

Words of Love: Peace I leave with you, My peace I give to you; not as the world gives do I give to you. Let not your heart be troubled, neither let it be afraid. John 14:27

DAY 363
BANKING YOUR RICHES HIGHER THAN THE ATTIC

Scripture: And He said to them, "Take heed and beware of covetousness, for one's life does not consist in the abundance of the things he possesses." Luke 12:15-21

I heard a funny story of a husband who asked his wife to bury him with his riches. She obediently obliged by placing a check in his pocket, with the instructions to cash it whenever he was ready.

One morning a friend called me for an update on another friend, which led to a conversation about wealth management. She shared the following story with me: "This couple had been married for many years, and the husband was extremely tight with his wealth. Even though God had blessed him tremendously with good skills, great work ethics and good health to earn and accumulate much wealth; he was not very generous toward his wife, or anyone else, for that matter.

"Shortly after retirement, this husband, who professed to know Christ, even though his life did not show it, began to suffer ill health. Months passed and he steadily got worse. Still thinking about his wealth, he called his wife in for a serious conversation. His lack of knowledge about Bible truths became evident by the instructions he gave her. 'When I die,' he told her, 'I want you to put my riches in a particular corner in the attic, so I can retrieve it on my way up to heaven.' The wife agreed, but on further thought decided to place it in the basement, so he could retrieve it on his way down to hell."

These stories, while intending to be humorous, are quite poignant. No amount of wealth, whether stored in the attic, the basement, the bank, or buried in the grave with the deceased, is of any benefit to a person after the breath leaves the body. If we want our wealth to be deposited in "Heaven's Bank," we must spread it far and wide to alleviate suffering, and bring men and women, boys and girls into a saving relationship with Jesus Christ. This kind of investment will produce rich returns long after we exit this earth, and the interest will be paid from heaven's bank account. In the words of Biddy Mason, who touched lives by her generosity in the nineteenth century, "The open hand is blessed, for it gives in abundance even as it receives."

Words of Love: And when Jesus saw that he became very sorrowful, He said, "How hard it is for those who have riches to enter the kingdom of God! For it is easier for a camel to go through the eye of a needle than for a rich man to enter the kingdom of God." Luke 18:24–25

DAY 364

WHO SAID YOU COULDN'T?

Scripture: I can do all things through Christ who strengthens me. Philippians 4:13

I had two desires at the tender age of four or five years old. One was to become a teacher, and the other, to become a writer. At the age of twenty years old, I fulfilled the first dream, when I graduated from teachers' college, and now in my retirement years I am fulfilling my second dream. Both of these goals have been attained amidst doubts and hardships. Under the guidance of the Holy Spirit, and with hard work and determination, however, obstacles can fuel success. When others say you can't, tell them that with Christ, you can. Prove them wrong, but don't take the credit for yourself. Acknowledge that you could not do it alone. Remember from whom your strength comes.

I have a few questions for you: What challenges have you had to overcome? Did you have naysayers? Have you proved them wrong, or with God's help are you planning to prove them wrong? Let no man put limits on your accomplishments. Remember, with Christ all things are possible, if you only believe, and apply yourself to the dream.

Words of Love: And let us not grow weary while doing good, for in due season we shall reap if we do not lose heart. Galatians 6:9

DAY 365

WARM REGARDS

Scripture: Grace and peace to you from God our Father and the Lord Jesus Christ. I thank my God every time I remember you. In all my prayers for all of you, I always pray with joy. Philippians 1:2-4

"Warm Regards" is a beautiful, personal, and tender ending to written communication. It is intimate, and conveys affectionate sentiments for those who are special to you. I imagine our Lord and Savior, at the end of all His words to us, saying: "Until we talk again, just rest in my love, assured that you are the apple of my eye." Warm regards, my beloved.

Even when Christ's words are of reproof, we know they are offered in love, and intended for our growth. How I love a God who does not sugar coat my wrongs. He meets me where I am, but in love He does not leave me there. He works with me constantly to elevate me to the level that is fit for His kingdom. He even sacrificed Himself to make this a reality. With this knowledge, my heart sings, "O how I love Jesus, because He first loved me."

My dear readers, the Savior is eager to reside in our hearts, and invites us to open wide the door and let Him in. When we open the door of our heart to Him, He will open heaven's gate for us. What a glorious reunion that will be, when our blessed Savior's face we see. As we look upon His loving face, with eyes that tell of His saving grace. I can hardly wait... how about you? Until next time, be it here or there. Warm regards!

Words of Love: For God so loved you and me, that he gave his only Son, that if we believe in him, we should not perish but have eternal life. John 3:16 (Paraphrase)

CPSIA information can be obtained
at www.ICGtesting.com
Printed in the USA
BVHW04s2139100718
521353BV00006B/63/P